Hell, the Devil, and Karma

HELL,
THE DEVIL,
AND
KARMA

Samael Aun Weor

GLORIAN

Hell, the Devil, and Karma
A Glorian Book / 2011

Originally published in Spanish as *Si hay Infierno, Si hay Diablo, Si hay Karma* (1974)

This Edition © 2011 Glorian Publishing

Print ISBN 978-1-934206-51-5
Ebook ISBN 978-1-934206-65-2

Glorian Publishing is a non-profit organization. All proceeds further the distribution of these books. For more information, visit gnosticteachings.org

Contents

Illustrations

Chapter One
Hell

Question: In this day and age—according to scientists—we can no longer acknowledge the hell of fire and flames of which the Catholic religion speaks to us, since this is nothing more than a religious superstition. Is this true, Master?

Samael Aun Weor: Respectable gentleman, allow me to tell you that any religious type of inferno is exclusively symbolic.

It is not irrelevant in these moments to remember the Nordics' glacial inferno; the Yellow Springs (huángquán), the Chinese hell with all of its torments; the Buddhist hell; the Mohammedan hell; or the Infernal Island of the inhabitants of the ancient city of Gob of that part of Asia called Maralpleicie, whose civilization is today found hidden within the sands of the Gobi dessert. Unquestionably, these various traditional infernos emphatically allegorize the submerged mineral kingdom.

Remember, good friend, that Dante found his inferno in the living bowels of the Earth; read *The Divine Comedy*.

Question: Master, you speak to us about a world within the submerged mineral kingdom, nonetheless, all of the drilling into the crust of the Earth by all types of mining, oil companies, etc., have not revealed signs of a living world even in the first layer of the Earth. So, where is that submerged mineral world?

Samael Aun Weor: Great friend, allow me to tell you that the tridimensional world of Euclid is not everything.

Clearly, there are various superior dimensions above this world of three dimensions (length, width, and height); obviously, in accordance with the law of polarity, submerged infradimensions of various mineral types exist below this tridimensional zone. It is indubitable that the Dantesque type of hells correspond to the infradimensions.

Question: I beg your pardon for insisting, Master, but in all the books that I have searched within, driven by my longings, I do not remember any writing or document that talks about those infradimensions, much less that indicates how to discover them. Therefore, I ask you: what is the purpose of talking about infradimensions which, as far as I have been able to verify, no human being has been able to see or touch?

Samael Aun Weor: Respectable gentleman, your question seems very significant to me, however, it is worthwhile to clarify that the universal Christian Gnostic Movement has systems, methods of direct experience, by means of which we can verify the crude reality of the infradimensions of nature and the cosmos.

Thus, we can and must locate the nine Dantesque circles below the epidermis of the Earth, within the interior of the planetary organism on which we live. Obviously, the cited nine circles intelligently correspond with the nine natural infradimensions.

It is clearly evident that the nine heavens of Dante's *Divine Comedy* are nine superior types of dimensions that intimately correlate with nine inferior types of dimensions.

Whosoever has studied *The Divine Comedy* from the esoteric point of view cannot ignore the reality of the infernal worlds.

Question: Master, what is the basic difference between religions' hells, i.e. Catholicism, and those mentioned in the Gnostic Movement?

Samael Aun Weor: Good friend, the difference between symbolic hells from one or another religion, is like the difference between one flag and another of different nations; as each country allegorizes its existence with a national flag, likewise each religion symbolizes the infernal worlds with an allegory of an infernal type. Nevertheless, all Christian, Chinese, or Buddhist hells, etc., are fundamentally nothing but mere emblems that analogically represent the crude reality of the atomic hells of nature and the cosmos.

La Divina Commedia di Dante (Dante and the Divine Comedy), by Domenico
di Michelino. Fresco in the nave of the Duomo of Florence, Italy.

Question: Why do people have nightmares, as we commonly
say? What happens in this case? Do they travel to those infradimensional worlds?

Samael Aun Weor: I will gladly answer this interesting question from the audience. Ladies and gentlemen, I want you to
comprehend what nightmares are, indeed.

Occult anatomy teaches us that in our lower abdomen there
are seven inhuman chakras or negative vortices of sinister
forces: seven infernal doors.

It could happen that someone with indigestion because of
a heavy meal may activate the infernal chakras by means of
the digestive disorder; then those abysmal doors open, as it is
clearly taught by the religion of Mohammed. Thus, that night,
the individual enters with his personality into the infernal
worlds. This is how is possible for the detached personality to
penetrate into hell. Yes, it is not difficult for the ego to penetrate into the abode of Pluto.

The monsters in nightmares really exist. They originally derived [devolved] from archaic times; this is why they normally inhabit the infradimensions of the submerged mineral world.

Question: Venerable Master, does this mean that not only those who die without having saved their soul enter into hell?

Samael Aun Weor: It is evident, clear, and manifest that the living ones also penetrate into the infernal worlds, as is being demonstrated by nightmares. Clearly, the human infraconsciousness is naturally infernal. By all means it could be stated that all the abysmal horrors are within the atomic infernos of the human being. In other words, we emphasize the following: not in the slightest are the infernal abysses divorced from our own subconsciousness and infraconsciousness.

Now the audience will comprehend why it is so easy for anyone to penetrate into the nine Dantesque circles at any time.

Question: Beloved Master, indeed, I do not comprehend why you first stated that the infernal worlds are in the infradimensions of the Earth, and thereafter you mention that those atomic infernos are also found within oneself. Would you be so kind to clarify this for me?

Samael Aun Weor: Excellent question. Whosoever wants to discover the laws of nature must find them within himself, since the one who does not find within himself what he seeks, will never find it outside of himself. The ancients stated:

Man, know thyself thus you will know the universe and its Gods.

We must find within our interior everything that exists in nature and in the cosmos. Therefore, the nine infernal Dantesque circles are within us, here and now.

Question: Master, I have had nightmares in which I have seen many monsters within a world of darkness. Could it be that I have entered into those infradimensional or infernal worlds?

Samael Aun Weor: This is an important question. It is necessary for the audience to comprehend that those infradimensions are within the submerged depths of our own nature.

Obviously, I repeat, located in our lower abdomen, the seven doors to our atomic infernos are opened during nightmares, and through them we descend into the submerged worlds.

People who have not visited the kingdom of Pluto in their life are very rare.

Nevertheless, it is good, ladies and gentlemen, while studying this subject-matter, that we think about the raw, natural reality of those worlds that are situated in the infradimensions of the planet on which we live. So, let us think for a moment about worlds, regions that penetrate and co-penetrate each other without confusion. So, let us think for a moment about these densely inhabited regions, etc.

By no means should we interpret religious allegories literally. Let us seek within them the spirit that vivifies and gives life. The diverse religious infernos allegorize raw, natural realities; thus, we must not confuse the symbols with the cosmic phenomena in themselves.

Question: Master, would you explain to me a little more about those infernal worlds, since in the nightmares I have had, I have never seen light or beautiful faces. Why?

Samael Aun Weor: I will gladly answer this question. The infernal darkness is another type of light; this indeed corresponds to the range of the infrared. Thus, the inhabitants of such subterranean realms perceive the diverse color variations corresponding to that zone of the solar spectrum.

Friends, I want you to comprehend that all the color varieties that exist in the ultraviolet also exist in the infrared.

There is a variety of yellow in the ultraviolet. This is remarkable, however, a variety of yellow also exists in the infrared, yet in a different manner, and likewise happens with the rest of the colors; therefore I emphatically repeat the following: darkness is another type of light.

Unquestionably, the inhabitants of the submerged mineral kingdom are found too distant from the sacred Absolute Sun, and for that reason they indeed become terribly malignant and frightfully ugly.

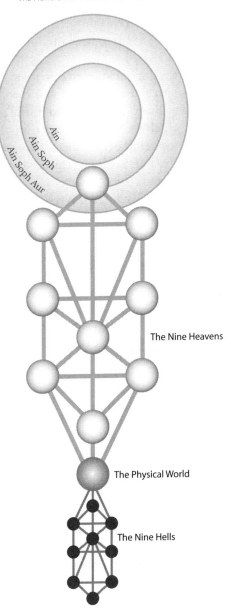

Question: I understand, Master, that in the submerged worlds of the Earth are all types of monsters and that they live there, but how is it possible that within my very self, who is so small in comparison to the planet, I can find those worlds?

Samael Aun Weor: My good friend, allow me to tell you that any molecule of cotton, iron, or copper, etc. is like a complete solar system in miniature. Precisely, a disciple of Marconi imagined our solar system looking like a great cosmic molecule.

Therefore, whosoever does not discover within a simple molecule the movement of the planets around the sun is indeed very far from comprehending astronomy.

Nothing is unlinked in the universe; indeed, there is no effect without a cause, nor a cause without an effect. Likewise, within each of us there are forces and atoms that correlate one moment with the celestial spheres and in the next with the infernal spheres.

It is good to know that within our organism are psychic centers that place us in contact with either the nine superior dimensions of the cosmos or the nine inferior dimensions.

I have already clearly stated that this tridimensional world in which we live is not everything, since above us we have the superior dimensions and below the inferior dimensions.

Unquestionably, all these heavenly or infernal dimensions are related with the distinct zones of our own psyche, and therefore if we do not discover them within our very selves we will not discover them anywhere.

Question: Master, you frequently mention the words "atomic abysses;" why atomic?

Samael Aun Weor: This question is remarkable; therefore I will gladly answer it. First of all I want you to know that any atom is a trio of matter, energy, and consciousness.

Now, let us think for a moment about the atomic intelligences. Obviously, there are solar and lunar intelligences; yet, terribly perverse, malignant, atomic intelligences also exist.

Within our organism, the atoms of the secret enemy are controlled by a certain malignant atom located exactly in the coccygeal bone. These types of atoms cause illnesses and originate within us distinct manifestations of perversity.

Let us expand a little more on this information and let us think for a moment about all the malignant atoms of the planet Earth. Obviously, the heaviest atoms, the more demonic atoms, inhabit the abode of Pluto; that is, these atoms inhabit the infradimensions of the world in which we live.

Now you will comprehend the reason why we talk about atomic abysses, about atomic infernos, etc.

Question: Master, I understand that the majority of us—when we think in terms of the atom—we imagine something infinitely small; therefore, when we are told that all the suns and planets of the cosmos constitute an atom; this somewhat overwhelms the order of our process of reasoning; is this congruent?

Samael Aun Weor: Respectable gentleman and friend, it has never occurred to me to think of reducing the entire universe or universes to a simple atom. Allow me to tell you that planets, suns, satellites, etc., are constituted by sums of atoms, and this is different, right? If in any portion of my lecture I compared the solar system with a big molecule, I did it based upon the law of philosophical analogies, but I never meant to reduce the solar system to a simple atom.

Chapter Two

The Three Aspects of the Earth's Interior

Question: Master, based on what you have previously explained to us, should we then understand that the infradimensions only exist below the interior layers of the Earth, since the supradimensions, which are associated with the heavens, are only found above the terrestrial crust?

Samael Aun Weor: Respectable gentleman, your question is combined quite significantly; thus, I will give a quick answer.

It is good for all of you to understand that this planetary organism on which we live has three clearly defined aspects in its interior:

First: the merely physical mineral region

Second: the supradimensional zone

Third: the infradimensional zone

Question: Even supposing that these three aspects of the interior of the Earth which you have spoken about to us exist—since, I clarify, in my case, I agree with it only hypothetically—we would have to arrive at the conclusion that the nine heavenly spheres co-exist with the hells that correspond to the infradimensions. Is it perhaps congruent that the heavens are to be found in the same location as the hells?

Samael Aun Weor: Respectable gentleman, it is urgent for you to comprehend in an integral manner that everything in nature and in the cosmos is reduced to additions and subtractions of dimensions that interpenetrate each other without disorder.

There is an hermetic postulate that states, "That which is above is as that which is below." Apply this postulate to this subject-matter under discussion.

Clearly, according with the law of correspondences and analogies, the nine heavens have their correspondences within the interior of our planetary organism; these nine heavens within the interior of the planetary organism in which we live are intelligently correlated with the nine profound zones of the planet Earth.

However, allow me to explain this subject-matter in depth; what really happens is that these nine heavens have a gravitational atomic center that is exactly located in the center of the planet Earth. In other words, I want to tell all of you, ladies and gentlemen, that the nine heavens that gravitate around such a gravitational atomic center of the planet Earth are extended far beyond the whole solar system. This same process is repeated in each of the planets of the solar system of Ors.

Question: Venerable Master, your exposition strikes me as very lovely and fits perfectly within the hollows of my understanding; notwithstanding, I must admit that according to the precepts of formal logic, the explanation that you just gave cannot be clearly demonstrated. Therefore, in this case how can we verify your affirmation?

Samael Aun Weor: Respectable gentleman, your question is indeed intriguing. Unquestionably, formal logic leads us unto error; therefore, we cannot reach at the experience of the reality by means of such logic. We need a superior logic, which fortunately exists. Ouspensky has already written *Tertium Organum* or "the third canon of thought." It is clear that there is a sense of unity in the mystical experience of many transcended individuals; those humans—by means of the development of certain cognitive faculties—have been able to directly verify for themselves the reality of the infernal worlds in the interior of the planet on which we live. What is most intriguing about all of this is that the data enunciated by one and many other adepts are similar despite the fact that such individuals dwell in distinct parts of the Earth.

Question: Then Master, are you telling us that only certain reduced number of adepts who have had the fortune of being endowed with those cognitive powers, are the ones who have been able to verify the infradimensions and the supradimensions of the planets and the cosmos, as well as within the human being?

Samael Aun Weor: In the field of direct experimentation, in the field of practical metaphysics, a great diversity of individuals exist with psychic faculties more or less developed. Obviously, there are disciples and there are masters; disciples can give us more or less incipient information; yet, the adepts or masters have immensely superior faculties at their disposal, which make them more capable of in-depth investigations, therefore, such faculties allows them to speak in a more clear, precise, and detailed manner.

Question: Master, according to what you have taught us, we must verify through our own experience what the Adepts and enlightened ones affirm. Consequently, is it possible for us, the profane, to verify through our own experiences, the reality of the infernal worlds, beyond the experiences of a simple nightmare caused by stomach indigestion?

Samael Aun Weor: Dear friend, it is obvious that the direct experimentation in the field of metaphysics is only accessible to individuals who have developed the latent faculties in the human being. Nevertheless, I want to tell you with complete clarity that every person can briefly experience the crude reality of such atomic infernos when experiencing those disgusting nightmares. Indubitably, I did not mean to state that the complete verification of the crude reality of the infradimensions of nature is permissible through the aforementioned nightmares. Whosoever wants to truly experience that which is below the tridimensional world of Euclid must develop certain very special psychic faculties and powers.

Question: Is it possible for all of us to develop those faculties?

Samael Aun Weor: Respectable gentleman, allow me to inform you that the International Gnostic Movement possesses methods and systems by which every human being can develop their psychic powers in a cognizant and positive manner.

Question: Master, what can you tell us so that we may understand about that demon who dwells in a hell full of flames imbibed in a tremendous odor of sulfur, and where the souls who behaved badly while they were alive are punished?

Samael Aun Weor: Gentleman, I will answer your questions in order. Unquestionably, within the submerged regions of the mineral kingdom beneath the very epidermis of the planet Earth different zones exist. Let us briefly remember the igneous zone; it is clear that volcanic eruptions have demonstrated its existence. Let us now mention the aqueous zone; no one can deny that water exists within the interior of this planetary organism. Now for a moment, let us think of the aerial element, even if this seems incredible, air currents, special aerial zones, also exist within our planet Earth. Moreover, it has been said with completely dazzling clarity that a certain vast aerial region, better said, a totally hollow region, exists within the interior of this world. And not in the slightest can we deny the reality of stones, sand, rocks, metals, etc.

Now when thinking about the concept of that demon or demons, let us also reflect upon lost souls; since this is indeed intriguing. Many inhabitants of the infernal worlds inhabit the region of fire, yet others live in the aerial regions, and finally others inhabit the aquatic regions and the mineral zones. Therefore, it is obvious that the inhabitants of the terrestrial interior are quite related with sulfur, since sulfur is an integral part of volcanoes; nonetheless, specifically, it is evident that only those who inhabit the fire can be associated with sulfur. Consequently, I want you respectable gentleman, honorable public, ladies, and gentlemen, to comprehend the inferno or "infernus" in a crudely natural manner, without any type of artifices.

Question: Master, can you tell me how is it that—since the region of the lower abdomen is associated with the infernal worlds—the silver cord is located in that infernal area? Does this mean that such a cord is constantly connecting us with our infernal worlds?

Samael Aun Weor: Respectable sir, I will give you a precise clear answer. Much has been said about the silver cord; it is indubitable that every soul is connected to the physical body by means of this magnetic thread. However, we have been told that a section of this cord or thread of life is found related to the heart and another to the brain. Diverse authors emphasize the idea that seven sections are derived from the silver cord and that these are found connected with seven specific centers of the human organism. In any case, this thread of life, this cord which you mentioned to us that is the very basis of your question, is in no way connected to the seven chakras of the lower abdomen. It is interesting to know that during the hours of sleep, the essence, the soul, escapes from within the physical body in order to travel to different places of the Earth or the cosmos; when this happens the magnetic thread of our existence is loosened and stretches infinitely; thereafter it pulls us towards our physical body so that we awaken in bed.

Question: Master, can you expand on what you have just said with respect to the seven chakras that are found in the lower abdomen, since we have been told in other lectures and even in your own books that the seven chakras are found located in different parts of our organism?

Samael Aun Weor: Honorable gentleman, I understand your question and I will answer it with great pleasure. I understand that you, sir, are mistaking the seven chakras of the lower abdomen with the Seven Churches of the Apocalypse of St. John, which are located on the dorsal spine. Indubitably, in no part of my explanations, which we have been developing here in Mexico City, have I mentioned that the [lower] magnetic centers or vortices of force are located on the staff of Brahma or spinal canal. We have only cited or mentioned the seven infernal doors, which the religion of Mohammed talks about, which are seven specific centers or chakras located in the lower abdomen and which are related with the infernal worlds. That is all; understood?

Question: Venerable Master, based on everything that has been previously explained, can we infer that the physical aspect of the center of the Earth belongs to the tridimensional world; however, the supradimensional or infradimensional aspects which are located in the same subterranean regions of the planet cannot be verifiable by means of the intellectual tridimensional, sensorial perceptions of the rational animal?

Samael Aun Weor: Respectable gentleman, allow me to tell you and, in general, to everyone in this audience that listens, that our five senses only perceive the tridimensional aspects of existence; however, our five senses are incapable of perceiving the supradimensional or infradimensional aspects of the Earth and of the cosmos.

Obviously, the subterranean regions of our world are comprised by three fundamental aspects. Yet, again, our ordinary senses only perceive in a superficial manner what is physical, tridimensional. However, if we want to know the superior or inferior dimensions of the interior of the Earth, we must develop other faculties of perception, which are found latent in the human race.

Question: Beloved Master, should we understand that living beings inhabit both the supradimensions as well as the infradimensions?

Samael Aun Weor: My friends, unquestionably, the three zones of the interior of our world are inhabited. If the lost souls live within the infradimensions, then many Devas, elementals of a superior order, dwell in the supradimensions within the planetary interior, i.e. Gods, Masters, etc. who work intensely with the intelligent forces of this great nature. We could talk very extensively about the populations of the central zones or supradimensional or infradimensional zones of the interior of our world, however, these themes shall be addressed in future lectures. Good night.

Chapter Three

The Seven Cosmoses

Friends, we are gathered here again with the purpose of studying the Ray of Creation.

It is urgent, indispensable, and unpostponable to clearly and precisely know the exact place that we occupy within the vivifying Ray of Creation.

First of all, respectable gentlemen, dear ladies, I beseech you very kindly to follow my lecture with infinite patience.

I want you to know that there are seven cosmoses, namely:

1. Protocosmos

2. Ayocosmos

3. Macrocosmos

4. Deuterocosmos

5. Mesocosmos

6. Microcosmos

7. Tritocosmos

Unquestionably, the first cosmos is formed by multiple, transcendental, divine, spiritual suns.

Much has been spoken about the sacred Absolute Sun, and it is obvious that every solar system is governed by one of these spiritual suns. This means that our planetary system possess its own sacred absolute sun, just like all the other solar systems of the unalterable infinite.

The second order of worlds is formed by all the millions of suns and planets that travel throughout space.

The third system of worlds is formed by any galaxy; i.e. this great Milky Way that has the Sun Sirius as its central cosmic capitol.

The fourth order of worlds is represented by our solar system of Ors.

The fifth order corresponds to our planet Earth.

The sixth order is the Microcosmos, man.

The seventh order is in the infernal worlds.

Let us extend our explanation even better:

I want you, ladies and gentlemen, to understand with complete clarity what the first order of worlds is. These are extraordinary spiritual suns that sparkle with infinite splendors in space; these are radiant spheres that astronomers can never perceive through their telescopes.

Now, reflect on the order of the billions and trillions of worlds and stars that inhabit infinite space.

Now, consider the galaxies themselves; any of them when looked at separately is certainly a Macrocosmos, and our galaxy, the Milky Way, is not an exception.

What would we now say about the Deuterocosmos? Unquestionably, every solar system—regardless which galaxy it belongs to, or whether it is a galaxy of matter or anti matter—is obviously a Deuterocosmos.

In space, Earths are as numerous as the sands of the immense sea. Indubitably, any of these Earths, any planet in itself, is a Mesocosmos (it does not matter which center of cosmic gravitation it might have).

Much has been spoken about the Microcosmos, man. We emphasize the transcendental idea that each one of us is an authentic and legitimate Microcosmos. Nevertheless, we are not the only inhabitants of the infinite; it is obvious that many inhabited worlds exist; thus, any inhabitant of the cosmos or of the cosmoses is an authentic Microcosmos.

Finally, it is convenient to know that the submerged mineral kingdom with its own atomic infernos exists within any planet. The atomic infernos are always situated within the interior of any planetary mass and within the infradimensions of nature, below the tridimensional zone of Euclid.

Thus, ladies and gentlemen, let us understand that the first order of worlds is completely different from the second, and that each cosmos is absolutely dissimilar and radically distinct.

The first order of worlds is infinitely ineffable and divine; not a single mechanical principle exists within it, since it is governed by one law.

The second order is unquestionably controlled by the three primary forces, which regulate and direct any cosmic creation.

The third order of worlds—our galaxy or any galaxy in the sacred space—is indubitably controlled by six laws.

The fourth order of worlds—our solar system, or any solar system of the infinite space—is always controlled by twelve laws.

The fifth order—our Earth, or any planet (all planets are similar to ours) in whichever orbit around any sun—is absolutely controlled by twenty-four laws.

The sixth cosmic order—any human organism—is definitely controlled by forty-eight laws. We can see that this is totally proven in the human germinal cell, since this is constituted—as it is already known—by forty-eight chromosomes [Editor: modern scientists have recognized forty-six, but have yet to discover two chromosomes related to the fourth dimension].

Finally, the seventh order of worlds is under the total control of ninety-six laws.

Now, I want you to know in a precise manner that the numbers of laws in the abysmal regions are scandalously multiplied. It is evident that the first Dantesque circle is always under the control of ninety-six laws. However, this number of laws is duplicated in the second circle, producing one hundred and ninety two laws. The ninety-six laws triples in the third, quadruples in the fourth, thus, in like manner the 96 laws is multiplied successively: 96 x 2, 96 x 3, 96 x 4, 96 x 5, 96 x 6, 96 x 7, 96 x 8, 96 x 9; so therefore in the ninth circle, when multiplying 96 x 9, we get 864 laws.

If you were to profoundly reflect on the first cosmos, you would then perceive that the most absolute freedom exists there, since there everything is governed by a single law.

Complete happiness still exists in the second cosmos, due to the fact that it is completely controlled by the three primary laws of the entire creation.

However, a mechanical factor is introduced in the third cosmos, because in it the three primeval, divine laws duplicate themselves, thus becoming six. Obviously, a certain cosmic automatism already exists in the third cosmos, since the three primary forces no longer work in unison, for upon duplicating

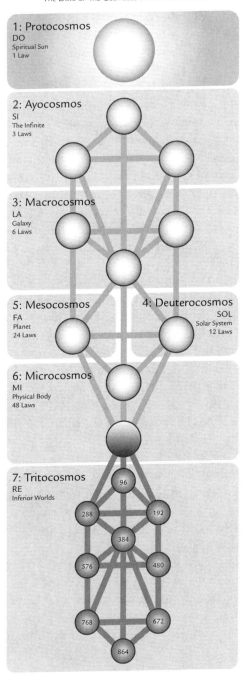

1: Protocosmos
DO
Spiritual Sun
1 Law

2: Ayocosmos
SI
The Infinite
3 Laws

3: Macrocosmos
LA
Galaxy
6 Laws

5: Mesocosmos
FA
Planet
24 Laws

4: Deuterocosmos
SOL
Solar System
12 Laws

6: Microcosmos
MI
Physical Body
48 Laws

7: Tritocosmos
RE
Inferior Worlds

themselves they have originated the mechanical system of any galaxy.

Now, look at what any solar system is. It is clear that in it, the six laws have once again duplicated themselves, thus becoming twelve, which increase the mechanicity, the automatism, the complication, etc.

Let us now limit ourselves to any planet of the infinite, and very especially to our terrestrial world. Obviously, a planet is more heterogeneous and complex due to the fact that in it the twelve laws of the solar system have become twenty-four laws.

Let us now bluntly look at the Microcosmos, man. Let us examine his germinal cell, and in it we will find forty-eight chromosomes, which are the living representation of the forty-eight laws that control our entire physical body. Obviously, when duplicating themselves, these forty-eight laws originate the ninety-six laws of the first Dantesque circle.

Hence, I want you, ladies and gentlemen, to comprehend the place that we occupy in the Ray of Creation.

Someone who knew that the word inferno is derived from the word "infernus" (which in Latin means inferior region) emphasized the idea that the place that we occupy in the tridimensional zone of Euclid is the inferno, which according to him is the inferior place of the cosmos. Regrettably, the person who made such an unusual affirmation in fact did not know the Ray of Creation. If he had more information, if he had studied the seven cosmoses, he would have utterly realized that such an inferior place is not this physical world in which we live, but is the seventh cosmos, which is situated exactly within the interior of the planet Earth, within the natural infradimensions, below the tridimensional zone of Euclid.

Question: Master, after having listened with attention and patience to your scientific exposition on the Ray of Creation, I have observed that when you address the first order of worlds— that is, the Protocosmos—you mentioned that movement, life, corresponds to the first law where absolute freedom reigns. Now, quoting the words of the great Kabir Jesus, he taught us:

> *And ye shall know the truth, and the truth shall make you free.* - John 8:32

By following the law of analogies and correspondences, should we understand that since we are those who move and have our Being in the sixth order of worlds—that is, the Microcosmos— in order for us to vividly know the truth and thus to be completely free, we must strive to become inhabitants of the worlds governed by a single law?

Samael Aun Weor: I will most gladly answer the question of the gentleman. Respectable ladies and gentlemen, it is indispensable to comprehend that the greater the number of laws, the greater the degree of mechanicity and pain; the lesser the number of laws, the lesser the degree of mechanicity and pain.

Unquestionably, in the sacred Absolute Sun, in the central spiritual sun of the solar system in which we live, move, and have our Being, there is no mechanicity of any type, and therefore, it is obvious that the most absolute bliss reigns in there.

Undoubtedly, we must fight in an inexhaustible manner in order to free ourselves from the 48, 24, 12, 6, and 3 laws, so that we can return into the sacred Absolute Sun of our system.

Question: Master, based on what you have formerly explained, we can then deduce that worlds with a greater number of laws are more mechanical and consequently by logic more dense and materialistic. Does this mean that the infradimensional or infernal worlds will cause greater suffering, and this is why they are called the regions of penalties and punishments?

Samael Aun Weor: This question from the audience seems somewhat intriguing, thus I am very glad to quickly answer it. Respectable gentleman, I want you and everybody to know and understand that the greater the number of laws, the greater the degree of mechanicity and pain.

The ninety-six laws of the first infernal zone are terribly painful; however, as this amount of laws are multiplied according to each of these infradimensional zones, pain, mechanicity, materialism, and weeping also become multiplied.

Question: Venerable Master, I have observed that previously you spoke to us about the nine concentric circles in the region of the infradimensions, which correspond to the nine circles of the supradimensions of the cosmos; however, now when addressing the Ray of Creation, you have only enumerated and explained seven cosmoses. Is there something incongruent in this?

Samael Aun Weor: Respectable sir, it is indispensable for you to make a clear differentiation between the seven cosmoses, the nine heavens, and the nine Dantesque circles from the natural infradimensions.

Obviously, the nine heavens are related, as we have already explained, with the nine submerged regions below the epidermis of the Earth. This is how Enoch saw them while in a state of ecstasy upon Mount Moriah; a mount where he later built a subterranean temple with nine interior levels in order to allegorize the transcendental reality of his vision.

It is unquestionable that the nine heavens are utterly concretized in the spheres of the Moon, Mars, Venus, the Sun, Mars, Jupiter, Saturn, Uranus, and Neptune. It is therefore clear that all of these nine heavens correspond to the Deuterocosmos.

Is it therefore clarified in your mind that the seven cosmoses are not the nine heavens?

Question: Master, when you explained to us that as the ray descends to a greater number of laws—from the first cosmos down to the infernal regions—each time the mechanicity, the automatism, the materialism, becomes greater. So, this makes me think that as we move away from the three primary laws, we sequentially separate ourselves from the direct will of the Father, thus lingering under our own miserable fate. Is this the case?

Samael Aun Weor: Respectable gentleman, honorable ladies who listen to me in this audience, I want you to know in a clear and precise manner that the solar, sacred Absolute gloriously shines beyond this system of worlds that form our solar system. It is indubitable that the unalterable happiness of the eternal living God exists in the central Spiritual Sun, governed by the unique law. Unfortunately, as we move farther and farther away from the sacred Absolute Sun, we then penetrate into worlds that are each time more and more complicated, worlds where automatism, mechanicity, and pain is established.

Obviously, the bliss within the cosmos of three laws is incomparable, because the materialism is less. In this region, any atom possesses within its inner nature only three atoms of the Absolute.

Yet how different is the third cosmos! There, the materialism increases, since any of its atoms possesses within its inner nature six atoms of the Absolute.

Let us now penetrate in the fourth cosmos. There, we find denser matter, due to the concrete fact that any of its atoms possesses within its inner nature twelve atoms of the Absolute.

Let us concretize a little farther; if we carefully examine the planet Earth, we will see that any of its atoms possesses within its inner nature twenty-four atoms of the Absolute.

Let us now carefully specify and by means of divine clairvoyance study in detail any atom of the human organism, and we then will perceive within it forty-eight atoms of the Absolute.

Let us descend a little more and enter into the kingdom of the most crude materialism, that is, into the infernal worlds, below the crust of the planet on which we live. There, we shall discover that in the first infradimensional zone, the density has terrifyingly increased, because any inhumane atom possesses within its inner nature 96 atoms of the Absolute.

Farther down, in the second infernal zone, every atom has 192 atoms. And in the third zone, every atom possesses within its interior 384 atoms of the Absolute, etc. Thus, one after another the materialism increases in a dreadful and terrifying manner.

Obviously, when submerging each time within laws that are more and more complex, we become progressively distant from the will of the Absolute, and fall into the mechanical complication of this great nature. Therefore, if we want to re-conquer freedom, we must free ourselves from so much mechanicity and so many laws and thus return to the Father.

Question: Beloved Master, if divine will is not exerted within the Microcosmos, man, then why is it stated that not a single leaf of a tree moves without the will of God?

Samael Aun Weor: Respectable gentleman, as we have already stated, only a single law governs in the sacred Absolute Sun. Likewise, the will of the Father is still exerted in the cosmos of three laws because in it everything is governed by the three fundamental laws. Nevertheless, undoubtedly, in the world of six laws there already exists a mechanicity which—in a certain way—makes it independent of the will of the Absolute.

Now, consider the worlds of 24, 48, and 96 laws. It is obvious that within such orders of worlds, mechanicity multiplies independent of the solar, sacred Absolute.

This former assertion allow us to suggest that the Father is excluded from all creation; nonetheless, it is good for everyone to know that every mechanicity is previously calculated by the sacred Absolute Sun, since the different orders of laws with their diverse mechanical processes could not exist if these had not been previously arranged by the Father.

This universe is a whole within the intelligence of the solar, sacred Absolute, and these phenomena crystallize in a successive manner, little by little. Understood?

Question: Master, could you tell us why you relate the number seven with the laws of creation, the human organism, and the worlds? Is this a tradition or is it really a law?

Samael Aun Weor: This question from the gentleman deserves an immediate answer. I want all of you, ladies and gentlemen, to comprehend with completely dazzling clarity what the laws of three and seven are.

It is urgent for you to know that at the dawn of creation, the Cosmocreators (the creators of this universe in which we live, move, and have our Being) each one of them, under the direction of their particular Cosmic Divine Mother Kundalini, worked, developing in space the laws of three and seven, so that everything might have abundant life. Only in this manner was our world able to exist.

It is not therefore strange that every natural cosmic process is developed in accordance with the laws of three and seven. By no means should it seem unusual the fact that such laws are correlated in the infinitely small as well as in the infinitely large, in the Microcosm and in the Macrocosm, in all that is, in all that has been, and in all that shall be.

Let us think for a moment on the seven chakras of the dorsal spine, on the seven principal worlds of the solar system, on the seven rounds that ancient and modern Theosophy talks about, on the seven human root races, etc. All these gigantic septenary processes—that is, every septenary manifestation of life—always has as its foundation the three primary forces: positive, negative, and neutral. Understood?

Question: Master, why is it that when you talk about the creation of worlds, beings, or galaxies, you express yourself using terms such as: it is clear, it is indubitable, it is obvious, it is natural, etc.? What are the bases of your assertions so that you can talk with such certainty?

Samael Aun Weor: I see amongst the audience someone who has elaborated a very interesting question, which I will gladly answer.

Ladies and gentlemen, I want you to know in a concrete, clear, and definite manner, that two types of reasoning exist. We must denominate the first one as subjective reasoning, and we must qualify the second as objective reasoning.

Unquestionably, external, sensory perceptions are the foundation of the first type of reasoning. Yet, the second type of reasoning is different. This can only be processed in accordance with the inner, vivid experiences of the consciousness.

It is obvious that the diverse functions of my own consciousness are found behind the terms quoted by the gentleman. In my speech, I utilize such terms as specific vehicles for the concepts of my sensory data. In other words, by means of certain emphasis, I tell the gentleman and the audience who listens to me, the following: I would never use the words quoted by the gentleman if I had not previously verified with my cognizant powers, with my transcendental cognitive faculties, the truth of all that I am asserting. So, I like to utilize precise terms with the purpose of making exact ideas to be known. That is all.

Question: Master, in your former exposition you mentioned the dawn of creation. Could you explain to us in which epoch this occurred and who performed such a work?

Samael Aun Weor: Respectable gentleman, there is no time in eternity. I want all of you who have attended our lecture to perfectly comprehend that time does not have a basic reality. Time does not posses an authentic, legitimate origin.

Certainly and in the name of the truth, I must tell you that time is merely something subjective. Time does not possess an objective, concrete, and exact reality.

Indeed, what really exists is a succession of phenomena: i.e. the sun rises and we exclaim it is six in the morning. It sets and we say it is six in the evening. Twelve hours have elapsed in between. Now, in which part of the cosmos can we find these twelve hours, this "time"? Can we perhaps hold that time in our hand and place it on the table of a laboratory? What color does such time have? Of what metal or substance is that time made?

Let us reflect, ladies and gentlemen; let us reflect a little. It is the mind that invents time, since, indeed, what truly exists in an objective manner is the succession of natural phenomena. Unfortunately, we made the blunder of assigning time to every cosmic movement.

We set our beloved hours between the rising and the setting of the sun. We invent them, we place them along with the movement of the stars, nevertheless, these are fantasies of the mind.

Cosmic phenomena are occurring one after another within the eternal instant of the movement of the great life. Our universe exists as an integral, unitotal, and complete whole within the sacred Absolute Sun. All the cosmic changes are processed within an eternal moment, within an instant that has no limits within the sacred Absolute Sun.

It is evident and manifest that when the different successive phenomena of this universe crystallize, regrettably, the concept of time then comes to our mind. Such a subjective concept is always placed between phenomenon and phenomenon.

Indeed, the Solar Logos, the Demiurge Architect of the universe, is the true author of all of this creation. Nevertheless, we cannot set a date to his work, to his cosmogenesis, because time is an illusion of the mind. Thus, creation is something that is far beyond anything that is merely intellective.

The inferno or the infernal worlds exist throughout eternity. Let us quote the phrase of Dante Alighieri in his *Divine Comedy:*

> *Through me you pass into the city of woe: Through me*
> *you pass into eternal pain: Through me among the people*
> *lost for aye. Justice the founder of my fabric moved: To*
> *rear me was the task of power divine, supremest wisdom,*
> *and primeval love. Before me things create were none,*
> *save things eternal and eternal I endure. "All hope*
> *abandon ye who enter here."* – Canto 3:1-9

Question: Venerable Master, according to what I have been able to read, the Master G. relates the world of ninety-six laws with the Moon. However you affirm that such region is found below the epidermis of the planetary organism in which we live. Can you explain this divergence of concepts?

Samael Aun Weor: Respectable sir, I will give you an immediate answer.

Certainly, Master G. thinks that the Ray of Creation ends with the Moon, and I emphatically affirm that it concludes in the submerged worlds, in the inferno. Listen, respectable ladies and gentlemen: the Moon is something different. The Moon is a dead world, a corpse that belongs to a past cosmic day of creation.

The voyages of the astronauts to our satellite have come to demonstrate in a conclusive and definitive manner, the irrefutable fact that the Moon is a dead world.

I do not know how the Master G. made this mistake in his calculations, since any moon of the infinite space is always a corpse. Regrettably, Master G. firmly believed that in our system the Moon was a new world that was being born, that was surging from within the chaos.

In the past cosmic day, the Moon had abundant life; yes, the Moon was a marvelous Earth in space. Nevertheless, now it is

SELENE, THE MOON OF THE EARTH

already dead, and in the future the Moon will become totally disintegrated. That is all.

Question: Beloved Master, according to Master G., our satellite, the Moon, was originated from a detachment of terrestrial matter due to tremendous magnetic forces of attraction within the laws of gravity, thus forming a new world where the lost souls certainly enter in order to suffer within the Avernus of those infradimensional regions. Consequently, Master Samael, does this mean that Master G. arrived at this conclusion because his cognitive faculties were poor?

Samael Aun Weor: I understood the question from the gentleman and I will gladly answer him with clarity.

By no means do I want to underestimate Master G's psychic faculties. Obviously, he fulfilled a marvelous mission and his work is splendid; nevertheless, the man has the right to make mistakes. It is possible that he took such information related with Selene, from some legend, from some source, from some allegory, etc. In any case, we emphatically affirm what we know, what we have been able to directly verify for ourselves, without underestimating any Master's labor.

That the Moon was the outcome of a collision between the Earth and another planet, or that it emerged from the Pacific Ocean, as it is declared by another respectable Master, are concepts that we respect but that we have not practically evidenced.

I affirm in a compelling manner and with certain emphasis, thus limiting myself exclusively to reveal with my objective reasoning what I have been able to see, hear, touch, and feel by myself: never in the entire cosmos have we known any moon to become an inhabitable world.

Any well-awakened initiate knows by means of direct experience that the worlds—like men, plants and everything that exist—are born, grow, age, and die. It is clear that any planet that dies, in fact and by its own right, becomes a corpse, a moon. Our planet Earth will not be an exception. Thus, you can be sure, ladies and gentlemen, that after the seventh human root race, our Earth will also become a new moon.

Therefore, let us be exact. I am mathematical in investigation and demanding in expression. We have methods, systems, and procedures by means of which we can and must come in contact with those infernal worlds. Only then we will recognize the reality of *The Divine Comedy* of Dante, who places the inferno below the epidermis of the planet Earth.

Chapter Four

Monads and Essences

Beloved friends, once again we are meeting here in this place in order to talk in a detailed manner about the different causes that lead intellectual humanoids downward along the descending, devolving path through the infernal regions.

Unquestionably, in these moments millions of devolving, descending creatures are crossing Acheron in order to enter the Avernus. After having completed their cycle of existences in the physical tridimensional world of Euclid, waves of humanoids cease to incarnate into human bodies in order to definitely submerge themselves into the mineral kingdom.

Indeed, the evil of the world has an dam; yes, no matter how monstrous evil might become, it has a defined limit. What would become of the universe if there was no insurmountable obstacle to evil? Then, obviously, evil would develop infinitely until reigning sovereign in all of the spheres.

Here, it is worthwhile to emphasize with completely dazzling clarity, the tremendous reality of the 108 existences that are assigned to every living essence, to every divine psychic principle.

The 108 existences bring to mind the 108 beads of Buddha's necklace, as well as the 108 turns that the Hindu Brahman performs around the sacred cow. It is indubitable that with the last turn he finishes his daily rite; he then introduces the tail of the aforementioned allegorical animal into the cup of water that he will drink.

Having understood all of this, let us now proceed.

It is obvious that the Divine Mother Kundalini, the igneous serpent of our magical powers, attempts to achieve the realization of our inner self during the course of the 108 existences that are assigned to each one of us. It is evident that within such a cycle of successive lives, we have innumerable opportunities for realization of the self. To take advantage of them is what is valuable. Regrettably, we incessantly slip back into errors, thus habitually, in the end, the outcome is failure.

It is obvious and evident that not all human beings want to tread the path that will lead them to final liberation.

The different messengers that came from above—i.e. prophets, avatars, great apostles— have always wanted to show us, with exact precision, the rocky path that leads to authentic and legitimate happiness.

Regrettably, people want nothing to do with divine wisdom. They have imprisoned the masters, they have assassinated the avatars, they have bathed themselves in the blood of the righteous. They mortally hate anything that has a flavor of divinity.

Nevertheless, all of them—like Pontius Pilate—wash their hands, given that they believe themselves to be saints, and presume that they march on the path of perfection.

We cannot deny the emphatic and definitive fact that millions of sincere but mistaken people exist who very honestly boast of being virtuous, thus thinking the best about themselves.

All kinds of anchorites live within the Tartarus—i.e. mistaken mystics, sublime fakirs, priests of many cults, penitents of all types—who would agree about many things, except the tremendous truth that they are lost and that they march on the path of evilness.

This is why the great Kabir Jesus stated in his own right:

> From a thousand who seek me, one finds me; from a thousand who found me one follows me, and from a thousand who follow me, I choose one.

Krishna textually said the following:

> Among thousands of men, one perchance strives for perfection; even among those who strive for perfection, one perchance attains perfection; and amongst the perfect, only one perchance knows me in truth. - Bhagavad-Gita 7:3

When emphasizing the difficulty of entering the kingdom, Jesus the great Kabir said:

> But woe unto you, scribes and Pharisees, hypocrites! For ye shut up the kingdom of heaven against men: for ye neither go in yourselves, neither suffer ye them that are

entering to go in. Woe unto you, scribes and Pharisees,
hypocrites! For ye devour widows' houses, and for a
pretence make long prayer: therefore ye shall receive the
greater damnation. - Matthew 23:13, 14

When the great Kabir Jesus addressed those many false
apostles who wander about, going everywhere founding diverse
sects that never lead to final liberation, he said:

Woe unto you, scribes and Pharisees, hypocrites! For ye
compass sea and land to make one proselyte, and when
he is made, ye make him twofold more the child of hell
than yourselves. - Matthew 23:15

Respectable friends, noble brothers, dear ladies, the gravest
thing of this subject-matter is that those who are lost, the
sincere but mistaken ones, always think that they are doing
well. How can we make these people comprehend that they
are doing wrong? How can we make them understand that the
path that leads to the abyss is paved with good intentions? In
what manner can we demonstrate to the people with sleepy
consciousness that the sect to which they belong or the tenebrous school to which they are affiliated will lead them to the
abyss and to the second death? It is unquestionable that no
one thinks the worst of his sect; all of them are convinced by
the words of their blind leaders of the blind.

Certainly, and in the name of truth, we shall say with great
frankness that only by awakening consciousness can we see the
narrow, straight, and difficult path that leads unto light.

How could those who sleep see the path? Could the mind
perhaps discover the truth? It is written with golden words in
the great book of universal life that the mind cannot recognize
what it has never known. Do you perhaps believe that the mind
has known, once upon a time, what the reality, the truth is?

It is clear that mind's understanding goes from the known
to the unknown. It moves within a vicious circle. Thus, it so
happens that (for the mind) the truth is unknowable from
moment to moment.

I beg you, beloved brothers, noble friends, and respectable
ladies, to reflect a little. The mind can accept or reject whatever

it pleases. It may believe or doubt, etc., but it can never know reality.

Observe carefully what happens in the different corners of the world. It is clear that the sacred books circulate everywhere and they serve as a basis for many religious cults. Notwithstanding, who understands the hidden concepts contained within those books? Who has complete consciousness of what is written in each verse? The masses only limit themselves to believe or to deny, and that is all.

As proof of what I am affirming, behold how many sects have been formed with the marvelous verses of the four Christian gospels. If the Christian devotees had full consciousness of the Christic gospel preached by the great Kabir Jesus, it is obvious that so many sects would not exist; truly, only one Christic religion of a universal cosmic type would exist. However, the believers are not able to achieve an agreement among them because they have their consciousness asleep; thus, they know nothing. Nothing is evident to them, since they have never personally talked with an Angel. They have never consciously and positively entered into the heavenly regions. They walk because others walk. They eat because others eat. They repeat what others say. Thus, in this manner, with blindfolded eyes, they march from the cradle to the sepulcher.

Regrettably, time passes with terrifying swiftness. The cycle of human existences finishes, and finally, the devotees, convinced that they walk on the upright path, enter the horrible abode of Pluto, where only weeping and gnashing of teeth are heard.

The descent of the human waves into the interior of the planetary organism is performed descending through the animal and plant stages, until definitely entering into the mineral stage in the very core of the planet Earth.

I want you to know, I want you to comprehend, that it is precisely in the very center of this planet where millions of humanoids pass through that second death, of which the Apocalypse (Revelation of St. John) spoke.

It is evident that the destruction of "myself," the annihilation of the ego, the dissolution of the self-willed within the submerged regions of the Avernus, is absolutely indispensable for the destruction of evil within each one of us.

Obviously, it is only through the death of the ego that the liberation of the essence is made possible. This is how the essence re-surges, emerges up to the planetary surface, to the light of the sun, in order to begin again a new evolving cyclical process within the painful wheel of Samsara.

The re-ascension always takes place in the mineral kingdom, ascending thereafter through the plant and animal stages until re-conquering the human state that was formerly lost. It is clear that when we reenter into the human state, 108 existences are once again assigned to us, which if we do not properly take advantage of them, will eventually lead us downwardly, through the descending path, thus once again returning into the Avernus. In any case, dear brothers, noble ladies that listen to me, it is good for you to know that 3,000 of these cycles of cosmic manifestation are always assigned to each essence, to each soul.

Those who definitely fail, those who do not know how to take advantage of the innumerable opportunities that these

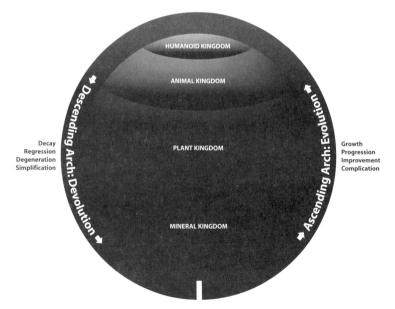

EVOLUTION AND DEVOLUTION THROUGH THE KINGDOMS OF NATURE ON THE WHEEL OF SAMSARA

3,000 periods confer upon us, grant unto us, will remain forever excluded from mastery. In the latter case, that immortal spark that all of us have within—namely, our sublime Monad—pulls back its essence, that is, its spiritual principles. It absorbs them into itself, and thereafter it submerges forever into the universal spirit of life. Thus, this is how the Monads without mastery, those sparks that did not achieve mastery or who definitely did not want mastery, remain excluded from any hierarchical rank. To that end, I clarify: not all the immortal sparks, not all the sublime Monads, want mastery.

Yet, when any Monad, when any Divine Spark truly wants to reach the sublime state of "Master Monad," it is indubitable that it then works its essence, its soul. In this case, such a Monad awakens in this soul infinite desires of transcendental spirituality.

Question: Beloved Master, based on what you have just explained, it seems to me, if I am not mistaken, that this is precisely what the Lord Krishna wanted us to know when he taught about the transmigration of souls, as well as the Master Pythagoras who taught about metempsychosis. Is this right?

Samael Aun Weor: I hear the statements involved in the gentleman's question and I will clearly give him a quick answer.

Friends, ladies, indeed what I am affirming tonight has documentation in India and in Greece. The first within the marvelous doctrine presented by that ancient Hindu Avatar called Krishna, and the second within the doctrine of Pythagoras. Obviously, the metempsychosis of the great Greek philosopher Pythagoras and the doctrine of the transmigration of souls taught by the Hindu Avatar Krishna are identical in their structure and in their depth. Regrettably, people distort the teachings in order to reject it in an arbitrary manner in the end.

Question: Respectable Master, what I do not comprehend is why eminent personalities, renowned as masters, such as the lady H.P.B. and Charles Leadbeater, as well as Annie Besant, founders of the Theosophical Society, who were people with faculties of clairvoyance, clairaudience, and other powers, never became aware of the facts that the great Kabir Jesus, as well as Krishna, Pythagoras, and you, Master Samael, have taught us. But on the contrary, they have proclaimed in huge treatises greatly renowned in the world by the pseudo-esoteric schools, that all humans inexorably walk on the ascending path of evolution until one day, with the passage of time, they will arrive to perfection and thus become one with the Father. Can you explain such incongruence?

Samael Aun Weor: I understood the gentleman's very important question, thus unquestionably, I will do my best to answer him right away.

Certainly, the laws of evolution and devolution work harmoniously and coordinately in all of nature. It is indubitable that everything that goes up will eventually go down. Every ascent is followed by a descent. Therefore, it would be an absurdity to assume that the law of evolution is something different.

If we climb a mountain, we will undoubtedly arrive at its summit. Yet, afterwards, we would need to descend. Thus, beloved brethren of mine, this is how the laws of evolution and devolution coordinate.

These two great laws constitute the mechanical axis of all of nature. If either of these two laws cease to function for just a moment, then all natural mechanisms would in fact become paralyzed.

Understand: there is evolution in the grain that germinates, grows, and develops. Yet, devolution exists in the plant when it withers and dies. There is evolution in the creature that develops within the maternal womb, in the child that is born, in the adolescent, in the growing youth. Yet, devolution exists in the one who ages and dies. Thus, the evolving and devolving processes are completely organized within this great creation.

Regrettably, those who have bottled themselves within the "dogma of evolution" are no longer capable of comprehending the infinite destructive and decadent processes of everything that is, of everything that has been, and of everything that will be.

Listen: neither evolution nor devolution can ever take us to the inner self-realization of the Being.

If we want to be truly liberated, if we seriously long for authentic happiness, we then need in an urgent and unpostponable manner to enter the path of the revolution of the consciousness.

It is not irrelevant to emphasize the transcendental and transcending idea that it is not possible to arrive at the great Reality as long as we continue incessantly turning amid the wheel of Samsara. Of what use is it, ladies and gentlemen, to incessantly return into this valley of tears, to constantly evolve and devolve and to descend again and again into the infernal worlds?

Our duty is to awaken consciousness so that we can see the path that will lead us with absolute precision to the final liberation.

Unquestionably, at the end of the nineteenth century and at the beginning of the twentieth century, many respectable, knowledgeable, occultist intelligences transmitted unto humanity a simple, elementary teaching. It is clear that such persons only proposed to publicly teach the first letters of the secret doctrine. At that time, they did not linger too much in the analysis of the evolving and devolving laws. Rudolf Steiner already affirmed, in 1912, that they, the initiates of that epoch, had only delivered an incipient, elementary knowledge, but that much later, a superior esoteric doctrine of transcendental nature would be given unto humanity. Now, we are delivering this type of superior esoteric doctrine. It is therefore indispensable to not condemn or criticize those who in the past worked in some way for humanity. They did what they could; now we must elucidate and clarify.

Question: Master, you stated that some Monads are interested in achieving self-realization yet others are not. Notwithstanding, all Monads emanate from the Absolute. I had understood that to search for self-realization was a compelled duty for all of them. Can you explain a little more about this?

Samael Aun Weor: I understood this young man's question thus, I will gladly answer. Friends, before anything else, I want you to comprehend: that which is divine, God, the Universal Spirit of Life, is not dictatorial. If that which is the reality, if that which is the truth, if that which is not of time, were dictatorial, what fate could we expect?

Friends, God individually also respects his own freedom. With this I want to state that within the bosom of the Divine there do not exist dictatorships. Every virginal spark, every Monad, has the complete liberty of accepting or rejecting mastery. Understood?

Question: Master, based on what you have just explained, we can then state that the Monad is responsible for the essence to fall into hell?

Samael Aun Weor: I see amidst the audience a lady who, with full sincerity, has asked this question which, evidently I will gladly answer:

Ladies and gentlemen, when a divine Monad wants mastery, it is clear that it achieves it by working its essence incessantly, from within, from its inner most profundities. Yet, it is clear and evident that if the Monad is not interested in mastery, the Monad will never awaken any intimate longing within the incarnated essence. Obviously, in this case, the essence—being deprived of every longing, and imprisoned within the ego, stuffed within the "myself"—will eventually enter into the infernal worlds. Therefore, I emphatically answer: the Monad is guilty of the failure of its essence. Since, if indeed the Monad profoundly worked its essence, it is unquestionable that the essence will never descend as a failure into the Tartarus.

Question: Master, it terrifies me to think that as an essence I would have to pass through suffering for 108 lives multiplied by 3,000 or rather 324,000 humanoid existences, so that finally in the grand scheme of things—as an essence—I will have to live within the Absolute as a failed Monad—in other words, without self-realization. Under these circumstances, it is worth it to make all possible efforts and sacrifices in order to achieve self-realization, no matter how much suffering this might imply, since these will be absolutely nothing in comparison to those which nature will impose on me if I choose the path of failure. Do you think so?

Samael Aun Weor: Respectable sir, great friend, allow me to emphatically tell you that every Divine Spark, every Monad, can choose the path.

It is indubitable that trillions of absolutely innocent Monads—beyond good and evil—exist in the infinite space. Many of them attempted to attain mastery but regrettably, they failed. Millions of others never wanted mastery. Regardless, now they are submerged within the bosom of the Universal Spirit of Life enjoying authentic divine happiness, because they are flashes of divinity. Unfortunately, they do not possess mastery.

It is clear that the gentleman who asked the question has enormous longings. This is because your interior Monad is motivating you; it is working on you incessantly. Your duty is therefore to proceed with firmness on the path of the razor's edge until achieving the inner self-realization of the Being.

Question: Master, is it because of this impassiveness that many people to whom we talk about the Gnostic teachings—even when they perfectly grasp what we are explaining to them—do not choose to follow the path of the revolution of consciousness? Does this mean that their Monad is not working on them to follow the path of self-realization?

Samael Aun Weor: I will answer this young man's question.

We need to profoundly reflect so that we can focus this subject-matter from diverse angles. It so happens that many Monads like to march slowly with the risk that their essences fail in each cycle of human existences. Other Monads prefer to work their essences in an intermittent manner, in fits and starts. Lastly, we have Monads that definitely never ever work their essence.

Therefore, this is the reason why not all the persons who listen to these teachings accept it. Nevertheless, it is convenient to know that someone who, for example, in this present existence did not accept the gospel of the new Age of Aquarius, could accept it in subsequent lives, as long as they have not yet reached the 108th life.

Question: Master, do the Monads that are never interested in working their essence belong only to the planet Earth or do they also exist in other planets?

Samael Aun Weor: Young friend, remember the law of philosophical analogies, the law of correspondences, and of numerology: "as above, so below."

Planet Earth is not the only inhabited planet in the starry space. The plurality of inhabited worlds is a tremendous reality. This invites us to comprehend that the Monads from other planets also enjoy complete freedom in order to accept or to reject mastery.

Notwithstanding, the personality is different. Thus, I want to emphatically state the following about it: not all of the existing human personalities who live in other inhabited worlds of the infinite space have fallen as low as we, the inhabitants of the planet Earth.

Friends, in the diverse spheres of the infinite exist marvelous planetary humanities who march in accordance with the great cosmic laws. However, again, I repeat, not all the Monads want mastery.

Infernos exist within all the planets from all the galaxies. Nevertheless, not all the planetary hells are inhabited. For instance: our sun is a marvelous star whose light illuminates all the planets of this solar system of Ors, and it is interesting to know that the infernal worlds of our king star are completely clean. Obviously, in this brilliant sun it is impossible to find cosmic failures; not one of its inhabitants march in submerged devolution. The creatures that live in the king star are completely divine, they are Solar Spirits.

It is convenient to not forget that any cosmic unit that emerges into life inevitably possesses a mineral kingdom that is submerged within its natural infradimensions. Albeit there are worlds whose submerged mineral kingdoms are densely populated; among them is our planet Earth. This indicates or shows us the failure of many Monads.

However, we need to delve a little more into this subject-matter, and understand with complete clarity that the descent of any essence into the horrible abode of Pluto does not always signify a definite failure. It is clear that the final failure is only for the essences, the Monads, that did not achieve inner self-realization through the 3,000 cycles or periods of existences—better said, in the 3000 turns of the wheel of Samsara—since when arriving at the last of these cycles—as I have stated many times—the doors are shut.

Chapter Five

The First Infernal Circle, The Sphere of the Moon

My friends, we are meeting here once again in order to study the first Dantesque circle from the infernal worlds.

It is indubitable that Limbo, the Orcus of the classics, mentioned by Virgil, the poet of Mantua, corresponds to this first submerged region.

We have been told with complete, dazzling clarity that this mineral zone is vividly represented by all of the caverns of the world, which, astrally united, compose the boundaries of the first submerged region.

Dante, the ancient Florentine, states that in such a region he found all of those blameless ones who died without having received the waters of baptism. All of this should be understood in a strictly symbolic manner.

If we carefully study *The Ramayana,* the sacred book of the Hindustanis, we can evidence with mystical astonishment the irrefutable and definitive fact that the sacrament of baptism is much older than the Christian era. In *The Ramayana* we can verify the remarkable case of Rama, who indeed was baptized by his Guru.

Unquestionably, in ancient times, no one received the baptismal water without first having been completely educated about the mysteries of sex, since the sacrament of baptism represents a pact of sexual magic.

It is remarkable that the sacrament of baptism was the first rite that was performed when entering into any school of mysteries.

It is indispensable, urgent, to transmute the pure waters of life into the wine of light of the alchemist. Only thus is possible to achieve the inner self-realization of the Being.

In the Orcus of the classics, in Limbo, we find many righteous people who died without having received the waters of baptism. They were sincere but mistaken people, filled with magnificent but mistaken ideas, people who believed that liberation was possible without the need of sexual magic.

Thus, the cold and sepulchral dead dwell in the first sublunar region, below the epidermis of this planet on which we live.

One feels true sadness, supreme pain, when contemplating so many millions of disembodied people wandering around in the region of the dead with their consciousness asleep.

Behold them there! They look like cold shadows with their consciousness profoundly asleep; they look like specters of the night!

Everywhere, the shadows of the dead come and go within the first Dantesque circle. They occupy themselves in the same activities of the physical life they just had. Thus, they dream within their memories of yesterday. They live totally in the past.

Question: Master, you have explained to us that the souls of those who have not been baptized dwell in the first subterranean sub-lunar region called Limbo. Since we understand that baptism represents a pact of sexual magic, this moves me to ask the following question: do all the beings who have not practiced sexual magic automatically enter into this region when they die?

Samael Aun Weor: Respectable friend, your question is quite intriguing, thus I will answer it immediately.

I want you to comprehend that the first submerged region is like the antechamber of hell. Thus, obviously, within it dwell the shadows of our beloved relatives, along with millions of human beings who never transmuted their seminal waters into the wine of alchemy.

Indeed, the essences, the souls, who—after passing away— gain some vacations within the superior worlds, are really few. It is indubitable that greater numbers of human beings return immediately into a new human organism. However, they spend a period of time within Limbo before re-incorporating themselves once again.

Notwithstanding, due to the critical state in which we actually live, innumerable deceased people are definitely submerged into the infernal worlds in order to pass through the tenebrous spheres of the Moon, Mercury, Venus, the Sun, Mars, Jupiter, Saturn, Uranus, and Neptune.

The last of these regions is definitive, since there the lost ones experience a final disintegration, or the second death that is so indispensable. Thus, thanks to this horrifying annihilation, the essence, the soul, manages to be liberated from those regions of the Tartarus, in order to ascend once again up to the

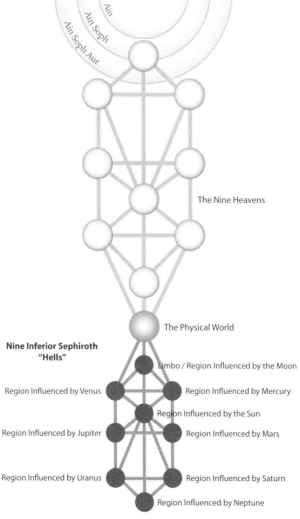

THE INFERNAL CIRCLES ON THE TREE OF LIFE

planetary surface, initiating a new evolution which will inevitably begin from the mineral kingdom.

Question: Venerable Master, the Roman church states in their doctrine that the ones who enter Limbo are the innocent children. How should we understand this?

Samael Aun Weor: Respectable friend, this subject-matter about "innocent children" must be understood in a symbolic and allegorical manner. You must not interpret the word "innocent" in its pristine original form, but as a radical ignorance. Indeed, those who ignore the mysteries of sex are ignorant, even if they boast of being wise, and even if they possess a vast erudition. Remember that many learned ignoramuses exist who not only ignore, but moreover they ignore that they ignore. Understood?

Question: Master, do you mean to state that the person who has not built his solar bodies has not been baptized?

Samael Aun Weor: Respectable young man, I am glad with your question, since this gives me a basis for a beautiful explanation.

The sacred scriptures speak clearly about the wedding garment of the soul, To Soma Heliakon, "the golden body of the solar man," the living representation of the suprasensible bodies that every human creature must elaborate. In our previous publications, we have clearly explained about the work related with the creation of the existential bodies of the Being, and therefore I assume that our Gnostic students can now understand the following.

It is indubitable that the intellectual animal mistakenly called "human being" does not possess the existential bodies of the Being, and therefore he must create them by working in the flaming forge of Vulcan (sex).

In these moments comes into my memory the case of a friend who passed away some years ago. He was a convinced Gnostic, however he did not manage to create his existential bodies of the Being. This I was able to verify within the region of the dead, within Limbo. While being out of my physical body, I found him. He had a gigantic appearance, and his spectral face was indeed a face from a pantheon or cemetery.

I wandered around with him through different places, through diverse streets of a city, which, unquestionably, was in Limbo, beneath this tridimensional region of Euclid.

"You are dead," I told him.

"What? That is impossible! I am alive," was his answer.

When strolling near a regal mansion, I took him inside so that he could see himself in a mirror. When he followed my suggestion, I saw him very much astounded. Then, I continued, telling him, "Try to hover by executing a little jump, thus, in this way, you will be convinced for yourself that you are deceased..."

Thus, that phantom obeyed and tried to fly, but instead of ascending like the birds, I saw him precipitating himself downward, headlong. In those moments, he assumed different animalistic figures. "You now have the shape of a horse, of a dog, of a cat, a tiger," thus, I described to him his different animalistic aspects as they stood out. Indeed, such a phantom was made up of a conjunction of quarrelsome and noisy "I's" that were interpenetrating each other without integration. But my efforts were useless. That deceased person did not understand me. He was already an dweller of the region of the dead, a sum of "I's" personifying psychological defects.

Thus, despite the fact that this friend had known Gnosis, he had not achieved the fabrication of his Astral body. All that I had before my sight was a mass of phantoms, which gave the impression or appearance of a personality. It is obvious that such an individual did not receive the sacrament of baptism. In other words, we must state that he did not transmute the "pure waters of life" into the "wine of light" of the alchemists.

Question: Master, does this mean that those who inhabit the region of the dead or Limbo will always have the opportunity to return into a new womb?

Samael Aun Weor: Respectable friend, do not forget that with his caduceus the God Mercury always takes out the souls that are submerged within the Orcus, with the purpose of reincorporating them into new organisms. Thus, only in this

Sarpedon's body carried by Hypnos and Thanatos (Sleep and Death), while Hermes (mercury) watches.

way is it possible for us, any given day, to be truly baptized. Understood?

Question: Beloved Master, I understand that the essence and the "I's" of the deceased enter into Limbo, but this is not a region of suffering. Am I correct?

Samael Aun Weor: Respectable gentleman, since you speak of the essence and "I's," it is good that we put the cards upon the table once and for all in order to clarify concepts and to define doctrinal positions.

Many believe that the ego, the "I", "the myself," the self-willed, is something very individual. This is how the multiple authors of modern psychology erroneously suppose. We, the Gnostics, go farther. We like to be profound. We like to delve within all of these mysteries, to inquire, to inspect, etc.

The "I" does not possess any individuality whatsoever. The "I" is a sum of psychic aggregates, which personify our psychological defects. The "I" a bunch of errors, passions, hatreds, fears, vendettas, jealousy, anger, lust, resentments, attachments, covetousness, etc.

These diverse aggregates have various animalistic forms within the hypersensible regions of nature. After death, all of this conjunction of quarrelsome and noisy "I's", all of this gamut of varied psychic aggregates, continue beyond the sepulcher. Our psychological essence, the psychic material, is bottled within such negative values. It is therefore clear that such psychic material—inserted within the ego—submerges itself into the Orcus, into Limbo, in order to return a little later into this physical world.

Question: Master, for an incognizant, common, and ordinary person, would Limbo be a continuation of his life?

Samael Aun Weor: Young friend that asked, I consider that your question is a little wrongly structured; it is necessary to structure it in a better manner in order to clarify.

Listen: there is no tomorrow for the personality of the dead, since every personality is a child of its time, is born in its time, and dies in its time. That which continues beyond the sepulcher is the ego, a sum of diverse, animalistic, and brutal psychic aggregates.

When in my former narration I contemplated my friend, with pain I understood that his physical personality had been annihilated; thus, all that which I had before my sight was a sum of grotesque animalistic figures, which were interpenetrating one another, giving the false appearance of a sepulchral, cold, and spectral personality.

What had become of my friend? Where was he? Since he had not built the Astral body, it is obvious that he had ceased to exist. If my friend had fabricated an Astral body by means of sexual transmutation, if he had really practiced sexual magic, it is clear that he would have fabricated the sidereal vehicle, thus he would then have been able to continue with his Astral personality within the hypersensible regions of nature. Regrettably, this had not been the case.

To be baptized, then, implies having practiced sexual magic. Thus, whosoever has not proceeded in this manner has not received the sacramental waters. Conclusion: he is an inhabitant of Limbo.

Question: Master, could this false personality formed by those grotesque "I's—which was once your friend—become your enemy in that region without a future?

THE BAPTISM OF CHRIST, BY ANNIBALE CARRACCI.
S. GREGORIO, BOLOGNA, ITALY

Samael Aun Weor: Young friend, it is urgent for you to comprehend that the ego is constituted by many "I"s and that some can be our friends or our enemies. Indubitably, some of those "I's" of the phantom to whom I have referred continue being my friends; yet others, obviously, can be enemies or simply grotesque, indifferent phantoms. Whatever the case, it is the ego that returns from the region of Limbo into this physical world in order to repeat all the painful dramas of his past existences.

The personality, as I already stated, is perishable. It does not ever return. This is something that you must clearly comprehend. Know how to differentiate between the ego and the personality. Understood?

Question: Master, should I understand that the true sacrament of baptism can only be received by the one who becomes initiated on the path of the razor's edge?

Samael Aun Weor: Respectable sir, the authentic sacrament of baptism, as I already stated in this lecture, is a pact of sexual magic. Regrettably, people undergo the baptismal ceremony, they go through the rite, but they never fulfill the pact; thus, this is why they enter into Limbo. If people were to fulfill that religious pact, they would then enter completely into the path of the razor's edge, that path cited by Christ when he said:

> *Because strait is the gate, and narrow is the way, which leadeth unto life, and few there be that find it.* - Matthew 7:14

Thus, it is indispensable to know that the secret path which leads the souls to the final liberation is absolutely sexual.

Question: Master, this means that only the deceased who have begun to practice sexual magic are the ones who have the right to some vacations?

Samael Aun Weor: Respectable lady who asks the question, I invite you to comprehend that the ego can never enter into the heavenly regions. The only thing the psychic aggregates can expect is the abyss and the second death, understood?

Nevertheless, let us delve deeper in order to elucidate and clarify this lecture. When the ego is not too strong, when the psychic aggregates are very weak, then the pure essence, the soul, manages to free itself for some time in order to enter the heavenly regions and thus enjoy some vacations before returning into this valley of tears. Regrettably, in this day and age, the animal ego has become very strong in many people, thus for such a reason now the human souls no longer have the happiness of such vacations. Indeed, in this day and age, the souls who succeed in entering into the Causal world or the Devachan —as the Theosophists state—are very rare.

So, I want all of you to comprehend the concrete fact that the souls—which, by the way, are very rare nowadays—that (between death and a new physical birth) can enjoy for a certain time some happy "vacations" are those who we can call in this world "very good people." Thus, because of this, the Great Law rewards them after their physical death. Understood?

Question: Master, those souls who managed to escape from within their ego in order to enjoy some vacations, when they re-enter into a new womb, do they have to become bottled into their ego again?

Samael Aun Weor: Friends, listen. The ego can only be destroyed, annihilated, in two manners. Firstly, by means of a conscious work on ourselves and within ourselves, here and now. Secondly, by undergoing horrible sufferings through the submerged devolution within the infernal worlds.

Unquestionably, heavenly vacations do not dissolve the ego. Thus, once the essence, the soul, exhausts the fruits of his reward, it will have to remain bottled up within its ego, its "I"s, "the myself," and like that it returns into this valley of tears.

Question: Master, when after its vacations the essence once again bottled into the ego returns into a new womb, does not it bring the longing for liberation in order to achieve its self-realization?

Samael Aun Weor: Respectable lady, your question is magnificent. I want to emphatically tell you the following: the ascension into the superior worlds comforts and helps us. When the essence returns from some vacation in the superior worlds of cosmic consciousness, it returns fortified and with great enthusiasm. Then it fights inexhaustibly in order to attain its total liberation. However, any effort will be useless if it were not to fulfill the pact of sexual magic contained in the sacrament of baptism.

Question: Master, can you tell us how the regions of the first Dantesque circle or circle of the Moon are, how life is, and what they do there?

Samael Aun Weor: I will quickly answer the gentleman who asked the question. When seen internally, the first Dantesque sub-lunar circle, represented by all the caverns of the Earth, is very interesting. There we find the first submerged counterpart of our physical cities, streets, villages, counties, and regions. It is not strange therefore that a life similar to the physical one that we lived is experienced. In no way should we be astonished by the fact that the deceased visit the houses where they lived, or that they wander around through the same places that they frequented before, and occupy themselves in the same chores or jobs that they used to perform.

I remember the pathetic case of a wretched carrier of heavy bundles. After his death, his ego continues carrying around a load, package, or bundle on his back. When I tried to make him comprehend his situation, when I tried to make him understand that he was already physically dead and therefore he had no reason to continue carrying around heavy bundles on his body, he looked at me with the eyes of a somnambulist, since his consciousness was asleep. Thus, he was incapable of comprehending me.

So, deceased people continue selling in their stores, or buying merchandise, or driving cars, etc. Every deceased one is occupied in those tasks in which they were occupied in life. It is very astonishing to see those bars filled with deceased drunkards, or prostitutes after death still fornicating within those houses of prostitution, etc.

Question: Master, what is the process the souls who inhabit Limbo have to follow in order to return into this tridimensional world?

Samael Aun Weor: The souls who dwell within Limbo must recapitulate the life they just went through; they have to slowly re-live it. Once such a retrospective process is concluded, all the actions of our previous life are simply reduced to mathematics. Then, the judges of Karma make us return into this valley of tears with the purpose of making amends for our errors, as well as for us to search for the path that will lead us to the final liberation. That is all.

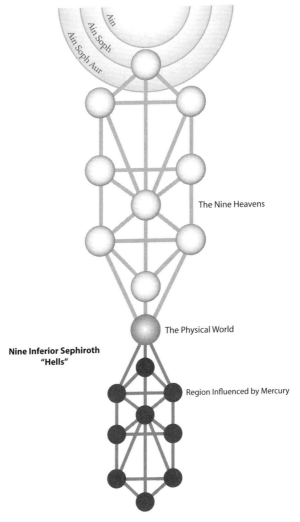

The Nine Heavens

The Physical World

Nine Inferior Sephiroth
"Hells"

Region Influenced by Mercury

THE SECOND INFERNAL CIRCLE, THE SPHERE
OF MERCURY, ON THE TREE OF LIFE

Chapter Six

The Second Infernal Circle,
The Sphere of Mercury

My friends, let us now carefully study the second Dantesque circle. I am emphatically referring to that negative aspect—or better said, that submerged aspect—of the planet Mercury. We are not going to speak about the heaven of Mercury. I repeat: it is indispensable that we investigate a little the submerged aspect, which relates strictly to the antithesis of that brilliant heaven.

When we penetrate with the astral body into the interior of the Earth, we can perfectly and straightforwardly verify for ourselves what the hell of Mercury is. When we penetrate into this submerged region, we feel in the depth of our soul the perpetual turbulence of those negative passionate forces that stormily flow and re-flow in that subterranean zone. It is not irrelevant to state that there we feel the stormy winds of Mercury, a certain aerial element. This subterranean zone is the place where the fornicators breathe. Fornicators are those who enjoy extracting the sacred sperm from their organism.

These miserable creatures from the underworld—sunk in the carnal vice—desperately come and go, here, there, and everywhere. One is astounded when seeing these lost ones incessantly cohabiting within the atomic infernos of nature. Such egos blaspheme incessantly and hate to death anything with the flavor of chastity.

There we find Semiramis, the terrible fornicator empress, who by promulgated decree made the enjoyment of animal passions lawful in her country. In that abode of Pluto we also find Queen Dido, who in amorous fury slew herself after breaking her vow of fidelity to Sicheus' ashes. There we also find Paris of ancient Troy, who kidnapped beautiful Helen, and Achilles, the impetuous warrior, destroyer of citadels.

Tartarus of misfortunes, abysses of iniquity, fright, horrors!

In the second Dantesque circle we also find with profound grief the fallen Bodhisattvas, those who murdered the God Mercury, unhappy souls who exchanged their birthrights for a pottage of lentils. What grief we feel in the depth of our consciousness when discovering within those Mercurial abysses the fallen angels, cited by ancient religious theogonies! So, those who exchanged their scepter of power for the distaff of Omphale, come and go through the black air within that submerged region, a region where human understanding is turned away by lust, a world of brutal instincts, where lasciviousness mires with the impetus of violence.

Behold the frightening profundities of the mysteries of Minos or Mina, where the black tantric ones who developed the abominable Kundabuffer organ (the cause of so much wickedness) breathe. Alas! how different the future of this wretched suffering humanity would have been if the glorious Archangel Sakaki with his sacred commission could had foreseen with mathematical exactitude the fatal outcome of

MINOS AND HIS TAIL, THE KUNDABUFFER

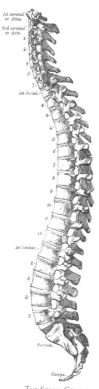

THE SPINAL COLUMN

that satanic tail, of that organ of abominations, whose development was allowed with definite planetary purposes in times of yore in this humanity.

It is clear that each human being is a creature that captures distinct cosmic forces in order to transform them and thereafter transmit them into the interior layers of the Earth. In view of the fact that some 18 million years ago the Earth trembled incessantly since its volcanoes on the Lemurian continent were erupting fire and lava, the development of the abominable Kundabuffer organ (a terribly negative, Luciferic force, projected from the coccyx downwards towards the atomic infernos of the human being) was allowed by certain sacred individuals led by the Archangel Sakaki. It is not irrelevant to remember that such a negative fohat grew covered by a physical tail, similar to the tail we see in apes. Hence, the dwellers of the Earth carried on their common presences such an appendage or projection of their spinal column. Thus, the forces that in that epoch passed through the human organisms, suffered, as a result, categorical modifications that permitted the stabilization of the terrestrial crust.

In later periods during the history of the centuries, when other sacred individuals considered that there was no longer any need for the abominable Kundabuffer organ (Satan's tail) to continue to exist, they eliminated that appendage from the human body. Unfortunately, the awful consequences of that organ of witches' Sabbaths remained in the five cylinders of the organic machine, known as intellect, emotion, movement, instinct, and sex. By profoundly delving into this subject-matter, we can discover for ourselves that such tenebrous consequences are perfectly defined as psychic aggregates or quarrelsome and noisy "I's" that personify our errors and constituting the ego, the myself, the self-willed.

So, within the submerged sphere of Mercury live millions of humans creatures with the abominable Kundabuffer organ completely developed.

I am not affirming in the former paragraph that the physical tail of apes is found presently developed in the physical anatomy of those three-brained or three-centered bipeds. Yet, indeed at the base of their spine in their human physical anatomy exists a very incipient osseous residue of that abominable tail. Nevertheless, the psychic aspect of such an organ is found in the metaphysical presence of millions of rational humanoids. This we have evidenced in a clear manner when (dressed in our Astral body) penetrating into the submerged realms of the Mercurial type, beneath the epidermis of the planet Earth.

Question: Beloved Master, I would like to know if the personages and acts that appear in your exposition when describing the second Dantesque circle are real or simply mythological, since although Dante also mentions them, we understand that Dante's work is simply a literary work of great merit.

Samael Aun Weor: Noble gentleman, respectable ladies, allow me to solemnly affirm that *The Divine Comedy* of Dante Alighieri is an initiatic and esoteric text that very few human beings have understood. The mythological personages cited in that text and that appear as the dwellers of the submerged sphere of Mercury, symbolically represent the living animal passions in such a region. The impetuous Achilles with his terrible sexual licentiousness, the adulterous Helen, and the ever libidinous Paris, clearly personify the inhabitants of the tenebrous zone of Mercury. However, I want just to mention one of these personages in particular, who is Helen kidnapped by Paris. Helen, the cause of so many maladies in ancient times, has other positive symbolisms, which are more beautiful. Yet, I do not want to talk about her positive symbols in these moments. Right now, let us look at Helen only in her abysmal aspect, the antithesis of her resplendent aspect, that is, her tenebrous Mercurial phase.

Ladies and gentlemen, remember that each symbol can be interpreted in seven different manners. Tonight we are only studying this very particular abyss of Mercurial type, which is beneath the epidermis of the planet on which we live.

Question: Master, can you tell me if this Mercurial circle is of a denser degree and if souls undergo a greater suffering than in the first circle?

Samael Aun Weor: Friend, in regard to your question, remember what we have already stated in past lectures when we studied the Ray of Creation. It is evident that the greater the number of laws, the greater the degree of mechanicity and pain. The submerged sphere of the Moon is governed exclusively by 96 laws. However, the tenebrous aspect of Mercury within the planetary mass on which we live is constituted by 192 laws, thus its mechanicity is even greater, and therefore undergoing suffering is much more intense. Besides, the atoms of this tenebrous Mercurial sphere are much heavier, since every atom contains within their interior 192 atoms of the Absolute. This means that the tenebrous Mercurial region is even denser than the lunar one.

Question: Master, do the souls that enter into this submerged zone of Mercury have any possibility to resurface?

Samael Aun Weor: Dear lady, honorable gentlemen, do not forget that justice is always beside mercy. Know that some Masters of the great White Lodge, great initiates, divine beings who have chosen renunciation to all bliss in order to help the lost ones, dwell within these tenebrous abysmal regions. Thus, when some soul repents within the abode of Pluto, undoubtedly it is always assisted by these saints. Unquestionably, such beings instruct, admonish, and show the path of light to all of those souls who indeed have repented of their perversities. When this happens, those who were condemned to perdition, return, reenter a womb; that is, they reincorporate into a new organism.

Question: Master why do you emphasize that the dead belong to the first submerged lunar region and nonetheless, when addressing the second, that is, the submerged zone of Mercury you do not affirm likewise?

Samael Aun Weor: Okay sir, listen to me: you must carefully scrutinize *The Divine Comedy* of Dante. Investigate, experience, and verify for yourself. Learn how to consciously and positively move in your Astral body.

Obviously, the Orcus of the classics, the Limbo of the Christians, is only the antechamber of hell, even though it corresponds to the first Dantesque circle. Every initiate knows that after death millions of us human beings live in that region.

The encounter with Minos, the demon who with his tail considers what circle in hell the defunct most go according as how oft his tail encircles him around, can only be found in the submerged sphere of Mercury. I am not stating this on my own whim. I repeat: any one who in a direct manner wants to investigate by themselves will corroborate my affirmations.

Question: Master, I do not understand what you have just stated. Why is it that the fornicator "I's," which also constitute part of "the myself" or the "self-willed" live in the underworld of Mercury, whilst in the first Dantesque circle occurs likewise?

Samael Aun Weor: Okay sir, undoubtedly almost all of the three-brained or three-centered bipeds, mistakenly called humans, are deep down, more or less fornicators. Nonetheless, as I have stated in former lectures, the Great Law assigns to each soul 108 existences in every cycle of cosmic manifestation. It is evident, clear, and manifest that no one can be cast into the abysses of perdition without having completed their cycle of existences. Normally, the dead reside in Limbo, which physically is represented by all of the caverns of the world. However, only those fornicators who have already exhausted their cycle of 108 humanoid existences are the ones who definitely enter into the submerged negative region of Mercury.

Nevertheless, please, I beg you, comprehend the following: sometimes there exist on the Earth true monstrous humanoids who no longer offer any possibility of redemption. These are cases that are definitely lost. Thus, after death, unquestionably they enter into the infernal worlds, even when they have not exhausted their complete cycle of 108 existences.

Question: Master, we know that the sphere of Mercury relates to fornicators. Does this signify that the "I"s are divided among the different Dantesque circles in accordance with the different types of psychic aggregates?

Samael Aun Weor: Regarding the question of this young man, it is clear that the ego is a sum of diverse psychic aggregates that personify errors. Some of them specifically correspond to certain Dantesque circles, and others are found intimately related with more submerged circles. However, the totality, the sum of all these negative values, precipitately devolves in their conjunction within the mineral kingdom, towards the center of planetary gravity. Understand that the consciousness of the condemned must experience each descending circle, each infradimension of nature beneath the tridimensional region of Euclid, through its corresponding psychological defects. Yet, tonight we are talking exclusively about the second circle. Regardless, soon after having reviewed the nine Dantesque circles we will study in detail the law of perpetual movement. Then all of you ladies and gentlemen will be able to delve a little more into this subject-matter related with the question that this young man asked today.

Question: Master, was it intended to state that in this circle that corresponds to lust, fornication has become terribly mechanical and therefore painful and disgusting?

Samael Aun Weor: Well, my friend, listen: within that black and fatal air, lust tends to mingle with violence, thus everything is instinctive and brutal. Understood?

Question: Venerable Master, what astounds me tremendously is that in spite of the tortures that are suffered in this circle, the souls who dwell there think that they go very well. Would you be so kind as to explain this subject-matter to us?

Samael Aun Weor: Noble sir, the people from the abyss always think the best of themselves. They firmly believe that they march on the path of righteousness and love, and consider us—the ones who walk on the path of the revolution of consciousness—as those who march, they say, "towards our own destruction." Likewise, I want all of you to know that the tenebrous ones—moved by good intentions—tempt us incessantly, with the purpose of, as they say, "saving" us. So, in these abysmal regions we see many anchorites, penitents, fakirs, mystics, monks, etc., admonishing diverse human groups, since they are totally convinced that they are doing very well.

Question: Master, do these souls who are so convinced that they are doing very well know that they are in hell?

Samael Aun Weor: Respectable lady, in regard to your question, know that the word inferno is derived from the Latin infernus, which signifies inferior region found within the interior of the Earth, where we also find the world of natural elements. Thus, it is unquestionable that the lost ones never consider those elements or such submerged regions as a place of perdition.

Normal, ordinary, and common people have their consciousness asleep; nonetheless, those who enter the abysmal regions awaken in evil and for evil. Such people develop a very special psychological idiosyncrasy, a different fatal type of logic. Thus, do not be surprised, do not all be astounded to know that for the abysmal lost ones, white is black and vice-versa. For example, to name Jesus the great Kabir or the Divine Mother Kundalini in those submerged regions is a blasphemy, something unforgivable to such condemned people, and consequently to name them is equivalent to provoking their anger. Then we will see them attacking us furiously.

Moreover, the lost ones do not ignore the concrete fact that they have to pass through the second death, however they are not afraid of it. Instead, they beseech for it, they ask for it, for they know that the second death is the doorway of escape in order for them to return to the surface of the Earth and thus re-initiate a new evolving ascension that begins in the stone and ends in man. Understood?

Question: Master, a person like me, who observes an absolute sexual abstention, would I perhaps be free from entering into the second Dantesque circle?

Samael Aun Weor: Friends, brothers and sisters, it is indispensable, it is urgent and unpostponable to know that lust processes itself within the 49 regions of the subconsciousness. Many saints who reached supreme chastity in the merely intellective level failed when they were submitted to sexual ordeals within the more profound regions of their subconsciousness. For example, someone could have achieved chastity in 48 subconscious regions and nonetheless to fail in the 49th. Many men and virtuous women who self-qualified themselves as being chaste and innocent are now inhabitants of the second Dantesque circle. Millions of religious people, priests from all beliefs, who thought that they had attained the most absolute chastity, live now in the inferno of Mercury. Therefore, let us none of us qualify ourselves as being chaste. "Whosoever feels sure of himself, let him look behind and not fall."

Question: Master, you have mentioned 49 regions in the subconsciousness, and frankly let me tell you that it is the first time that I have heard about the subconsciousness having such a number of regions. All the treatises of psychology, parapsychology, and psychoanalysis where the processes of the consciousness, subconsciousness, and infraconsciousness, etc. are mentioned and studied do not mention these 49 divisions or regions that you mention. Why is this so?

Samael Aun Weor: Respectable gentlemen and ladies who listen to me, it is convenient for us to remember the septenary constitution of the authentic human being. Nonetheless, the three-brained or three-centered bipeds mistakenly called human beings only possess subconscious and subjective states, since they have not awakened their consciousness yet, and since they have not created the existential bodies of the Being. So, multiply the septuple aspect by itself and you will have the 49 subconscious regions of every humanoid. Obviously, when we awaken the consciousness, these 49 subconscious and subjective states become cognizant. Thus, only then, will we have objectivity, an integral cognizance.

We need to transform the subconsciousness into consciousness. This is only possible by disintegrating the psychic aggregates that constitute the ego, the myself, the self-willed. Let us remember that the consciousness is bottled up within such aggregates. Thus, when these aggregates are disintegrated, the consciousness awakens as an outcome.

Lust, fornication in the submerged circle of Mercury underneath the terrestrial crust, is indeed the very foundation, the basis of the existential ego.

Question: Master, in some of your books you explain that in order to be able to awaken the consciousness, the "I" or psychological defect that was chosen for elimination has to be first dissected with the intellect, and that this procedure must be done in the 49 departments of the subconsciousness. But how can we penetrate with the intellect into these 49 regions, if we do not have our consciousness awakened yet? Would you be so kind to explain this to us?

Samael Aun Weor: Friends, to be able to radically disintegrate the ego in an instantaneous manner and simultaneously within all the 49 regions the subconsciousness is not possible. Thus, I invite you to reflect and to investigate this subject-matter clearly and perfectly.

When we want to annihilate any psychological defect, i.e. lust or any other defect, we must first of all to comprehend it. However, understand: the unitotal comprehension of the defect in question cannot be an immediate act within the 49 subconscious regions. This comprehension means a progressive advancement on the path of understanding. So, gradually we must advance, comprehending and eliminating the "I"s of the defect in question, in each of the subconscious regions. This will mark a methodical, profound, and orderly development of the consciousness. As the consciousness awakens, comprehension becomes clearer and clearer until it reaches its final 49th stage. There, the defect is radically annihilated.

Chapter Seven

The Third Infernal Circle, The Sphere of Venus

Friends listening to me on this night, we are going to talk about the Venusian infernos, which are located, as is already known, within the infradimensions of nature, beneath the epidermis of the Earth. Unquestionably, this Venusian region is much denser, much grosser than the former two regions, since every atom of its matter contains within its interior 288 atoms of the Absolute. Obviously, these are much heavier atoms, and therefore the materiality is much greater. Moreover, the very fact that this sphere is governed by 288 laws makes this subterranean zone very complicated, frighteningly difficult, and painful.

Yet, now let us carefully observe the taverns, cabarets, brothels, etc., from our tridimensional world of Euclid. Unquestionably, the vital shadow of all of this—that is, the sinister aspect of great orgies and bacchanalia—can be found in the submerged sphere of Venus. Those who always live from orgy to orgy, from tavern to tavern, submerged within the mud of great feasts, banquets, and drunkenness, know very well the effects following a night of grogginess. Thus, after boozing, many of them, wanting to drown with wine the disastrous characteristics of their hangover, continue on the path of vice until arriving at the total devastation of their organism.

Thus, by expanding this subject-matter, by delving a little more within this theme, I can emphatically affirm to you that this is how pain comes after pleasure. Now you can explain to yourselves how life will be or how existence will be for the lost souls within the submerged region of Venus. No wonder Dante found incessant rain, frightful cold, mud, sewage, rottenness, etc. within the submerged abysses of the third infernal circle. Equally, the frightful wide triple-throated barks of Cerberus, the infernal dog, are heard with revulsion by the defunct in those regions. This symbolic three-headed, cruel, monster dog

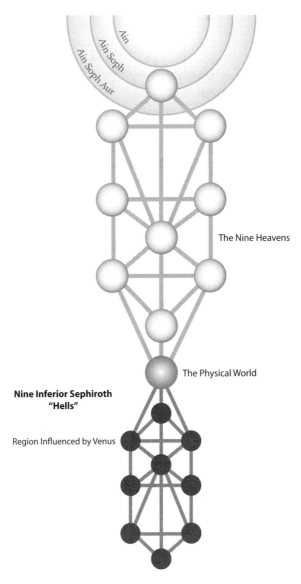

Ain

Ain Soph

Ain Soph Aur

The Nine Heavens

The Physical World

**Nine Inferior Sephiroth
"Hells"**

Region Influenced by Venus

THE THIRD INFERNAL CIRCLE, THE SPHERE
OF VENUS, ON THE TREE OF LIFE

represents the luciferic, violent, animal passions, completely out of control.

Behold there the leisure of the ancient Rome of the Caesars transformed into fatal consequences. Behold there Petronius who faced death as a last pleasure in the midst of a rowdy party, loved by all the women and crowned with roses and laurels. Behold also there the Goddess Lesbos amidst her lesbians; among them is found the poetess Sappho, who poetically sang of the infatuations of all the degenerated people of her epoch. There also is found the lyre of Nero broken into pieces, and the arrogant lords of great feasts, grotesque dwelling of the men of Heliogabalus, famous gluttons, true peacocks who gloriously shone at ancient jamborees. What happened to their goblets of fine baccarat?

Alas! What was the end of the swords of those gentlemen along with their oaths of love, the kisses of their lady, their sweet words, the applause of guests, the compliments, the praises, the regal dresses, the perfumes of the ladies, the pompous dances, the soft carpets, the brilliant mirrors, the regal poems, the damned purple, and exquisite silks? Now only the pestilence of the underworld, where Ciacco prophesied to Dante the fall of the victorious party in the beautiful Florence and the rise of the oppressed, which afterwards, newly defeated, were dominated in an even more tyrannical manner by the same party.

In this abominable zone of bitterness that poet, disciple of Virgil, unexpectedly asked for "Farinata and Tegghiaio, they who were so worthy of Giacopo Rusticcuci, Arrigo and Mosca, and others who bent their minds on working good" and who now dwell in even more profound regions within the infernal worlds.

Many sincere but mistaken people who terrifyingly devolve within these abysmal regions were people who livened with their lyre the fastuous rooms of great lords. Likewise, beautiful virtuous maidens that sang poems and unhappy wine drinkers from the suburbs of many cities, etc. now live within these infernos of the third Dantesque circle.

Question: Beloved Master, you mentioned that in this third Dantesque circle of Venus dwell many sincere but mistaken people, in other words, many souls that undoubtedly performed good deeds and nonetheless regardless, they suffer in those infernos. So, I ask, why is it that the sincerity of those souls does not constitute an extenuating element that saves them from such tenebrous punishment?

Samael Aun Weor: Friend, regarding your question, we are sure that if in life we practice a lot of good, such good deeds will always be paid back with increases. The divine never fails in rewarding good deeds. It always pays back every person according to their deeds.

Regardless, I beg you to patiently pay attention in order to understand the course of this lecture. So pay attention, listen to me: whosoever has exhausted his cycle of 108 existences and has not achieved the inner realization of his Being enters into the submerged devolution within the infernal worlds. However, it is clear that first we are paid for our good deeds before entering into the abode of Pluto.

Now you will comprehend, ladies and gentlemen, the reason why many perverse people in their present life live in opulence, while some saints or people who are working on their self-realization scarcely have food, clothing, and shelter.

Thus, it is unquestionable that after the good deeds have been well paid, those who are without self-realization enter into the subterranean abysses.

Likewise, there are pious people with secret unspeakable transgressions; nonetheless that which they have of good will always well paid by the law of Karma, yet regrettably their secret unspeakable transgressions take them into the abyss of perdition.

So, then my friend, understand what the law of retribution is. So, all of you comprehend, please comprehend.

Question: Venerable Master, I want you to be so kind to explain to me why the fornicators inhabit the region of Mercury, whereas the gluttons and drunkards inhabit the region of Venus, which is even denser than the region of Mercury, since this is a zone less dense than the zone of Venus.

Samael Aun Weor: Ladies and gentlemen, respectable sir who asks the question, please comprehend me.

We have been emphatically told that the original sin is fornication, thus fornication is the foundation of devolving waves within the infernal worlds. I am not stating that drunkards and gluttons breathe exclusively within the third infernal circle; it is obvious that the lost ones are 100 percent unredeemed fornicators. Now you will comprehend for yourselves why Dante found the dog Cerberus, living symbol of the sexual forces, barking lugubriously within the tenebrous regions. This clearly means that the inhabitants of the submerged regions are never free from lust, thus they suffer frightfully. However, we must specify, and this is what Dante, the disciple of Virgil, does, thus we must do the same. Listen: certain defects that we carry within stand out within each of the nine circles or infradimensional regions of nature, and that is all.

Question: Master, we have learned when studying the Egyptian Tarot cards that the dog symbolizes the Holy Spirit, since the dog guides us so that we can go out from within the infernos when we have decided to self-realize ourselves. Nevertheless,

the Cerberus of which Dante talks, and based on what you have just said, symbolizes lust. Would you be so kind to clarify your dissertation?

Samael Aun Weor: Gentleman, allow me to inform you that the dog of Mercury is strictly symbolic, since this clearly allegorizes the sexual potency. Hercules took this dog out of the abyss so that it would serve him as a guide, and

TWILIGHT

The Arcanum 18 of the Tarot

HERCULES CONVERTS CERBERUS INTO HIS GUIDE. GREEK.

we do likewise when we achieve chastity. That is, by working in the forge of Cyclops, by practicing sexual magic, by transmuting our creating energies, we advance on the path of the razor's edge until achieving the final liberation.

Woe to the gentleman who abandons his dog! He will be mislead from the path and will fall into the abyss of perdition.

Regrettably, the intellectual animal mistakenly called human has not achieved chastity; in other words, the intellectual animal has not taken Cerberus out of the infernal domains. Now you will comprehend for yourselves the reason why the defunct suffer within the Plutonian abysses when they hear the frightful barks of Cerberus, the dog with the ravenous, wide, threefold throat. It is obvious that the lost ones suffer the insatiable thirst of lust within the frightful Tartarus.

Question: Master, could you tell us about the bacchanalian feasts and orgies of the third Dantesque circle or submerged regions of Venus?

Samael Aun Weor: Ladies and gentlemen, this question brings into my memory the times of my youth, so listen to me. In my youth, I (as a fallen bodhisattva) also participated in great feasts where nights of sprees that shone amidst the pandemonium of orgies only left bitterness and remorse within my conscience. Thus, one night, after one of those parties, I—dressed in my astral body and absolutely conscious—was taken into the third Dantesque circle. There, I sat at the head of a fatal table with a party of demons.

This was the crude reality of a terrifying materialism, whose mere remembrance shivers the innermost parts of my soul.

The table of the feast was covered of bottles of liquor and filthy food, very especially for gluttons; in the center of the table was a great tray, upon which the head of a pig stood out.

Horrified by the macabre horrifying feast, I was looking with pain at the place of the orgy, when unexpectedly, everything changed; my divine Real Being, my Innermost—that Angel of the Apocalypse of St. John, who has the key of the bottomless pit in his hands—forcefully as if by magic laid hold of me by one of my arms, and snatched me out of that room. He then threw me upon a white mortuary sheet on that muddy, loathsome floor; there, he flogged me with a great chain while saying, "You are my Bodhisattva, my human soul, and I need you in order to deliver the message of the new age of Aquarius to humanity; are you going to serve me or not?"

Then I, with a lot of remorse in my heart, answered, "Yes, my Lord, I will serve you, I repent, forgive me."

Thus, my friends, this is how I came to abhor all that filth that is liquors, feasts, gluttony, drunkenness, etc., since the only thing that comes from all that filth are tears, which are symbolized by the rain. Those pestilent waters of bitterness and horrible mud of misery shone within that horrible region.

Chapter Eight

The Fourth Infernal Circle, the Sphere of the Sun

Respectable friends, on this night we are going to study with cognizance the fourth Dantesque circle, located within the natural infradimensions, underneath this tridimensional region of Euclid.

Yet first, we who have passed through the diverse esoteric transcendental processes within the superior dimensions have been able to directly verify the crude reality of the submerged mineral kingdom of the Sun for ourselves. Thus, unquestionably, we do not see the grotesque Dantesque spectacles of the terrestrial infernos within the solar infernos of the resplendent star that gives life to our entire solar system of Ors, since it is obvious that the most perfect mineral purity exists within the submerged solar mineral kingdom. So, it is indubitable that only the solar spirits happily dwell within that radiant star, which is the very heart of this great solar system in which we live, move, and have our Being. Then, given that in the Sun only exist sacred and eternal individuals, it is not possible to think of evident and definitive failures like those within our terrestrial world. The concrete fact is therefore evident, that tenebrous dwellers do not exist within the natural infradimensions of the solar world.

On the other hand, the infradimensions of our planet Earth are indeed a very different case for any esoteric investigator, since the devolving states of the fourth circle underneath the geologic crust of our planet Earth are strikingly clear and manifest.

Now, in accordance with the eternal, common, cosmic Trogoautoegocrat Law, the Sun is the source of all life and the marvelous agent that sustains any existence; thus, obviously, we come to find as a tangible fact the fatal and negative antithesis of this cosmic law within the antithetical solar aspect of the fourth submerged terrestrial zone.

JUSTICE

The cosmic scale in the Arcanum 8 [∞] of the Tarot.

So, within that tenebrous region, within those atomic infernos of nature, we find two specific types of devolving people. I am emphatically addressing the squanderers and hoarders. These are two types of individuals who on either side can never be conciliated, since they again and again attack each other incessantly.

By analyzing this subject-matter in depth, we must solemnly affirm that squandering is as absurd as cupidity. Thus, regarding the scales within the merely common, cosmic Trogoautoegocrat process, we must always remain in equilibrium. It is clear that the violation of the law of equilibrium brings about painful karmic consequences, since in the area of practical life we can consciously verify the disastrous consequences that come from the violation of the law of the scales. It is indubitable that the prodigal people, the squanderers who misuse their money, violate the law even when within their very depth they might feel very generous. The avaricious people, who do not circulate their money, those who egotistically retain their money in an improper manner beyond the norm, are indeed harming the collective, they are snatching bread from many people, they are impoverishing their fellowmen. Thus, for that reason, they are violating the law of equilibrium, the law of the scales. Even when the squanderers are apparently doing good by making money circulate intensely, it is logical that they are producing imbalance not only within themselves but also within the general movement of values; so, their squandering eventually causes tremendous economic harm to people.

Therefore, prodigal and avaricious people become beggars; this has been proven. Thus, it is indispensable, it is urgent, to cooperate with the eternal, common, cosmic Trogoautoegocrat law, in order to not alter the economic equilibrium, in order to not harm oneself, and in order to not harm the neighbor.

Now, since many people ignore what the eternal, common, cosmic Trogoautoegocrat law connotes, it is convenient to clarify its means. This great law manifests its means through the reciprocal nourishment of all organisms.

Thus, if we carefully observe the entrails of the Earth, we will find copper as the center of gravity for all the evolving and devolving processes in nature. If we apply a merely positive force to that metal, we will then see by means of objective clairvoyance extraordinary evolving developments. Yet, if we apply the negative force, we can then directly evidence the devolving descending forces within all of the atoms of that metal. Moreover, if we apply the neutral force, we will then see processes of atomic stabilization within that metal. So, for the esotericist investigators it is very intriguing to contemplate the metallic radiations of copper within the living entrails of our planetary organism. One is astounded when seeing how the emanations of that metal animate other metals, while in turn as a reward it receives nourishment through the emanations of those other metals. There is therefore an exchange of radiations among the different metals within the interior of the Earth. This is the reciprocal nourishment among the metals.

Even so, what is most astounding is the interchange of radiations between the metals that exist within the interior of our planet Earth and those metal radiations that exist within the submerged mineral kingdom of other planets of our solar system. Lo and behold the eternal, common, cosmic Trogoautoegocrat law in complete manifestation. So, the eternal, common, cosmic Trogoautoegocrat law allows the coexistence among the planets. This reciprocating nourishment among planets, this exchange of planetary substances, originates the equilibrium of the planets around their gravitational centers.

Likewise, we must affirm the following: there also exists reciprocal nourishment among minerals, among plants, among all types of organisms, etc. Moreover, the economic and human processes, the fluctuations of currency, the financial earnings and expenditures, the interchange of merchandise and currencies, the particular economy of each one of us, what one earns and spends, etc., also belong to the great eternal, common, cosmic Trogoautoegocrat law.

Again, we repeat, it is clear and evident that the radiant star that illuminates us in our solar system is in fact the administrator of this supreme, eternal, common, cosmic Trogoautoegocrat law. Thus, the function of that law would be impossible if all equilibrium is violated.

Now we can clearly explain to ourselves the fundamental reason by which prodigal and avaricious people alter the scales of payments, and cause therefore unfortunate consequences within the cosmic and human equilibrium. Therefore, whosoever violates the law in some way must receive their punishment. It is not strange then to find in the solar antithesis, which is the fourth Dantesque circle, the squanderers and the hoarders.

Question: Master, you have given us a truly transcendental explanation about the fourth Dantesque circle; you told us that within it dwell the squanderers as well as the hoarders. Would you be so kind to explain to us what type of sufferings the beings that dwell there undergo?

Samael Aun Weor: My friend, this is an interesting question that motivates me to an immediate answer, listen.

Since only consequences are what we see within the submerged worlds, I invite you to reflect; thus ask yourself, what is avarice, in which way is a hoarder similar to a beggar, what kind of life does a hoarder have, what kind of illnesses, what kind of sufferings, in which way do they die?

Conversely, let us go to the opposite. Let us think for a moment of a person who has squandered all of his fortune; how does he end up? What fate will his children have? What fate will his family have, in general, etc.? There were many cases of suicide in the Monte Carlo casino. Gamblers, who ended up in misery, who lost their millions, end up committing suicide from one day to the next.

What could we say now about these two types of people? Friends, only their catastrophic, terrible, and frightening consequences are what exist within the infernal worlds.

Squanderers and hoarders within the Avernus desperately blaspheme against divinity. Squanderers and hoarders utter maledictions. They fight each other while sinking themselves into a frightening desperation.

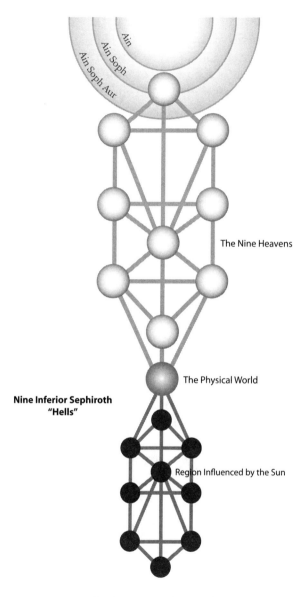

THE FOURTH INFERNAL CIRCLE, THE SPHERE
OF THE SUN, ON THE TREE OF LIFE

Question: Master, recognizing that squanderers and hoarders commit so much harm, I do not however understand the following: if the fourth Dantesque circle is much denser and materialistic than the second, and bearing in mind that in the second dwell those guilty of lust, the greatest sinners against the Holy Spirit, do not you think that the greater punishment should be for them?

Samael Aun Weor: Sir, ladies and gentlemen, I will repeat now what I emphatically and clearly affirmed in a former lecture. The original sin is lust and this serves as a basis for all the devolving descending processes within the nine Dantesque circles submerged within the entrails of our planet. However, it is evident that within the sum total of all of these descending processes within each of the nine natural infradimensions, certain specific defects, which are intrinsically correlated with their corresponding circle, stand out. Thus, friends, ladies and young people who listen, it is good for you to know that in the fourth circle the squanderers and hoarders are found perfectly defined, and that is all.

Question: Master, since—from my point of view—squandering and hoarding are directly related with the hunger of individuals and populaces, and since the great eternal, common, cosmic Trogoautoegocrat law relates to equilibrium, it seems to me that this can lead us directly to the problem of nourishment, since indeed this also has to do with the suffering that we endure within the fourth Dantesque circle if we do not maintain equilibrium on the scales of our nutrition. Thus, can you teach us something in regard to this subject-matter?

Samael Aun Weor: Respectable sir, regarding your question, we already made emphasis on the case of gluttons in our former lecture related with the third circle. Undoubtedly, gluttons violate the eternal, common, cosmic Trogoautoegocrat law within themselves and by themselves when excessively engorging foods and drinks into the interior of their organisms. It is clear that any violation of the law of the scales originates disequilibrium, thus the outcome is pain.

Question: Master, the beings who enter into the fourth circle are only those who have already exhausted their cycle of 108 human existences?

Samael Aun Weor: Respectable lady, regarding your question, allow me to emphatically, categorically, and definitively inform you that whosoever enters into the submerged devolution within the infernal worlds, including the inhabitants of the fourth Dantesque circle, have, in fact, already exhausted the cycle of 108 existences. Nevertheless, I have already stated in a former lecture that there are exceptions. At that time, I was specifically addressing the definitely perverse ones, those who because of their excessive malignity had to enter into the submerged infernal devolution without having yet exhausted their cycle of existences.

Question: Master, based on what you have just explained, I have made a synthesis from the purely economic point of view, which is: in the fourth solar Dantesque circle dwell all those who disequilibrate the scales of universal economy; am I right?

Samael Aun Weor: My gentlemanly friend, your question is correct. Indeed, one cannot violate with impunity the law of the scales of world economy without receiving the deserved penalty. The law is the law and the violation of any law brings pain.

Question: Beloved Master, when you addressed the gluttons in regard to the disequilibrium of the scales, can we by analogy say the same about those who ignorantly yet voluntarily lack adequate nutrition, especially because of their unawareness about the eternal, common, cosmic Trogoautoegocrat law. Can we therefore consider that the orthodox parishioners who have created a religion within their kitchen, or rather the vegetarians, will dwell within the fourth circle which you are bringing up in this lecture?

Samael Aun Weor: Respectable gentleman, in regard to your question, allow me to tell you with completely dazzling clarity that everybody is free to feed themselves as they please. There are unbearable vegetarians who have created a religion out of food, likewise on the Earth there are bloody, carnivorous, near cannibals, who have also destroyed their organisms. So, there are variety of nonsensicalities in this life. Thus regarding disequilibrium, everybody is guilty, since everyone violates the law of the scales, and the outcome of any violation is not pleasant.

However, it is not irrelevant to repeat that everyone is free of nourish themselves as they please. Nevertheless, we must not forget the law. If we destroy our bodies, we will have to endure the consequences. Regardless, it is convenient to specify that many vegetarians exist within the abysses. However, none of them suffer there because of the crime of eating vegetables, but because of many other causes and motives. Again, about nutritional matters, let everybody eat whatever they please. What is important, I repeat, is not to break the law, and that is all.

Question: Master, can you show us a procedure or a system, if there is one, which can teach us how to have perfect equilibrium on the scales?

Samael Aun Weor: Respectable lady, it is good for you to understand that the eternal regulator of the eternal, common, cosmic Trogoautoegocratic process is your Inner Monad, your Immortal Spark, or as the Christic gospel states, your Father who is in secret. Yes, within us God has the power of giving and the power of taking away. Therefore, if we act in accordance with the law, if we live in harmony with the infinite, if we learn how to obey our Father who is in secret, on earth as he is obeyed in heaven, we shall never lack our daily bread. Remember the Pater Noster, a magnificent prayer. Meditate profoundly on it, listen...

Question: But Master, how can we do the will of the Father if we are asleep, if we cannot see him nor hear him?

Samael Aun Weor: Lady, gentlemen, friends, remember the written law, the Decalogue of Moses. Do not break the written commandments. Live by them, and respect them. Yes, if every one of those here present, if every people of goodwill determines to live in accordance with the law and the prophets, they will then perform the will of the Father on earth as it is in heaven. Thus, the day will arrive when the devotees of the real path will awaken their consciousness; then they will be able to see their Father in order to receive his commands directly and to consciously fulfill them. Yet, first we must respect the written law and thereafter we will know the commandments of the Blessed One.

Question: Master, what can you tell us about the materiality and about the laws that govern the fourth Dantesque solar circle?

Samael Aun Weor: Respectable gentleman, friends, listen to me well: the fourth Dantesque circle is constituted by atoms much denser than those that give form and structure to the three previous circles. It is evident that every atom of the fourth tenebrous circle carries within its belly 364 atoms of the Absolute. These specific types of atoms give unto the fourth submerged region a terribly gross and material aspect, immensely heavier and more painful than the aspect that is lived and breathed within the three previous circles.

However, it is not surprising when one sees stores, shops of all types, markets, cars, objects of all types within those regions, objects which in the end are nothing more than simple gross mental forms, which are crystallized by the minds of the defunct. Regarding this, I still remember a very curious case.

One night, I entered with my astral body within that tenebrous region of the Tartarus, then before the counter of a luxurious store (a mere mental form from a submerged merchant) I called Bael. That dreadful magician of darkness, dressed in a blood-colored robe and wearing an oriental red turban, came to me, seated in a palanquin. In the rear his followers were pushing and carrying his carriage. This leftist personage, a fallen angel, luminary of the firmament from ancient times, looking at me with hatred, hurled himself against me and bit my right hand. It is obvious that I conjured him at once, thus that phantom became lost within the darkness of that horrible abode of Pluto in the end.

Alas friends! One is astounded when seeing within those regions so many exploiters of bodies and souls. There we find the lottery and decks of cards of gambling people, likewise many priests and hierarchs, mystics who insatiably covet their neighbor's goods. Indeed, one is filled with amazement when seeing so many prelates and anchorites, penitents and devotees who, despite their covetousness, loved humanity, moreover, astonishingly, all of these lost souls live within the fourth submerged region, still believing that they are doing very well, and what is the most grave aspect of this subject-matter is that they will never accept the concrete fact that they are doing evil.

Question: Master, can you tell us if there are Masters of the White Lodge within this fourth Dantesque circle who instruct those who dwell there with the purpose of making them to comprehend that they are doing evil?

Samael Aun Weor: Hierophants of the light, Nirmanakayas of compassion, splendorous Kabirs, Children of the Flame, abide everywhere, and many of them have renounced all bliss in order to live within the profundities of the abyss with the purpose of assisting those who are decidedly lost. Regrettably, the inhabitants of the Tartarus hate the Children of the Light. They classify them with the name of "white demons." They curse them. They will never accept their warnings that they are doing evil, since those who are decidedly lost always believe that they march on the path of righteousness, truth, and justice.

Question: Master, can you tell us what element is found within the fourth Dantesque circle: air, fire, water, earth, or what?

Samael Aun Weor: Respectable lady, those who are very avaricious are people who have metallized themselves very much; thus, I invite you to comprehend that the fourth Dantesque circle is essentially metallic or mineral. It is extremely dense. Obviously, just as the creatures that live in water, the fish, do not see the element in which they live, likewise, we who dwell within the element air do not see that element. Similarly, those who live in the mineral element see mental forms, shapes of stores, bars, taverns, banks, etc., but they do not perceive the element within which they live. For them, that element is as transparent as the air.

Now, what can we state about the element water? Obviously, it is by means of this element that the eternal, common, cosmic Trogoautoegocratic process is crystallized. Yes, the reciprocal nourishment of all creatures is made possible by means of the element water. Therefore, if the Earth were to remain without water, if the seas were to dry up, if the rivers were to disappear, then all the creatures that inhabit the face of the Earth would die. Thus, the concrete and definitive fact that water is the agent by means of which the eternal, common, cosmic Trogoautoegocrat law is crystallized is completely demonstrated.

In the fourth Dantesque circle, the waters are black, and I repeat, mineral is its fundamental element.

Do not the squanderers and hoarders violate the law? Do they not alter the equilibrium of the economic scales of people? Do they not alter the modus operandi of the eternal, common, cosmic Trogoautoegocrat law? So, dear friends, ladies and gentlemen, reflect upon all of this.

Chapter Nine

The Fifth Infernal Circle, the Sphere of Mars

Friends, ladies and gentlemen, now we are going to talk a little bit about the fifth natural infradimension, which correlates to Mars, and that is located underneath the geological crust of our terrestrial world. So, we emphatically clarify in advance that we are not addressing the submerged mineral kingdom of the very planet Mars. We are exclusively addressing the fifth infradimensional section located underneath the epidermis of our planet Earth, which is related with a Martian type of vibration. I am not going to talk about the heaven of Mars, or about that planet, either. What I am going to state exclusively involves the fifth infradimension of our planet Earth, and that is all. The purpose of clarifying all of this in advance is in order to avoid erroneous interpretations, since the mind, as it is already known, can fall into many subtle misapprehensions.

Listen: the ironical, infuriated people, the arrogant, haughty, and conceited people, unquestionably stand out within the fifth Dantesque circle. Now, in our book entitled *The Three Mountains,* we have studied that within the hells of the very planet Mars the esotericist-investigator discovers awful Witches' Sabbaths, frightening warlocks, tenebrous covens, harpies, or whatever else they are called. On the other hand, underneath the epidermis of our planet Earth, within the fifth Dantesque circle, which is a kind of Martian-like section, the witches (followers of Selene) with their disgusting warlocks (which in the Strophades Islands of the Aegean Sea were frequently frightening the Trojans) certainly do not stand out, since within the turbid waters and the filthy mud of the fifth circle (what Dante Alighieri, the old Florentine disciple of Virgil, the poet of Mantua only sees) are many arrogant people, who upon the face of the Earth ostentatiously show off amidst rich palaces and fatuous mansions.

Our consciousness has become divided into many contradictory parts that fight amongst themselves, and that in hell, must be dissolved.

The most painful experience for the lost souls within this abominable region is to have to self-confront their very millenary diabolical creations. Unquestionably, the consciousness has to confront itself in all of its components, which are all of those psychic aggregates that constitute the ego, the myself, the self-willed within which it is bottled.

I saw much mud, stagnant waters, and supreme pain within those submerged regions.

I still dreadfully remember a certain desperate creature submerged within that feculent, bitter, slimy place, slobbering in despair, trying to hide from the sinister stares of certain horrible monsters that—in the depth of her own psyche—were parts of herself, "I's" personifying her violence.

Alas, to flee from ourselves; the "I" fleeing from the "I"? This is frightfully horrifying! The consciousness facing, confronting, her very selves is a Machiavellian torture, impossible to describe with words.

Those "I's"—parts of that living creature who was trying to flee from them—did not have (as other mortals) their eyes in front of their head, but ominously, they were visible on the right and left, like the eyes of birds. Those "I's" were psychological aggregates of violence, armed with symbolic rifles, who wanted to attack that creature who was desperately hiding; astoundingly, the creature and the assailants were all psychic aggregates, component parts of the same ego; they formed the pluralized "I" in its totality.

To wallow within so much sludge, to flee from ourselves, to feel terror facing oneself, the "I" confronting the "I," parts of oneself confronting other parts of oneself, is indeed the horror of horrors, the indescribable, a terror that cannot be expressed with words. Thus, this is how the consciousness of the defunct within the fifth infradimension of the planet Earth becomes aware of its own maladies, its own horrors, its bizarre violence, its ominous anger.

Question: Beloved Master, I observed that when addressing the fifth Dantesque circle you told us there are convulsions of anger, and that within the infradimensions of the planet Mars there are Witches' Sabbaths; however, when you addressed the fourth Dantesque solar circle you informed us that with respect the infradimensions of the Sun, these are clean of "I's." Notwithstanding, in the process of initiation, Mars corresponds the next step ahead; if my question was understood, can you please clarify it?

Samael Aun Weor: Respectable friend, I have stated that within the submerged Martian mineral kingdom—meaning, within the infernos of the planet Mars, neither in its heaven nor on its planetary surface—the esotericist investigator can certainly find the tenebrous harpies and their frightful Witches' Sabbaths. I have also said that in the submerged mineral kingdom of the Sun that illuminates and gives us life, within its merely natural infradimensions, everything is clean; there we do not see the followers of Selene nor the horrible warlocks, nor the followers of Simon the magician. It would be an absurdity to suppose just for a moment that the left-hand adepts and the fortune-tellers of Python could live within the entrails of the radiant Sun. It is clear that the solar vibrations would destroy, would annihilate instantaneously, any impure creature...

Again, I repeat what I previously stated: only solar spirits, ineffable beings that are beyond good and evil can solemnly dwell within the Sun.

Question: Master, you stated that within the fifth infradimension of our planetary organism, the "I's confront other "I's" and that the consciousness also confronts those "I's" which are terribly malignant because of their wrathful nature. Does this signify that the consciousness that forms part of the myself is a third party in discordance?

Samael Aun Weor: Respectable sir, your question is important, thus I will gladly clarify it immediately. First of all, it is urgent to know that the ego, the "I", the myself, the self-willed is not something individual. Certainly, the ego is a sum of psychic aggregates, which we can also be denominated as "I's." Therefore, our "I" is a sum of small, irritable, and noisy "I's" that we carry within. If we name them demons, we will not commit any specific definitive error whatsoever. Thus, by carefully analyzing this subject-matter, we can arrive at the logical conclusion that such demon "I's" clearly personify our psychological defects.

So, I invite you, ladies and gentlemen, to concretely comprehend that each one of those devil "I's" carry within their interior a certain well-defined percentage of our own consciousness.

It so happens that in the fifth natural infradimension of our planet Earth, the consciousness confronts its very self. By looking at itself through many eyes from diverse angles, in accordance with each one of its "I's the consciousness acquires knowledge of itself.

It is indubitable that the consciousness tries to flee from itself, to flee from its own defects, representations of its own diabolic creations.

For the defunct, it is not pleasant to feel horror for themselves, thus they try to flee from themselves; one part of themselves tries to hide from the terrifying and frightening stare of another part or parts of themselves.

Listen, by using this time a very exact similarity, I want to assist all you to understand what I am stating. Here in Mexico, at the entrance of the Castle of Chapultepec, there is a hall of mirrors; on the surface of each one of those mirrors the visitors see their image in a completely different manner. Some of those mirrors break down our image, depicting us as giants of ancient times; others depict us with the appearance of insignificant dwarfs; another mirror depict us as having chubby figures, frighteningly obese; other mirrors depict us as having elongated, deformed figures, and horrifyingly thin; other mirrors deform our images depicting them with monstrous arms and legs, etc. So, imagine for a moment that each one of these images were one of our "I's," living personifications of our errors. What would become of all those creatures within those multiple mirrors, parts of oneself, parts of the myself, parts of the ego that we carry within, if each one of them becomes horrified of the others and each one of them wanted to independently flee from the others? Imagine each of us, transformed into all of those multiple "I's" and each one of our parts, frightened of every part of our parts; each horror frightened of each horror! That is a torture worse than that of Tantalus. Behold therefore, the torture within the fifth Dantesque circle.

Indeed, ladies and gentlemen, the ego that we carry within is constituted by thousands of demon "I's" that represent our psychological defects. It is clear that here in this physical world that swarm of devils controls our organic machine, yet they do not keep any concordance whatsoever among themselves. All of them struggle for supremacy; all of them want to control the capital centers of the organic machine. When one of them achieves to govern the organic machine for a moment, he then feels as if he is the master, the boss, the only one. However, afterwards he is dethroned and another one becomes the boss. Now ladies and gentlemen you will understand for yourselves the reason why we human beings are filled with inner contradictions.

So, if we could see ourselves in a full length mirror the way we really are, we would feel horrified of ourselves. This experience is a concrete fact within the fifth natural infradimension of the planet Earth. Nevertheless, in the cited tenebrous region, the shock is even cruder, more real, to the point that each one of the terrified parts flees without succor, trying to hide from each one of the other parts.

The consciousness divided into multiple pieces, horror of the Avernus, mystery, terrible things of the darkness of Minos! Woe! Woe! Woe!

Question: Although it is evident that this fifth natural infradimension of our planet Earth is even more dense and material

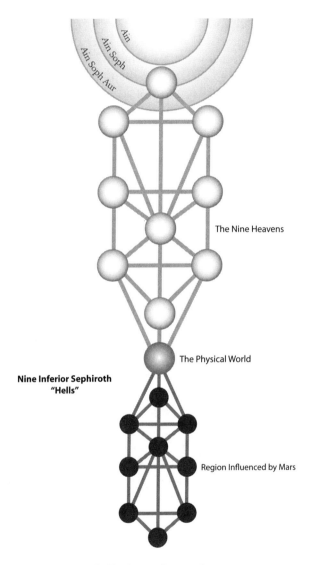

The Nine Heavens

The Physical World

**Nine Inferior Sephiroth
"Hells"**

Region Influenced by Mars

THE FIFTH INFERNAL CIRCLE, THE SPHERE
OF MARS, ON THE TREE OF LIFE

than the former ones, can you please explain to us what elements are characteristic of its density?

Samael Aun Weor: Gentleman, friends, indeed the fifth Dantesque circle is denser than the four previous ones due to its atomic composition. It is understood that each atom of the fifth submerged region carries in its womb 480 atoms of the sacred Absolute Sun. It is therefore evident that the fifth submerged region is even more gross than the previous ones; consequently, the suffering within it is greater.

Millions of condemned souls inhabit this zone of the Earth, people who hurt each other, i.e. blasphemers that utter maledictions against the eternal living God, people filled with hatred and revenge, arrogant, irate, impetuous people, assassins, and the wicked.

Astoundingly, all of these people believe that they are doing very well. None of them suppose even for a moment that they walk on the path of darkness and horror, and that they are doing badly. All of them feel holy and virtuous. Some of them pity themselves, classifying themselves as victims of injustice. To that end, all of them, in general, presume to be just.

Question: Regarding the nine works that are performed in the Second Mountain or Mountain of Resurrection, would you be so kind as to tell us the difference between the work within the fifth infradimension of the planet Mars and the one within the fifth Dantesque circle of our planet Earth?

Samael Aun Weor: Friends, friends, I invite you to comprehend what the work of the dissolution of the ego is. Undoubtedly, when submerging by means of meditation into our own atomic infernos with the purpose of comprehending these or those psychological defects, it is unquestionable that we place ourselves in contact with this or that natural infradimension. Now, since the fifth submerged region is the fundamental section related with anger, obviously, when we are trying to comprehend in an integral manner the diverse processes of annoyance, wrath, violence, arrogance, etc., we place ourselves in contact with the cited fifth Dantesque circle.

On the other hand, it is indispensable to make a clear differentiation between those inhumane elements that are related to the nine Dantesque circles of our planet Earth, located underneath the epidermis of this afflicted planet, and the infra-conscious elements, which within our psyche retain an intimate relation with the infernos of the Moon, Mercury, Venus, the Sun, Mars, Jupiter, Saturn, Uranus, and Neptune.

But please ladies and gentlemen, listen to me well so there will be no confusion: you must make a distinction between heavens and hells. The heavens of each one of these cited planets is totally different from their hells. Thus, you have to always learn how to locate any planetary inferno within the submerged mineral kingdom of the same planet. Heaven is different; this is a region of light, harmony, happiness. We cannot enter into any of those planetary heavens without previously having worked within their corresponding infernos. Therefore, looking these things from this angle, it is clear that we can never enter into the heaven of Mars without previously having worked within the Martian infernos, which are located within the living entrails of Mars own submerged mineral kingdom. So, within the infernos of the planet Mars, within its natural infradimensions, we must eliminate certain infra-conscious, inhumane, psychic, witch-like states. Listen, this type of work is only possible to be performed by those sacred individuals known as Potentates; these are those individuals who are preparing themselves to attain the state of Virtue within the heaven of Mars.

On the other hand, comprehend that any psychological work within the entrails of these other worlds of our solar system maintains a certain relationship with their corresponding infernal sections within the planet Earth. Yes, ladies and gentlemen, do not forget the laws of correspondences, analogies, and numerologies. Whatever the case, it is urgent to know that in the infernos of the planet Mars, the Potentates must eliminate infra-conscious, witch-like, psychic states; yet, we, within the corresponding Martian fifth infernal section of our planet Earth, are limited to eliminating the processes of anger, arrogance, etc.

Chapter Ten

The Sixth Infernal Circle, the Sphere of Jupiter

Respectable friends, today we are going to study with complete clarity the sixth Dantesque circle, which relates to Jupiter, and that is submerged underneath the epidermis of our planet Earth. Unquestionably, it is good to know that this infradimensional region is even denser than the five previous ones because of its atomic constitution, given that each atom of the sixth Dantesque circle carries in its womb 576 atoms of the Sacred Absolute Sun. Undoubtedly, such extremely heavy atoms are the *causa causarum* of a tremendous materialism. Obviously, the people that live submerged within this infernal region are controlled by 576 laws, which make their existences extremely complicated and difficult. In this region, time is frighteningly slow; each minute seems to be a century and therefore, life becomes tedious and intolerable.

If we carefully analyze the Jupiterian vibration in its transcendental, planetary aspect, we then discover that mysterious force which grants the scepter to the kings and the miter to the hierarchs of diverse confessional religions. Therefore, the planet Jupiter within the infinite space is extraordinary, mystical, regal, and sublime.

On the other hand, its antithesis, located within that sixth submerged infradimension, underneath the geological crust of our planet, is in fact turned into the abode for the materialist atheists, enemies of the eternal. The blasphemers, those who hate everything with the taste of divinity, and the heretics, those who cultivate the dogma of separatism, also breathe in those regions.

Like Dante, one feels filled with pain when beholding so many mitered skeptics and atheists stuck within the sepulcher of their own passions, hatreds, and limitations. When we think about the great legislators, sovereigns, and lords who rule social conglomerates, we obviously discover tyrants and petty-

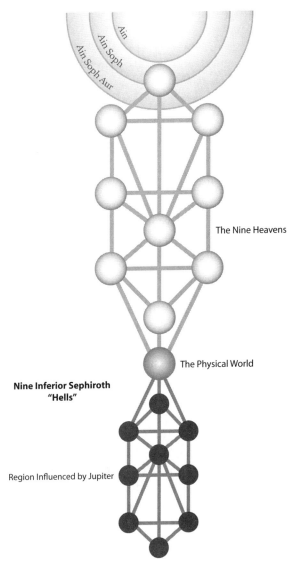

The Nine Heavens

The Physical World

Nine Inferior Sephiroth
"Hells"

Region Influenced by Jupiter

THE SIXTH INFERNAL CIRCLE, THE SPHERE
OF JUPITER, ON THE TREE OF LIFE

tyrants that originate complications and pain here, there, and everywhere. Thus, the outcome of such ominous proceedings corresponds exactly to the sixth Dantesque circle. Therefore, it is not surprising for the esotericist-investigator to find within this tenebrous region from the abode of Pluto all these types of hierarchs that abused their power. Accordingly, it is clear that such people suffer the unspeakable.

So, the always generous Jupiter, as a paternal friend, has its ominous antithesis in those terrible parents who, having plentiful wealth, deny bread, shelter, and refuge to their children. Undoubtedly, it is there, within that sixth ominous abysmal region, where those sinning shadows find their dwelling place after death.

The consciousness of the investigator is heartbroken when beholding those very cruel parents submerged within that tenebrous Jupiterian region; however, what is most astounding is that under the light of the Sun in this tridimensional world, they always believed themselves to be virtuous, just, and generous. Moreover, some of them were even profoundly religious. In that sinister abode also breathe family heads who—despite all their cruelties—aspired to the inner self-realization of the Being and whose contemporaries believed them to be very good; yes, from the doors of their house outward, their conduct appeared to be upright, although it is clear that within their private abode there was weeping and affliction. Indeed, they were extraordinarily pietistic people, pretending meekness, posing as stand-up comedians, unbearable vegetarians who make food a kitchen religion. Using the tone of the great Kabir Jesus, I say unto them: "Woe unto you, Pharisees, hypocrites! For ye are like unto whited sepulchers." However, the same would never be said by their partisans or those who had seen them in those beautiful pseudo-esoteric or pseudo-occultist types of halls.

It is not strange to find very honest and sincere but terribly mistaken heads of family within the sixth submerged infradimensional region. What these heads of family should have done they did not do, and what they should not have done, they did. Some of them were extraordinarily fanatical heads of family who—in the world where they lived—taught religion to their children with sticks and lashings, as if religion could be learned with floggings; ominous parents indeed who darkened homes by embittering the lives of their children.

Jupiter, generous as always, benevolent and altruistic, has its contrast underneath the epidermis of the Earth, within the sixth submerged infradimension. What is the antithesis of generosity? Egotism, usury, embezzlement; this is obvious. Therefore, it is not strange to find within this infrahuman region those who monopolize all the goods of the Earth to themselves, such as Sanagabril and his henchmen.

Thus, every religious antithesis, every Jupiterian contrast, is inevitably found within the sixth infernal circle underneath the epidermis of the Earth.

Question: Dear Master, I have observed that you mentioned that time is tremendously long, that minutes seem centuries due to the great density of this submerged Jupiterian region. Is time long because of the sufferings or are the sufferings long because of time?

Samael Aun Weor: Respectable gentleman, in regard to your question, allow me to inform you that time only exists from the merely subjective point of view, because indeed time does not have an objective reality. Thus, by relying on this basic principle, we arrive at the logical conclusion that time is a submerged subconscious creation. Unquestionably, within each infraconscious zone, or better said, within those inhuman parts that exist within each one of us, time has to become consistently slower within the most profound depths of materiality. In other words, I will state the following: in the merely intellective level, time is not as slow as in the deeper subconscious levels. Meaning, the more subconscious the region where we live, the slower is time. This will take a greater appearance of reality. Here in this physical world where we live, that is, on the surface of the Earth and under the sunshine, there are minutes that seem to be centuries, and there are centuries that seem to be minutes; everything depends on our mood. It is clear that when in complete happiness, twelve hours seem to be one minute. It is obvious that a moment of supreme pain seems to endure centuries. Now, let us now think about the abyss, about the submerged abysmal regions, about the city of Dis, the damned city located at the bottom of the tenebrous Tartarus; there, the lost souls feel that each minute is transformed into centuries of abominable bitterness. Thus, regarding the question of the gentleman, I think that now he will understand my answer in depth.

Question: This is how it is indeed, Master. However, since you mentioned states of consciousness, namely, subconsciousness, unconsciousness and infraconsciousness, does this mean to say that when we are talking about infradimensions we are also talking about states of consciousness?

Samael Aun Weor: The infradimensions of nature and of the cosmos not only exist in the planet Earth but also in any cosmic unity from the infinite space, i.e. suns, moons, planets, galaxies, stars, likewise in anti-stars, anti-galaxies of anti-matter, etc. These natural infradimensions are not therefore exclusive products of the subconsciousness or infraconsciousness of intellective humanoids, but the outcome of mathematical laws that have their origin in every ray of existential creation.

Question: Master, this means therefore that when we refer to the consciousness in itself we should think that this is free of time?

Samael Aun Weor: Gentleman, ladies and gentlemen, I want to emphatically tell you that in the Sacred Absolute Sun, time is 49 times faster that here on Earth.

By judiciously analyzing the former statement, we say: since time is a mere subjective creation of the intellectual humanoid, it is obvious that time is 49 times slower than in the Sacred Absolute Sun. In other words, I clarify: since the mind of the humanoid possesses 49 subconscious departments, based on this we state that time here amongst the tri-brained or tri-centered bipeds [see next page] mistakenly called humans is 49 times slower than in the Sacred Absolute Sun.

Sustained by the inductive process taught by Aristotle in his "Divine Entelechy," we conclude: if time in the Sacred Absolute Sun is 49 times more rapid than the intellective level

THE THREE BRAINS OR FIVE CENTERS

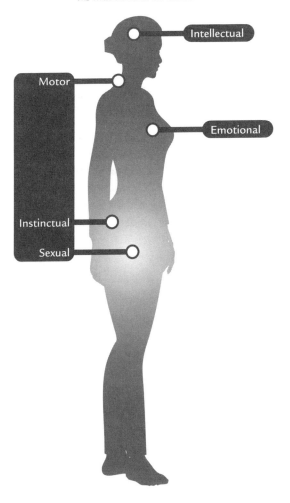

of the humanoid, obviously this means that in the Sacred Sun time does not exist; in it, everything is an eternal moment, an eternal now.

Now, when beholding that which is called consciousness, that is, when studying it wisely, we discover the original, virginal, paradisiacal Being, free from every subconscious process, beyond time. That is to say, the consciousness in itself is not a product of time.

Question: I beg your pardon Master, since I might appear a little insistent, but I have grasped the following concept: in the measure that we awaken consciousness, the infraconscious and subconscious states cease to exist because these become conscious states. Is this wrong?

Samael Aun Weor: Sir, your question is quite interesting. Evidently, when the submerged states of Pluto, namely, the infraconsciousness, unconsciousness, subconsciousness, are radically eliminated, then the consciousness awakens.

Time seems too long for us within the sixth submerged dimension due to the clear and evident fact of the subconscious, unconscious and infraconscious states; on the other hand, in Nirvana time does not exist due to the compelling and definite fact that neither the ego nor the subconscious, nor the aforementioned abysmal states, exist within that divine region.

Question: Based on this explanation that frankly surprises me, because I had never ever related time with states of subconsciousness, I arrive at the conclusion that the unconsciousness, the infraconsciousness, and the subconsciousness of which psychologists speak so much, are indeed negative and Satanic states, and therefore are the obstacles to humans' self-realization. Am I right, Master?

Samael Aun Weor: It has been solemnly told unto us that we need to transform the subconsciousness into consciousness; yet, we also include the infraconscious and unconscious states within these transformative concepts. Thus, to awaken the consciousness is what is radical. It is only in this manner that we can see the path that will lead us to the final liberation.

Obviously, the concept of time, which embitters life so much within the sixth submerged dimension and within the different Dantesque circles of the Tartarus, is definitely eliminated when the consciousness awakens.

Question: Master, you told us that the sixth submerged Jupiterian region is the antithesis of the planet Jupiter that orbits around the Sun. Yet, I observed that when you spoke about the other Dantesque circles you did not refer to them as the antithesis of the planets to which they correspond. Would you like to clarify this for us?

Samael Aun Weor: Sir, ladies and gentlemen, obviously, the nine infernal circles are always the negative antithetical aspect of the upper spheres, namely, the Moon, Mercury, Venus, the Sun, Mars, Jupiter, Saturn, Uranus and Neptune. I believe that I have already said something about this subject-matter in past lectures, in which we described the relationship between those planets and the nine zones submerged below the epidermis of our planet Earth. Now, when looking for a similarity to all of this, you see that every person under the sunlight projects his shadow everywhere; likewise, you find something similar with each of these nine planets of the solar system and their corresponding shadows, or obscure, tenebrous zones within the entrails of the planet in which we live. Understood?

Question: Master, could you tell us if the submerged zone of the planet Jupiter is inhabited?

Samael Aun Weor: Respectable lady, allow me to inform you and all the people listening to me that within the natural infradimensions of the submerged mineral kingdom of the planet Jupiter are terribly perverse demons, devolving creatures, people heading towards their second death. I clarify, I am not talking about the heaven of Jupiter; I limit myself exclusively to mention the submerged mineral kingdom of that planet.

Question: Master, can we consider that—despite the fact that within the infernos of the planet Jupiter exist terribly devolving malignant beings—the infernos of the planet Jupiter are antithetical to the infernos of the sixth Dantesque circle of the planet Earth?

Samael Aun Weor: Friends, the tenebrous corresponds with the tenebrous; therefore, between the infernos of the planet Jupiter and the sixth Dantesque circle submerged below the geological cortex of our planet Earth there is no antithesis whatsoever. We must look for antitheses exclusively between the luminous and obscure aspects of Jupiter. Indubitably, the Jupiterian splendors have their opposites, their shadows, not only within the entrails of that radiant planet, but also underneath the crust of our afflicted planet.

Question: Master, could you tell us what are the materials or elements which structure that tenebrous zone of the sixth submerged dimension of our planetary organism?

Samael Aun Weor: Friends, we have already stated in past lectures that the inhabitants of any natural element never perceive the element in which they live, i.e. the fish never see the water; we, the inhabitants of this tridimensional world of Euclid, never perceive the air that we breathe; we do not see it. The salamanders do not see the fire. Likewise, those who dwell within the petrous, rocky element never see such an element; they only perceive objects, persons, events, etc. Obviously, the petrous density of the sixth abode of Pluto is unbearable, terribly dense; now we will understand for ourselves the reason why Dante saw so many condemned souls within their sepulchers; these are not sepulchers in the literal sense of the word; what is meant to say with this is sepulchral states, that is, very narrow limited conditions of the subconsciousness and infraconsciousness, etc.; these are painful conditions of life within the sixth abysmal region.

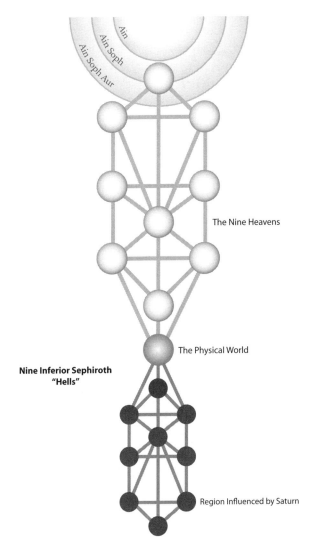

THE SEVENTH INFERNAL CIRCLE, THE SPHERE
OF SATURN, ON THE TREE OF LIFE

Chapter Eleven

The Seventh Infernal Circle, the Sphere of Saturn

Friends, once again we meet here so that we can talk profoundly about the submerged sphere of Saturn.

Indeed, we are not talking about eternal damnation or endless condemnation. Unquestionably, eternal damnation does not exist, since every punishment—as serious as it may be—has to have a limit, beyond which happiness reigns. So, in this sense, we radically differ from the clerical orthodoxy.

Indubitably, the devolving processes of life performed within the entrails of the Earth, within the submerged infradimensions, underneath the geological crust of our planet, conclude with the Second Death. Once the pristine purity of the psychic material has been restored through the Second Death, the essence is then liberated in order to inevitably re-initiate new processes of a completely evolving type. Therefore, our opposition to the dogma of an absolutely eternal damnation is obvious and evident. Thus, our means of comprehending the expiation of faults stands out at first glance.

We could never conceive that any expiatory debt—as grave as it may be—would not finally arrive at an end. It is clear that divine justice can never fail, since every fault—as serious as it may be—has its exact mathematical expiatory equivalent. Thus, it is not possible to pay more than what is owed, and if divinity would collect more than what is owed, it would obviously be unjust.

Thus, beloved friends of mine, with this clarification I have started our lecture of today, with the unavoidable purpose for you to comprehend our esoteric, occultist point of view, which is radically opposed to all sectarian dogmatism, this, as a mode of preamble before entering into the theme of the submerged sphere of Saturn. Let us now therefore delve a little bit more into this subject-matter related with the submerged spheres.

In our past lecture, we studied in detail the sixth Dantesque circle, and today it is convenient that we profoundly penetrate within the seventh, the circle of Saturn.

If we carefully read *The Divine Comedy*, we will find that Dante describes such a region converted into an ocean of blood and fire. Let us be granted the liberty of stating that Dante's point of view is completely allegorical or symbolic. Such a description signifies the concrete and definite fact that a certain reddish, bloody color, which highly characterizes violent animal passion, definitely prevails in that Saturnine region.

Regarding colors, we must know that above the solar spectrum, the entire ultraviolet range shines within the superior dimensions of nature and the cosmos. Yet, below the solar spectrum, the infrared range fatally shines. The infrared is the characteristic range of the infradimensions of nature, underneath the geological crust of our planet. Therefore, such a passionate, blood-red color of the submerged Saturnine region cannot be exhibited in our tridimensional world of Euclid, since in our tridimensional region, that color finds its opposite in a different yet similar one of the ultraviolet range.

It is intriguing to know that every lost one who enters the seventh Dantesque circle shows in their radiant aura that abominable bloody color, which certainly makes them compatible to that submerged zone of our planet Earth.

The seventh Dantesque circle is, therefore, occupied by the violent against nature, the violent against art, the fraudulent, the violent against God, the violent against themselves, against their own goods, and against their neighbor's goods.

Once—in my astral body—when moving around in a positive and conscious manner within that submerged region, I observed the reigning violence within such a frightening zone of bitterness.

I still remember two very notable demons whom I approached diplomatically, with the purpose of not hurting their susceptibilities or provoking unnecessary psychological reactions. These demons, feeling perversely satisfied with their miserable satanic condition, pronounced themselves against the Cosmic Christ, thus they denied Him emphatically.

THE SEVENTH CIRCLE AS SYMBOLIZED BY DANTE

Violence reigned everywhere; unnecessary destructions, frightening blows against things, against people, against everything, were seen here, there, and everywhere within that bloody, submerged atmosphere. In that region I felt as if the Saturnine influence with its definitive centrifugal forces were propelled to disintegrate, to reduce everything, people, furniture, doors, etc. to cosmic dust.

Then, I was very astounded when finding a very respectable creature, whose eyes still reflected the soft light of day; presently, he is a very famous doctor, a true Samaritan, who in life has only proposed to heal his patients with true love and without any exploitation. Now, what I just stated might cause bewilderment. Many of you could object and tell me, "How is it possible that one, being righteous, could end up within the region of the wicked?" Likewise, the subject-matter about life and death could be debated, since the good man in question is obviously still alive. Yes, he is still breathing under the sun. Then if that is so, why is he dwelling within the seventh Dantesque circle?

So, it is necessary to answer such enigmas, to clarify them, to inspect, to inquire, to investigate with precision.

If we think on the multiplicity of the "I," then it is not strange to consider that any of these, his psychic aggregates related with the crime of violence against nature, are breathing within its corresponding submerged region, even when his personality is still alive upon the face of the Earth. Thus, obviously, if that doctor does not dissolve his pluralized "I," he will have to descend with the devolving wave within the entrails of the planet in order to stand out very especially within the seventh Dantesque circle. Understand: there is a great deal of virtue within the wicked and a great deal of evil within the righteous.

Once the cycle of 108 physical existences that are assigned to every soul upon the face of the Earth concludes, it is unquestionable that we descend with the devolving wave, even if we are bestowed with beautiful virtues. It is not irrelevant that we remember now Brunetto Latini, that noble gentleman who with so much love taught the Florentine Dante the path that leads to the immortality of man, a noble creature who was submerged within that abyss because of the crime of violence against nature.

Question: Master, could you please explain to us: when do we commit the crime of violence against nature?

Samael Aun Weor: I am very glad to give an immediate answer to this lady's question. Violence against nature exists when we violate the sexual organs. Such a violent crime exists when a man forces his wife to copulate when she is not in the disposition to do it. Likewise, such a violent crime exists when a woman forces her husband to copulate when he is not in the disposition to do it.

Such a violent crime also exists when the woman forces herself to copulate when her organism is not really in the favorable condition to do it. Likewise, such a violent crime exists when the man obliges himself, thus violating himself, in order to copulate when his organism is not in the condition for it.

Such a violent crime exists when the woman obliges herself to copulate when her organism is not in the right condition to do it.

Such a violent crime exists in those who commit the crime of rape, that is, to force another person to submit to sexual intercourse against such a person's will.

Since crime is also hidden within the rhythmic flow of the verse. It is not therefore unusual that violence against nature is committed when a man forces his phallus to become erect when it is not really in a favorable condition for copulation.

Violence against nature exists when—with the pretext of practicing sexual magic or even with the best intentions of attaining Self-realization—the male obliges himself to perform the chemical copulation, or obliges his wife to perform it, when their creative organs are not in the precise amorous moment and in the favorable conditions that are indispensable in order to perform the copulation.

Violence against nature exists in those ladies who, knowing they need inner Self- realization, violate their own nature by pitilessly obliging themselves to perform the copulation when they are certainly not in the required condition to do it.

Violence against nature exists in masturbators or in those who perform the chemical copulation when the woman is menstruating. Likewise, violence against nature exists when spouses perform the sexual act when the woman is pregnant.

Violence against nature exists when the Vajroli Mudra is practiced vigorously several times during the day or during the night, when the sexual organs are not really in favorable and harmonious conditions.

Violence against nature exists when sexual magic is practiced two consecutive times, violating in this way the laws of the creative magnetic pause.

Question: Master, in the case when the spouse does not have complete potency and is practicing sexual magic, is nature also being violated in this manner?

Samael Aun Weor: I am very glad to give an immediate answer to this gentleman's question. It also happens that an organ that is not in use becomes atrophied. Thus, if anybody—in this case a male—were to remain abstinent in a radical and absolute manner, it is clear that he would harm himself because he would become impotent. Then, obviously, if that male wanted to be healed from that harmful condition, he could then attain it by practicing sexual magic, which is, the connection of the phallus and the uterus without the ejaculation of the semen. It is clear that—due precisely to the lack the of erection of the phallus—in the beginning the connection will be almost impossible. However, when attempting it, when placing the phallus close to the uterus, together with a mutual exchange of caresses, then there is no violation against nature, but an erotic medical therapy, which is indispensable in order to perform the healing. In the beginning, these types of patients can use some type of clinical medical treatment based on the advice of their physician, with the purpose of precisely achieving the first sexual connections. And it is clear that if the couple withdraws from the sexual connection before the orgasm in order to avoid the ejaculation of their semen, it will be reabsorbed within their organism, thus fortifying the sexual system extraordinarily. The exact outcome of this procedure will be the healing. So, I repeat, in this entire process there is no violation against nature.

Question: Master, when you talk about violence against nature do you exclusively address the violence of the human organism?

Samael Aun Weor: Respectable friend, I want you to know in a clear and definitive manner that when we talk about violence against nature, we are emphatically addressing all types of sexual violence, clearly specifying the sexual organs of human beings. With this, nonetheless, I do not want to state that there are not other types of violence against nature. If someone forced the inferior creatures of nature to perform contrived copulations, in this way violating their free will, there would then be violence against nature. Another: if someone artificially inseminated animals, as it is the custom in this day and age, there would then be violence against nature.

There is violence against nature when we commit adultery, or when we adulterate vegetables and fruits with the infamous hybrids that have been invented by the ignoramuses of this black age of Kali Yuga.

There is violence against nature when we castrate ourselves or when we force animals to be castrated.

Therefore, the transgressions that enter into this type of violence against nature are innumerable.

Alas! Friends, ladies, and gentlemen that listen to me, people that receive this 1973-1974 Christmas message, remember that crime is also lurking within the incense of the temple. Crime is also hidden within the beautiful paintings that the painter portrays on his canvas. Crime is also hidden within the most delectable harmonies with which the musician delights us on this planet Earth. Crime is also hidden within the perfume of litanies that are delightfully whispered within the temples. Crime dresses itself as saint, as a martyr, as an apostle, etc. and even when it seems incredible, it disguises itself with priestly robes and officiates at the altars.

Friends, ladies and gentlemen, remember that noble sire whom they called Guidoguerra—cited by Dante—the grandchild of the chaste Gualdrada, who in his lifetime achieved many noble acts both by his wisdom and his sword. Remember also Tegghiaio Aldobrandi, whose voice in the upper world should be appreciated; both noble males that now live in the seventh infernal circle because of the crime of violence against nature.

Question: Master, if we disintegrate the "I" of violence against nature, or almost all the "I's" that have bottled our essence, and if we still have some left, will we anyhow fall also into any of these Dantesque circles?

Samael Aun Weor: Respectable lady, I am glad to hear your question, since this is quite opportune.

Someone could eliminate from his psyche those psychic aggregates related with the crime of violence against nature, and nevertheless still fall into any of the other Dantesque circles, since while the animal ego exists within us, it is obvious that we are indisputable candidates for the abyss and the second death.

Question: Master, if we have already arrived at the last of the 108 existences that have been assigned to every human being, yet in it we are working on the path of the razor's edge, would another opportunity be given to us in order to finish our work?

Samael Aun Weor: Noble lady, I am very pleased to answer your question: You must know with complete clarity that the laws of nature are not governed by tyrants but by just and perfect beings. Therefore, if someone—despite having finished their cycle of 108 existences—starts to tread the path of the razor's edge and thereafter disincarnates while treading the regal path, obviously they will receive assistance. New existences will be assigned unto them so that they can achieve the realization of their Inner Self. Nevertheless, if they deviate from the secret path, if they apostatize, if they do not dissolve their ego, and backslide into their same transgressions, then they would inevitably fall into the abyss of perdition.

Question: Based on what has previously been stated during the course of this lecture, I have arrived at the conclusion that once we devolve within the atomic abysses of nature, we are indeed inhabitants of all of the Dantesque circles from our planetary organism. Am I right, Master?

Samael Aun Weor: I want to tell the gentleman that the statement of his question is indeed correct. When someone enters into the submerged devolution of nature, through time he slowly descends from circle to circle, standing out very especially within that zone where his worst transgression is specifically found.

Question: Master, what can you tell us about homosexuals and lesbians; do they commit violence against nature?

Samael Aun Weor: Respectable sir, your question is indeed quite interesting. It is urgent to comprehend that homosexuals and lesbians inevitably submerge into the seventh Dantesque Saturnian circle, precisely because of the crime of violence against nature.

I want you to comprehend that this type of degenerated people—enemies of the Third Logos—are indeed lost cases: seeds that do not germinate.

Question: Master, are lesbians and homosexuals born into the world as such due to the karmic law, or does the engendering of such children have some hereditary relationship? Which one of these two factors predominates?

Samael Aun Weor: I hear this question from the international Gnostic missionary Efrain Villegas Quintero who is visiting us here in the patriarchal headquarters of the Gnostic Movement in Mexico City. Ladies and gentlemen, it is convenient to know that those humanoids who in former lives violently precipitated themselves on the path of sexual degeneration, obviously downwardly devolved from existence to existence in order to finally appear as homosexuals or lesbians, before entering into the infernal worlds. Lesbianism and homosexuality are therefore the outcome of a processed degeneration through preceding lives, a fatal karmic consequence, that is all.

Question: Master, if any of those people would for a moment manage to know that their lesbian or homosexual condition is a punishment based on the karma of their degeneration from preceding lives, and thus asked the law for help, would the law concede them the mercy of recovering a normal state, or do they not have enough strength in order to ask for such benefit?

Samael Aun Weor: Ladies and gentlemen, there is a proverb that states, "Heaven helps those who help themselves." Divine Mercy is beside Justice, but "Actions speak louder than words." Thus, if any of these degenerates of infrasexuality were to truly repent, let them demonstrate it with concrete, clear, and definite actions. Let them immediately marry someone of the opposite sex, and let them really start treading the path of authentic and legitimate sexual regeneration. So, it is right for these types of delinquents to cry, pray, and beg, but let them also show their repentance with actions. Only in this manner is salvation possible for these types of creatures.

Nevertheless, it is very difficult for homosexuals and lesbians to have courage, a true longing for betterment. Undoubtedly, they are completely degenerated people, within which certain areas of the brain are no longer active. They are rotten seeds, where it is impossible to find any longing for regeneration.

Some individuals from this devolving class have made of their crime a mystique disguised with garments of sanctity. These types of individuals who promote human rottenness are even worse, and more dangerous. Thus, regarding this kind of people, we must not forge illusions, since they are lost cases, abortions of nature, complete failures.

Question: Master, sequentially, is every hope for self-realization lost for those who reject the opposite sex, or does any door remain open?

Samael Aun Weor: Respectable friend, listen. Infrasexuality is symbolized in ancient Kabbalah by the two wives of Adam: Lilith and Nahemah.

Lilith frankly allegorizes the most monstrous sexual degeneration. Within the sphere of Lilith we find many anchorites, hermits, cloistered monks and nuns who mortally hate sex. We also find in that sphere all those women who take abortive and who murder their newly born creatures, true hyenas of perversity. Another aspect of the sphere of Lilith corresponds to pederasts, homosexuals, and lesbians. Unquestionably, those who violently reject sex as well as those who abuse it, falling

ADAM AND HIS WIVES

thus into homosexuality and lesbianism, are lost cases, terribly malignant creatures. For these types of people all doors are closed, except the door of repentance.

The sphere of Nahemah is represented by another type of violence against nature: the irredeemable fornicators, the fornicators of abomination, etc., people who find themselves quite defined as Don Juan or Casanova types, and even the devil type, which is the worst of the worst.

Ladies and gentlemen, let us now continue talking a little bit about the violent against God. When reaching this point of our lecture I want to remember Capaneus, the ancient of Crete, one of the seven kings who sieged the Theban walls and who now breathes within the seventh submerged Saturnian zone, underneath the geological crust of our Earth. In his *Divine Comedy*, the Florentine Dante, disciple of Virgil, the great poet of Mantua, cites this terrible case related with this particular theme.

> *That shadow cried out: "Such as I was alive, such am I dead. Though Jupiter weary his smith, from whom in wrath he took the sharp thunderbolt wherewith on my last day I was smitten, or though he weary the others, turn by turn, in Mongibello at the black forge, crying, Good Vulcan, help, help!' even as he did at the fight of Phlegra, and should hurl on me with all his might, thereby he should not have glad vengeance."*

Their own rage and pride of those violent against the divine is the worst punishment within the seventh submerged infradimension.

There is violence against divinity when we do not obey superior orders, when we attempt against our own life, when we irately blaspheme.

There are many subtle moods of violence against the divine. Undoubtedly, those violent against God are those who do not want anything to do with mystical or spiritual subject-matters, those who suppose they can exist without divine mercy, and who at the bottom of their soul rebel against everything that has a smell of divinity.

There is violence against God in those self-sufficient people who in a skeptical manner smile stupidly when listening to some subject matters that in some way are related with the spiritual aspects of life.

There is violence against God within those scoundrels of the intellect, in those ignoramuses who deny any spiritual possibility to the human being, those who believe that they have monopolized the universal knowledge, in those "models of wisdom," in those learned ignoramuses who not only ignore, but moreover they ignore that they ignore, in those iconoclasts who make a clean sweep when they analyze religious principles and thereafter they leave their henchmen without any new spiritual base.

There is violence against God in the pseudo-sapient Marxist-Leninists, who have taken away the spiritual values from humanity. Regarding them, there comes into my memory in these moments an encounter with Karl Marx within the submerged worlds. I found Karl Marx within those tenebrous regions. That individual had awakened in evil and for evil. Nonetheless, he is a fallen Bodhisattva. Lenin, unconsciously and profoundly asleep like an ominous shadow, was following him. I questioned Marx with the following words, "It has been many years since you died, thus your body became dust within the tomb. Nonetheless here I find you alive within these regions. What happened then to your dialectical materialism?"

Karl Marx, while looking at his wristwatch, did not dare to give me any sort of answer, but turned around and withdrew. However, a few meters away he shouted a sarcastic and horrifying guffaw. By means of intuition I managed to capture the living essence of that sarcastic guffaw, since in it was his answer, which we could summarize in the following phrase: "That dialectic was nothing but farce, a dish in order to deceive naive people."

It is intriguing to know that when Karl Marx died, he received the religious funerary honors of a great rabbi.

In the First International Communist gathering, Karl Marx took the floor and said, "Gentlemen, I am not Marxist." There was surprise among the audience, loud shouts, and

KARL HEINRICH MARX (1818 – 1883)

from there many political sects were born, namely, Bolsheviks, Mencheviks, Anarchists, Anarchist-Unionist, etc. It is therefore quite interesting to know that the first enemy of Marxism was Karl Marx. In a magazine from Paris, one can read the following:

> *"By means of the triumphant worldly proletariat, we will create the Universal Soviet Socialist Republic with its capital in Jerusalem. In this way we will take possession of the wealth of all nations. This is how the prophecies of our holy prophets of Talmud will be fulfilled."*

Indeed, these were not phrases uttered by a materialist nor by an atheist, but by Marx, a Jewish religious fanatic.

Understand: I am not criticizing political matters through this lecture. I am emphatically and essentially addressing occult matters.

Indeed, Karl Marx, moved by religious fanaticism, invented a destructive weapon in order to reduce all religions of the world to cosmic dust. That weapon is without a doubt a "jargon" that can never withstand an in-depth analysis. By "jargon" I refer to the dialectical materialism.

The intellectual loafers know very well that Karl Marx manipulated Hegel's "metaphysical dialectic" in order to elaborate that deceptive "dialectical materialism." Evidently, Karl Marx took from Hegel's work all the metaphysical principles that Hegel gave to his work, and with the leftovers Karl Marx elaborated his deceptive dish. Thus, it is not irrelevant to repeat in this lecture that Marx, as the author of such a lie, of such a farce, of such Communistic dialectic, never believed in it, and therefore he did not have any inconvenience in confessing his feelings in the heat of the assembly when saying, "Gentlemen, I am not Marxist."

Undoubtedly, this gentleman fulfilled one of the Protocols of the Elders of Zion that literally states:

> *"When we come into our kingdom it will be undesirable for us that there should exist any other religion... We must therefore sweep away all other forms of religion. It does not matter if for our means, we have to fill the world with materialism and repugnant atheism, since the day we become triumphant, we will universally preach the religion of Moses that, by its codified and thoroughly dialectical system will bring all the peoples of the world into subjection to us."*

Concerning this, I am not condemning any race in particular. I am frankly addressing some Semitic personages with Machiavellian plans. They are Marx, Lenin, Stalin, etc.

Sequentially, from a rigorously occultist point of view, I could evince that the cited fallen Bodhisattva struggled in his own way on behalf of divinity, using for his means a cunning weapon in order to destroy the other religions. Marx was a priest, a rabbi from the Jewish religion, a faithful devotee of the doctrine of his ancestors.

Indeed, what is astounding is the credulity of the fools who—believing themselves to be erudite—fall into the skeptical snare set by Karl Marx. These naive people from the Marxist-Leninist dialectical materialism obviously become violent against divinity. Thus, for such a reason they enter into the seventh Dantesque circle.

Question: Venerable Master, in the Masonic Order to which I belong, it is stated that religion assists man for a good death and that Masonry assists man for a good living. Notwithstanding, I believe that the majority of Masons that I know do not know what religion means, and confuse it with something totally negative. Since we are dealing with violence against God, would you be so kind to give us the right concept about the meaning of religion?

Samael Aun Weor: Regarding your question, respectable sir and good friend, likewise people who attend this lecture, listen: Religion derives from the Latin word "religare," from re-, again, and ligare "to bind," and which means "to bind again the soul to God." Now, Masonry is not, properly said, a religion. It is rather a universal type of fraternity. Nevertheless, it is very commendable for such a meritorious institution to study the science of religion. By no means we are suggesting that some should be affiliated to such-and-such school, since everybody is free to think as they please. We only limit ourselves to advise the study of the science of religion. The science of religion is precisely Gnosticism in its purest form, a divine type of wisdom, profound analytical esotericism, transcendental occultism.

Question: Beloved Master, allow me to insist. I have heard in another lecture within the Gnostic teachings that the universe was created by seven Masonic Lodges, and this undoubtedly links Primeval Masonry with the Father. Consequently, I have the concept that in synthesis, Masonry is the common denominator of all religions, and therefore it proceeds from Gnosis. Would you be so kind to clarify this for me?

Samael Aun Weor: Respectable sir, those who have profoundly studied the Masonry of Ragon or Leadbeater know very well that occult esoteric Masonry existed not only under the porticoes of the temple of Jerusalem but also in ancient Egypt and in submerged Atlantis. Regrettably, in the age of Kali Yuga or the Iron Age in which we currently find ourselves, such honorable institution has entered into the descendent, devolving circle.

Nevertheless, it is clear that in the future great Root Race—precisely when the powerful esoteric civilizations of the past resurrect—that honorable institution will have to fulfill a brilliant mission. So, we do not deny the divine origin of that institution.

We know that the seven Cosmocreators officiated with holy liturgy at the dawning of the great day, when they fecundated the chaotic matter so that life could spring. From century to century, throughout the different cosmic rounds, the workshops became each time denser and denser, until finally reaching the state in which they are currently found.

We recommend the Masonic brothers to study in depth the esotericism of Solomon and the divine wisdom of the land of the Pharaohs. It is necessary, it is urgent, for the Masonic brothers to not fall into the Marxist-Leninist skepticism, into that dialectic for fools. Let the Masonic brothers not pronounce themselves against divinity, because this, besides being contrary to their esoteric order of divine origin, will inevitably lead them to the seventh Dantesque circle, the tenebrous region of the violent against God.

Question: Venerable Master, how can we classify the concrete fact of some Gnostics who, believing that they are identified with the doctrine of Christ, are also identified with the opposite side, which is the Marxist atheism?

Samael Aun Weor: Respectable gentleman, it so happens that within the occultist or esoteric currents some sincere individuals, who truly aspire to work for a better world, never cease to exist. It is unquestionable that these individuals become poisoned by the red propaganda. Thus, since they desire to create here in the Western world such a "Soviet paradise," they work with enthusiasm in order to achieve the total realization of this great longing of theirs. They are sincere but mistaken individuals, people with magnificent yet mistaken intentions. Remember that the path that leads to the abyss is paved with good intentions. If these individuals lived for a while as workers in the Soviet Union, I am sure that when returning to this region of the Western world, they would furiously demonstrate themselves as anticommunist.

It is very intriguing to know that there are more communists in the Western hemisphere than in the Soviet Union. This is because in the Soviet Union, behind the iron curtain, people already know about the Communist reality. They have lived it, and therefore they cannot be cheated by the red propaganda. On the other hand, since in the Western hemisphere we still do not have a Marxist-Leninist type of government, the red agitators can play with naive people in the same manner that a cat plays with the mouse before devouring it.

From a rigorously esoteric point of view, we can emphatically affirm the following: within the submerged worlds, within the tenebrous regions of the seventh Dantesque infradimension, Communists dress in black robes, since they are indeed leftist personages, priests of black magic. I will conclude stating the following: the venerable great White Lodge has classified Marxism-Leninism as authentic and legitimate black magic.

Therefore, those who have seen the secret path that leads to final liberation cannot avoid committing the crime of violence against God if they become active leftist members of leftism's ranks.

Question: Dear Master, albeit all of us know what fraud means, since we always relate it with economic types of matters, are all type of frauds included in this crime which is purged within the seventh Dantesque circle?

Samael Aun Weor: Friends, many types of fraud exist, thus it is good to clarify all of this. Dante symbolized fraud with an horrifying, tenebrous image. Dante depicted the monster of fraud in the following manner:

> *His face the semblance of a just man's wore, so kind and gracious was its outward cheer; the rest was serpent all: two shaggy claws reached to the armpits; and the back and breast, and either side, were painted o'er with nodes and orbits. Colours variegated more nor Turks nor Tartars e'er on cloth of state with interchangeable*

*embroidery wove, nor spread Arachne o'er her curious
loom.* - Inferno, Canto 17

Dante stated that such a monster had a terrible stinger at
the end of its tail. This symbolic monster expresses very well
the crime of fraud. Let us think for a while on the variegated
colored snares with which the fraudulent envelop their victims,
and the very kind and gracious faces with which the fraudulent
people appear, likewise their poisonous snake bodies, and their
horrible shaggy claws and the sting with which they hurt their
victims.

The types of fraud are so varied that one is really astounded.
There is fraud in the one who forms an esoteric circle and
thereafter abandons it.

There is fraud in those who open a Gnostic center and
thereafter disturb it with their crimes, namely, when falling
in love with the neighbor's wife, seducing members with the
purpose of practicing sexual magic, committing adultery in
hiding, coveting the Isis (priestess) in the temple, exploiting
the brothers and sisters of the sanctuary, promising what they
cannot fulfill, preaching what they do not practice, performing
the contrary of what they teach, creating scandals, drinking
alcohol in front of the surprised devotees, etc.

There is fraud in the man who promises matrimony to a
woman and does not fulfill his word, in the woman who gives
her word to a man and then disappoints him by falling in love
with another man, in parents of family who promise their son
or daughter such and such a gift or such and such help and
thereafter they do not fulfill their promise, etc.

All these forms of fraud are violence against the Father. This
is why Dante allegorizes them as that frightful monster with a
venerable face.

There is fraud in the individual who borrows money and
does not return it. There is fraud in the sellers of lottery and
gambling games, since the victims, convinced that they can
win, lose their money and feel deceived.

Question: Venerable Master, we understand that the seventh
Dantesque circle is denser than the former circles, so we would

like if you would be so kind to explain to us about the material constitution of such infradimension.

Samael Aun Weor: Friends, the seventh Saturnian submerged region is of an astounding material density, since each atom within this submerged region possesses 672 atoms of the Absolute within its womb. Obviously, these specific types of atoms are extremely heavy, and therefore the seventh submerged region is extremely gross and painful. In it, life is unbearably difficult, terribly complicated, and frighteningly violent, given that this number of laws (672) governs this tenebrous submerged zone, located underneath the geological crust of our planet.

Question: Master, I would like to know if the element or elements within which the inhabitants of such circle move about is also not seen by them and if they think that they are doing very well?

Samael Aun Weor: Respectable friends, I want you to know that this cavernous region of our planet is a mixture of mineral and fire. Nevertheless, there, the flames are only known by their effects, by the violence, by the rough, instinctive and brutal blows, etc.

I repeat what I already stated at the beginning of this lecture: what Dante symbolizes with blood is exclusively the bloody color of sexual violence shown in the aura of the lost ones and within the infrahuman atmosphere of that zone.

Undoubtedly, the inhabitants of this submerged Saturnine region never think bad about themselves, since they always suppose that they march on the path of righteousness and justice. Some of them know that they are demons, but they console themselves with the idea that on this Earth all "human beings" are demons. However, they who do not ignore that they are demons would never admit the idea that they are wicked, since they firmly believe they are good, just, and upright people. If someone were to reprimand them because of their crimes, if someone were to admonish them, if someone were to call them to repentance, they would feel offended, slandered, and would react with acts of violence.

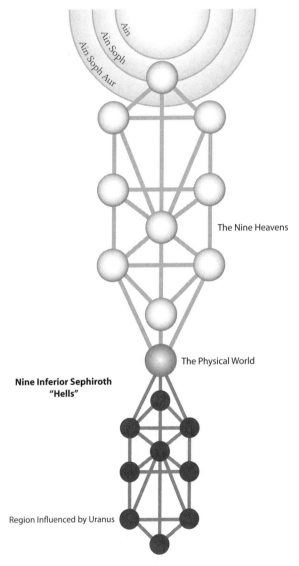

The Nine Heavens

The Physical World

**Nine Inferior Sephiroth
"Hells"**

Region Influenced by Uranus

Ain

Ain Soph

Ain Soph Aur

THE EIGHTH INFERNAL CIRCLE, THE SPHERE
OF URANUS, ON THE TREE OF LIFE

Chapter Twelve

The Eighth Infernal Circle, the Sphere of Uranus

Friends of mine, tonight, November the 18th, 1972, the tenth year of Aquarius, once again we are meeting, now with the purpose of studying the eighth Dantesque circle submerged underneath the terrestrial crust within the infradimensions of nature.

Regarding explanations, we have to start by reviewing what we have already said in other books in relation to Black Tantra. Obviously three types of Tantra exist, namely:

White Tantra

Black Tantra

Gray Tantra

Hindustanis speak frankly about the igneous serpent of our magical powers, about that solar electronic power that ascends through the spinal medulla of the ascetics.

It is clear that the transcendental fohat develops exclusively with White Tantra. We have already given the clue in our previous books. Nonetheless, we repeat it: "the connection of the lingam-yoni (phallus-uterus) without the ejaculation of the sacred sperm."

Black Tantra is different, since it has connection of the lingam-yoni and magical rites yet with seminal ejaculation. In this concrete case, the outcome is the awakening of the igneous serpent in its strictly negative form. It is evident that in Black Tantra the sacred fire is downwardly precipitated from the coccyx towards the atomic infernos of the human being; thus, when this occurs, the tail of Satan, the abominable Kundabuffer organ, appears.

Gray Tantra has another purpose, which is animal pleasure without transcendental aspirations.

Now, we will focus explicitly on the abominable Kundabuffer organ.

MOSES RAISES THE SERPENT OF BRASS

And the people spake against God, and against Moses, "Wherefore have ye brought us up out of Egypt to die in the wilderness? for [there is] no bread, neither [is there any] water; and our soul loatheth this light bread." And the LORD sent fiery serpents among the people, and they bit the people; and much people of Israel died. Therefore the people came to Moses, and said, "We have sinned, for we have spoken against the LORD, and against thee; pray unto the LORD, that he take away the serpents from us." And Moses prayed for the people. And the LORD said unto Moses, "Make thee a fiery serpent, and set it upon a pole: and it shall come to pass, that every one that is bitten, when he looketh upon it, shall live." And Moses made a serpent of brass, and put it upon a pole, and it came to pass, that if a serpent had bitten any man, when he beheld the serpent of brass, he lived. - Numbers 21

Two fiery serpents exist. The fiery serpent that awakens with White Tantra is the serpent of brass, which by victoriously ascending through the spinal medullar canal healed the Israelites in the wilderness. In contrast, there is the tempting serpent of Eden, which is the horrible Python that writhed in the mud of the Earth and that the irritated Apollo slayed with his arrows.

The first, the fiery serpent of brass, is the ascending fire that has the power of awakening the chakras of the dorsal spine. It opens, we might say, the seven Churches of the Apocalypse of St John, thus transforming us into terribly divine Gods.

The second fiery serpent opens the seven chakras located in the lower abdomen, which are the seven doors of hell, as Muslims call them.

Much has been said about the Kundalini, the annular, serpentine power that wonderfully develops within the body of every white tantric devotee. However, we solemnly affirm that no one can enjoy the powers of the luminous serpent without having been previously devoured by it. Now, friends, brothers and sisters of the Gnostic Movement, you will comprehend for yourselves the reason why the adepts from India have been qualified as Nagas (serpents). The great Hierophants of Babylon, Egypt, Greece, Chaldaea, etc., named themselves "serpents." In serpentine Mexico, Quetzalcoatl, the Mexican Christ, was devoured by the serpent, and therefore the title of Flying Serpent was granted unto him. Wotan was likewise a serpent because he had been swallowed by the serpent.

It is obvious and clear that the core of marriage—that is, the integral fusion of the Divine Mother with the Holy Spirit; in other words, the union of the igneous serpent of our magical powers with Shiva, the Third Logos, the Arch-Hierophant and Arch-Magi—is only possible when we have been devoured by the serpent. Then, the glorious resurrection of the secret Master within us here and now comes as a completion.

Now, I invite the entire audience and all the Gnostic Movements in general that listen to me, to an in-depth reflection on the antithesis... It is unquestionable that the horrible Python serpent is the negative and fatal opposite—better said, the shadow, the radical antithesis—of the serpent of light, since indubitably, truth disguises itself with darkness within the abyss.

If in the superior dimensions of nature and the cosmos we are devoured by the serpent of brass that healed the Israelites in the wilderness, obviously, within the eighth Dantesque circle the condemned are devoured by the horrible tempting serpent of Eden. Thus, this is how they are transformed into frightfully malignant, poisonous vipers.

I want you to integrally comprehend that the serpent will always have to devour us, whether in the luminous aspect or in the infernal tenebrous eighth circle.

The fatal feast of the horrible tempting serpent of Eden is pathetic when devouring the lost ones with the purpose of destroying them, of disintegrating them, of reducing them to cosmic dust, in order to liberate the essence, in order to restore the original pristine purity of the consciousness. It is only in this manner that the soul attains its emancipation from the painful Tartarus.

It is quite astounding to know that either through the luminous way based on conscious work and voluntary sufferings or through the tenebrous way within the eighth circle of fatalities, the serpent always destroys the ego. Thus, it is wonderful to know that the ego has to always be dissolved, no matter what our will may be—that is, according to our will or against our will. Thus, either as victors or failures the serpent must inevitably swallow us...

Thus, once the tempting serpent of Eden, that horrible Python, which is the negative aspect of the Divine Mother, completes her labor within the Avernus, she then returns to her positive polarization within the luminous region... Behold therefore, friends, in what manner the Divine Mother loves her child.

Therefore, those who go astray on the path of Black Tantra when developing the serpent of fatalities inevitably condemn themselves to the Second Death. Thus, the red turbaned Drukpas can never flee from the Divine Mother Kundalini. She will devour them inevitably, no matter what the cost might be.

Therefore, within the eighth infernal circle unluckily dwell the false alchemists, the devotees of Black Tantra, the falsifiers of metal. They are those who crystallized negatively. To be more precise, they are those who, instead of crystallizing the Sexual Hydrogen Ti-12 in the superior existential bodies of the Being, made it crystallize negatively in order to transform themselves in fact into Adepts from the tenebrous countenance who inevitably will be devoured by the horrible serpent of fatalities.

Hence, I want everyone to become aware that there are two types of alchemy, two types of death for the ego, and two types of banquets that the serpent engorges. You can choose the path... You must choose. Knowledge is given unto you. You are before the philosophical dilemma of "to be or not to be."

Woe of you, candidates for the Second Death! Your tortures will be frightful. Only in this manner can you die within the tenebrous Avernus. Otherwise, in what other manner can the essence be emancipated? In what other manner can the essence be free in order to re-initiate a new evolving cycle that undoubtedly has to begin from the hard rock?

Likewise, within the eighth infernal circle we find the money counterfeiters, the falsifiers, the impostors, the incestuous, the sowers of discord, the bad counselors, those who promise and do not fulfill their promises, those who create scandals, and also those who commit pilferage, false and lying people, etc.

The eighth submerged region is the antithesis, the opposite, the negative aspect of the planet Uranus. That planet of our solar system is very interesting. It has been told unto us that the North and South Pole of the planet Uranus alternately point towards the Sun. When the positive pole of that planet is oriented towards the Sun, then the masculine force is imposed upon the face of the Earth. Yet, when the negative pole of that planet is oriented towards the resplendent Sun, then the feminine force commands on our afflicted planet. Each cycle or magnetic period of Uranus lasts 42 years. Thus, this is how in cycles or periods of 42 years men and women alternate their command here on the Earth. The complete orbit of the planet

Uranus around the Sun endures 84 Earth years: 42 masculine types of years and 42 feminine types of years.

If we carefully observe the customs of people during history, we will see intensive epochs of masculine activity—such as piracy, for example, when all the seas of the Earth were full of corsairs—and feminine epochs like the present epoch [1972], or like that epoch in which the Amazons established their lunar cults and governed a large part of Europe, making the world to shake. So, each masculine cycle is proceeded by a feminine cycle and vice-versa. Everything depends on the polarization of Uranus and on the type of energy that comes to Earth from that planet.

It is good to know for the benefit of the great cause that the sexual glands are governed by the planet Uranus. We need to integrally comprehend that the feminine ovaries are also governed by the planet Uranus. This is why such planet, as ruler of the new era of Aquarius, brings a complete revolution to our afflicted world.

Therefore, it is not strange that the sexual aspects of the totally lost ones are defined and that the tempting serpent of Eden engorges the fallen ones within the submerged region of Uranus underneath the crust of the Earth in order to begin the destructive process on a great scale, which concludes with the Second Death.

In our book entitled *The Three Mountains*, we stated that within the submerged mineral kingdom of the planet Uranus, the initiate has to disintegrate the bad thief Cacus or Gestas as it appears in the Christian gospel. Whereas, Agatho or Dismas, the good thief, is that inner power that from the depth of our being steals the Sexual Hydrogen Ti-12 for our own Inner Self-realization. Caco or Cacus, the bad thief, the horrible Gestas, is that tenebrous, sinister power that steals the creative energy for evil. It is not irrelevant to inform you that the abominable Kundabuffer organ is the outcome of the bad use of the creative energy, stolen by Caco, therefore the Kundabuffer organ develops not only within the black alchemists or tenebrous devotees of Tantra, but also within the decidedly lost souls, even if they possess no magical knowledge.

THE TWO THIEVES BESIDE THE CRUCIFIXION OF THE LORD

Now, in regard to the antithetical sphere of the planet Uranus, which is located within the abysmal depths of the planet Earth, by the law of contrasts and analogy of the contraries and of simple correspondences the horrifying Caco must also be destroyed.

Behold then, ladies and gentlemen, in which manner these luminous and tenebrous antithetical aspects correspond and how they are developed...

Question: Master, is the tempting Serpent of Eden the same sacred serpent?

Samael Aun Weor: My estimable brother, I will quickly answer your very interesting question. It is clear that within the Avernus truth disguises itself with darkness. Thus, it is remarkable to know that the serpent can be polarized in a positive or negative manner. This means that the tempting serpent of Eden is the tenebrous contrast, the negative polarization of the serpent of brass, which healed the Israelites in the wilderness. So, it is intriguing to know that the radiating serpent become polarized in this fatal manner. Yet, this invites us to comprehend that the serpent does it for the good of its own child, in order to destroy—within the Avernus—the infrahuman elements that we carry within, and thus to liberate us from the frightening claws of pain. Thus, this is how the love of every Divine Mother is.

Question: Beloved Master, since it is evident that the majority of the inhabitants of this planet do not practice either White or Black Tantra but Gray Tantra—that is, sexual intercourse with the ejaculation of the Ens Seminis and without any transcendental longing—I ask you if all of these masses of souls automatically enter the Eighth Dantesque circle like those who practiced Black Tantra.

Samael Aun Weor: Respectable gentleman, your question is very intelligent, therefore, understand my answer. It is worthwhile for you to know that every Gray Tantra inevitably becomes Black. When someone descends into the Avernus, that one awakens negatively. That fatal awakening is based on the development of the abominable Kundabuffer organ. It is therefore urgent to know that any fornicator, even if they do not know Black Tantra, is in fact tantric, and inevitably becomes a tenebrous personality with the tempting serpent of Eden completely developed.

Question: Master, when you talked to us about the second infradimensional circle, you explained that the fornicators dwell within it. Thus, just in order to clarify the concept, I want to know what difference exists between the fornicators that inhabit the circle of Mercury and those who enter the eighth Dantesque circle.

Samael Aun Weor: Friends, lust is the root of the ego, of the "I," the myself, the self-willed. Thus, this invites us to comprehend that lechery, fornication, unquestionably exists within each one of the nine natural infradimensions underneath the geologic crust of our planet. Nonetheless, a difference exist in all of this. Within the submerged sphere of Mercury, the frightening Coatlicue or Proserpine, the tempting serpent of Eden, does not yet devour her children. Only within the submerged eighth region is where she has her frightful banquet. Now we can explain to ourselves why the Florentine Dante saw in the eighth circle millions of human beings turned into pieces, bleeding, tearing themselves with their nails and with their teeth, decapitated, etc. It is obvious that in such a submerged region begins the process of ossification, crystallization, mineralization, and the destruction of any ego.

Question: Venerable Master, it is truly impressive the narrative that you just gave us about the love of the Divine Mother, regarding how she, whether in her aspect of light or her aspect of darkness, inclusive through the most painful manner within the entrails of the Earth, liberates her child, the essence. Consequently, how is it possible that many black magicians with awakened consciousness, knowing the pain that they have to undergo, persist treading the path of Black Tantra and the Second Death?

Samael Aun Weor: Respectable gentleman, it is worthwhile for everyone here present to know—as I have already stated in former books—that some awaken in the light and others in the darkness. Nonetheless, a radical difference exists between those who awaken positively and those who awaken in a negative manner. Undoubtedly, the lost souls, those who have awakened in evil and for evil, even when they know that they must devolve within the entrails of the planet until the Second Death before achieving the restoration of the original pristine purity of their psychic matter, do not repent of the path that they have chosen because they have made of their devolution and of the fatal wheel of Samsara a religion, a mystique... Therefore, it is not irrelevant to inform this audience that the leftist adepts have temples within the submerged regions where they worship the negative aspect of the serpent. Certainly, those infrahuman beings are never unaware of the fate that is reserved for them. Moreover, they even wish to accelerate it so that they can quickly emancipate themselves and thus go out free towards the light of the Sun with the purpose of once again starting a new evolution that will be reinitiated—as I have already stated—from the hard rock, and continue through the vegetable and animal states until re-conquering the intellectual humanoid state.

When one converses with Jahveh, one can clearly evidence that the lost souls abhor the Solar Logos and that they are completely enamored of the wheel of Samsara (vicious and fatal circle).

Question: Venerable Master, I do not understand how it is possible that an inhabitant of that submerged infradimension, of that eight Dantesque circle, whose essence is bottled within the tremendous "I" of lust, cannot even briefly awaken the consciousness, since in order for this to happen the essence must be liberated from within the ego.

Samael Aun Weor: Respectable gentleman, again I repeat what I have already stated: some awaken in the light and others in the darkness. Regarding this aspect of our lecture, let us tonight cite a verse from Daniel the prophet. Let us read the Bible:

> And many of them that sleep in the dust of the earth shall awake, some to everlasting life, and some to shame and everlasting contempt. Ant they that be wise shall shine as the brightness of the firmament; and they that turn many to righteousness as the stars for ever and ever. But thou, O Daniel, shut up the words, and seal the book, even to the time of the end; many shall run to and fro, and knowledge shall be increased. - Daniel 11:12

Since we are already in the times of the end and since knowledge has scandalously increased, it is therefore convenient to take the seal from the book and clarify the prophecy. I repeat: the abominable Kundabuffer organ has the power to awaken the consciousness of those who enter the abyss, where only crying and the gnashing of teeth are heard.

We can therefore awaken our consciousness in a positive and luminous manner by means the voluntary dissolution of the ego, or awaken it in evil and for evil by means of the development of the abominable Kundabuffer organ. Everyone can choose their path. The prophecy of Daniel has been clarified.

Question: Venerable Master, I know many spiritual mentors who, with a lot of sincerity, live separated from sexual practices. In other words, they are celibate. Therefore, as I understand it, they are not classified within any of the three Tantras that you have explained to us. Will these persons perhaps not enter into this region of the Avernus?

Samael Aun Weor: *"Woe unto you, scribes and Pharisees, hypocrites! for you are like unto whited sepulchers, you perverted serpents, you generation of vipers, for you make clean the outside of the cup and of the platter, but are within full of all rottenness."*

The Pharisee "I" is found active in the depth of many devotees. They boast of being saints and sages, chaste and perfect, but in their depth they are frightful fornicators.

The Pharisee "I" blesses the food when sitting at the table. The Pharisee "I" has pietistic attitudes. The Pharisee "I" deceives himself when believing to be virtuous. Yet, within the profundity of himself, he hides unspeakable intentions and Machiavellian purposes that he justifies with good intentions.

So, such beatific devotees are irremediably devoured by the tempting serpent of Eden within the eighth Dantesque circle.

Question: Master, can you tell us about the density and elements that integrate that infradimension?

Samael Aun Weor: Respectable friends, the eighth Dantesque circle is simultaneously a petrous and igneous region. Fire really tortures the lost souls in it. This Uranian zone submerged underneath the geologic crust of the planet Earth has crystallizations of an unbearable materialism. It is not irrelevant to remember with complete astounding clarity that within that zone, each atom carries in its womb 768 atoms of the sacred Absolute Sun. Consequently, each atom of that zone is terribly dense, and therefore it is not strange that in such region materiality is even denser than in the seven former circles. Thus, an equal number of laws (768) control all the activities of the infernal eighth circle. Therefore, life is extremely complicated and difficult within this submerged zone of the Avernus. Hence, sufferings are terribly intensified within that tenebrous zone, the negative aspect of the planet Uranus, located underneath the epidermis of the Earth.

Chapter Thirteen

The Ninth Infernal Circle, the Sphere of Neptune

Worthiest friends, we meet here tonight with the purpose of studying the ninth Dantesque circle. Our purpose is to delve into the core of this subject, since through these lectures we have arrived at the very center of the Earth, which has a frightful inertia, given that it is the very nucleus of our planet. Thus, when reaching this inmost part, Dante in his *Divine Comedy* cites the spear of Achilles. It has been told unto us that if in the beginning that spear hurt and caused harm or bitterness, thereafter it became a true blessing. That spear clearly brings to our memory the lance with which Longinus the Roman centurion wounded the side of the Lord. That spear, grasped by Parsifal, the marvelous hero of the Wagnerian drama, manages to heal the wound in the side of Amfortas.

In our former books we spoke in a concrete manner about this weapon of Eros. Within these books we stated that the spear is a phallic type of weapon that when wisely handled can be utilized for the disintegration of the pluralized "I." Consequently, the fact that Dante mentions the spear of Achilles precisely in the ninth sphere is something outstanding. Thus, this is an incentive impelling us to meditate.

It is commendable to remember that the holy lance is the very emblem of the phallus, within which stands the principle of all life, the transcendental sexual electricity, which is the weapon with which we can disintegrate and reduce the pluralized "I" to cosmic dust.

In this lecture I want to also address the Holy Grail, that divine cup or miraculous chalice from which the great Kabir Jesus drank at the last supper. It is clear that such a jewel is the living symbol of the eternal feminine uterus or divine yoni.

Thus, given that in this lecture we have entered into the theme regarding the ninth sphere, we cannot avoid mentioning the chalice and the lance from the great archaic mysteries, since it is in the ninth sphere where the devolving creatures definitely disintegrate.

What happened to Nimrod and his tower of Babel? What will occur to the modern fanatics of that tower? Vain will be their attempt to assault heaven with their rockets, since cosmic travel is not allowed to intellectual animals. Thus, to attempt it is a sacrilege. Cosmic travel is an right exclusive to authentic, legitimate, and true human beings. Therefore, after the great catastrophe that is approaching, the intellectual loafers of the tower of Babel will enter into the infernal worlds, into the ninth sphere, in order to be reduced to cosmic dust.

What happened to Ephialtes? Great was his prowess when he brought alarm to the incarnated Gods from ancient Atlantis. Nonetheless, within the ninth Dantesque circle he was reduced to dust.

What happened to Briareus, the one with one hundred arms, living allegorical representation of the adepts of tenebrous countenance who inhabited the submerged Atlantis in the times of yore? He was dissolved. He became dust of the earth within the ninth infernal Neptunian circle.

Woe to Brutus, Cassius, and the interior Judas of every living creature! The traitors are reduced to dust within that submerged Neptunian zone.

DANTE'S SYMBOL OF LUCIFER IN THE NINTH SPHERE CONSUMING THE THREE TRAITORS

And what happened unto you, Alberigo de Manfredi, lord of Faenza? What were your good intentions worth? To what avail did you enter the order of the Jovial Friars? The divine ones and humans know very well the horrible crime that you committed. Were you not the one who slew your kindred in the midst of a banquet? The legend of the centuries states that pretending that you wished to be reconciled with your kindred, you invited them to an infamous banquet. Thus, precisely when the supper ended, in the very moment when the dessert was served, you ordered your servants to slay them. Nevertheless, you apparently continued to live. This is how it appeared to people, yet indeed, in the very moment in which your crime was committed, you entered into the ninth infernal circle. Who then remained, inhabiting your body? Was it perhaps a demon?

Woe to the traitors! Woe to those who commit similar crimes! They are immediately judged by the tribunals of objective justice and sentenced to death. The cosmic executioners perform the sentence. Thus, those unfortunate souls are immediately executed and sink into the ninth Dantesque circle, even when their physical bodies are not dead. It is known that the physical bodies of those unfortunate souls are immediately taken from them by a demon that thereafter rules it, thus replacing the traitor. That demon remains inside the body so that the karmic processes are not altered for the people or relatives who in one way or another are related to such perverse personalities.

Even though it might appeared incredible, presently there are many living dead who tread the streets of many cities, physical bodies whose true owners now live within the infernal worlds.

Question: Venerable Master, if the essence bottled within the pluralized "I" is what transmigrates into the infernal worlds—in the replacement that you spoke to us about—does this signify that another bottled essence takes over the body of the living dead?

Samael Aun Weor: Friends, I repeat: any demon can replace the ex-owner of the body. There can also be the case that the demon who becomes owner of that situation, that is, master and lord of such an abandoned vehicle, is one of the less harmful demons that formed part of the ego that was precipitated into the Avernus.

Thus, the judges of heavenly justice condemn the crimes of high treason with the death penalty.

Question: Master, what should be understood by "a crime of high treason?"

Samael Aun Weor: Friends, there are many genres of treason, yet there are some so grave that they are immediately executed with the death penalty.

To invite such and such person or persons to a banquet and then murder them at the same banquet, alleging such and such a motive, is a very grave crime that cannot be paid in any other manner. In this case, the traitor is taken from his body and immediately executed. Thus, his body is then controlled by the hands of some demon.

It is evident that in no way do people notice what has happened within the depth of the personality of the traitor, given that the judges of heavenly justice are only interested in the sentence being executed, and that is all.

Question: Master, I did not fully understand the subject-matter related to the essence, given that I do not comprehend how it is that the demon that replaces the ex-owner of the body of the traitor could have a physical life devoid of Essence. What does Master G. tell us about this?

Samael Aun Weor: Master G. states that many people devoid of Essence tread on the streets; they exist only with their personality, meaning, they wander around alive, yet they are dead.

Friends, there comes into my mind that little verse that states:

> Dead are not those who in peace rest within the cold tomb; dead are those who still are alive yet their souls are doomed.

The demon that replaces the owner of a given body can no longer have any type of essence; this completely clarified my explanation. These are the cases of those soulless people cited by H.P.B. in her *Secret Doctrine*, so I am not the first one to mention this subject-matter, neither I am the last, except that I am the first one who totally clarifies it.

Question: Venerable Master, would you be so kind as to give us an explanation in regards to what you formerly stated about the cosmic executioner?

Samael Aun Weor: I see in the audience an International Gnostic Missionary who very sincerely has posed this question.

The tribunals of objective justice—which are different from the subjective justice of this vain world in which we live—have cosmic executioners under their services. In these moments there come into my memory two very famous ones who worked in the ancient Egypt of the Pharaohs. This type of executioner acts according to the Great Law. They are beyond good and evil. They have power over life and power over death...

Regarding this, I remember with completely dazzling clarity something unusual that occurred to me in my present existence. After having concluded all the esoteric, initiatic processes, I was submitted to many ordeals, yet there was one under which I was always failing; I am emphatically addressing a sexual problem.

At that time, many years ago, the inevitable always happened to me. I failed in the decisive moments, thus unfortunately swallowing the apples of the garden of Hesperides... Yet, in the physical world I kept the most absolute chastity. The disaster always happened to me out of the body within the superior worlds. I was failing when in the presence of many ineffable ladies... Over and over again I was succumbing amongst the immodest processes of Gundrigia, Kundry, Salome, the seductive Eve of Hebrew mythology.

The grave aspect of my case is that, in spite of having become triumphant in all of the former esoteric, initiatic ordeals, these failures had come to happen to me precisely at the end of the Mountain of Initiation. Thus, my case was indeed lamentable, since in all of those scenes of an erotic type, under the tree of the science of good and evil, I was not the owner of myself: a demon was entering into my mind.

That demon was controlling my senses, controlling my will. Thus, this is why I was failing, unfortunately... I suffered the unspeakable. The wound of Amfortas bled on my side. Hence, my remorse was frightful.

Thus, finally one day, when mortally wounded to the core of my soul, it happened that I cried out to my Divine Mother Kundalini in request for her succor. Thus, her aid was not delayed... Then, one given night, my adorable Mother detached me from my physical body and took me before the tribunals of objective justice.

Great was my shock when I saw myself in the presence of the judges of the tribunal of Karma. Many people filled the hall. Terror was expressed upon their countenances. All of them were grieving in their hearts. I advanced some steps into the hall of Truth-Justice. Then, a judge opened a book and read, "Crimes against the Goddess Moon, adventures of Don Juan Tenorio during the epoch of the medieval troubadours and of the knights-errant and feudal cities." Then, with a thundering voice, he pronounced the sentence of death, and in an imperative manner he commanded the cosmic executioner to execute the sentence at once.

I still remember the unspeakable terror of those moments. My legs trembled in the precise moment when the executioner unsheathed his flaming sword and menacingly directed it towards my defenseless person. During those seconds—that to me seemed to be centuries of torture—through my mind passed all my sacrifices for humanity, my struggles for the Gnostic Movement, the books I had written, etc. Thus, I said to myself, "So, this is the fate that now lies ahead for me, after having suffered so much for humanity? Alas is this the payment that the Gods give me? Woe! Woe! Woe!"

Suddenly, as the executioner directed the tip of his sword towards me... I felt that something moved and agitated violently within my interior. Then, with mystical astonishment, I saw emerging from my body through the dorsal spine, a lustful, terribly perverse demon that assumed the shape of a neighing horse... The executioner aimed his sword towards the malignant beast, which was precipitated headlong down into the bottom of a dark precipice. Its legs and tail were seen turned upwards, when finally the whole body of that frightful abomination totally penetrated under the epidermis of the planetary globe, to become lost within the tenebrous entrails of the Avernus...

Thus, friends of mine, this is how I was freed of that lustful "I" that I created in the Middle Ages when, as a fallen Bodhisattva, I wandered from castle to castle on a regal mount, upon the rocky roads, on the lands of feudal lords. Thus, once I was freed of that abomination of nature, I felt happy, since I never failed in the sexual tests again. I became master of myself and thus I continued along the path of the razor's edge.

Lo and behold, ladies and gentlemen, the great benefit that the cosmic executioner performed for me... Unquestionably, these types of beings are beyond good and evil and they are terribly divine.

Understand: by no means do I want to demagogue, since I do not even remotely pretend to praise the infamous executioners of subjective justice, of earthly justice, of that vain justice that is bought and sold. In this lecture I am exclusively referring to those sacred individuals of objective justice, of heavenly justice, which are radically different...

Question: Master, at the beginning of your impressive narration regarding the souls that entered into the ninth Dantesque circle, you addressed the present builders of the tower of Babel, and mentioned the men of science who launch rockets into space. Can you clarify what these sages of modern science are guilty of?

Samael Aun Weor: Respectable gentleman, I will gladly answer your question at once.

Ancient texts of ancient wisdom state that when the Titans of submerged Atlantis wanted to assault heaven, they were precipitated into the abyss. I want you ladies and gentlemen to be fully aware that the sages of the twentieth century are not the first ones to launch rockets into space, neither are they the only earthlings that have been able to send astronauts to the moon. Nimrod and his henchmen, the fanatics of the tower of Babel, inhabitants of submerged Atlantis, created better

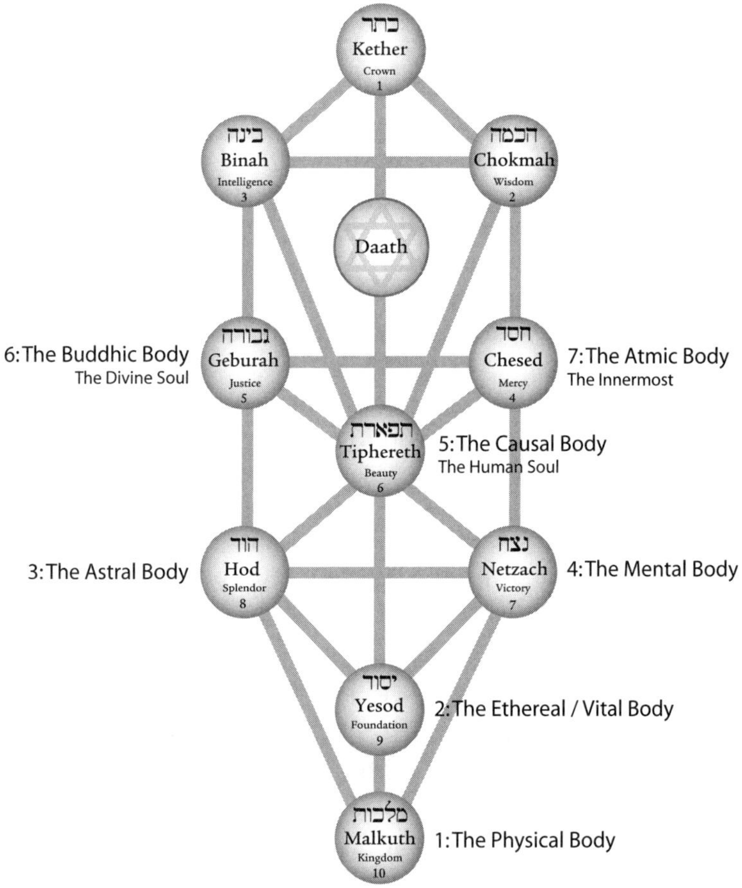
כתר
Kether
Crown
1
בינה
Binah
Intelligence
3
חכמה
Chokmah
Wisdom
2
Daath
גבורה
Geburah
Justice
5
6: The Buddhic Body
The Divine Soul
חסד
Chesed
Mercy
4
7: The Atmic Body
The Innermost
תפארת
Tiphereth
Beauty
6
5: The Causal Body
The Human Soul
הוד
Hod
Splendor
8
3: The Astral Body
נצח
Netzach
Victory
7
4: The Mental Body
יסוד
Yesod
Foundation
9
2: The Ethereal / Vital Body
מלכות
Malkuth
Kingdom
10
1: The Physical Body

The Tree of Life and the Bodies of the Being

rockets, propelled by nuclear energy, and also sent men to the moon. This is something I know. I saw it, and I give testimony of it because I lived in Atlantis. I still remember an airport of the submerged continent... Many times from a neighboring restaurant, "Caravancin or Asana," amidst the enthusiastic shouts of the excited multitudes, I saw many of those spaceships launched... What was the end of all of this? What happened to the Titans? Now we find only dust within the ninth infernal circle.

Friends, ladies, do not forget that space is infinitely sacred, and consequently, interplanetary navigation is controlled by very severe cosmic laws.

The error of these modern henchmen of the tower of Babel precisely consists in their self-sufficiency. These learned ignoramuses, these braggers, rely on the mistaken principle that they are already human. They do not want to realize that they have still not arrived at such a stature. They are only rational homunculi, intellective humanoids.

Listen: in order to be human, one needs to give oneself the luxury of creating for personal use an astral body, a mental body, and a causal body. Thus, only those who have created such suprasensible vehicles can really incarnate their Real Being, which would immediately place them within the realm of human beings.

It is therefore absurd for rational animals to escape from the zoo (planet Earth) in order to travel throughout the infinite space.

Therefore, it is necessary to know that these braggers of the tower of Babel will be fulminated by the terrible ray of cosmic justice and will perish within the ninth Dantesque circle.

Dressed with the Eidolon (astral body), I have spent entire hours within the entrails of the Earth, within the very center of permanent gravity, in the nucleus of our world. That region is terribly dense since each atom of the cited zone carries within its womb 864 atoms of the sacred Absolute Sun. An equal number of laws (864) control the unhappy creatures which in this zone are found in the process of complete disintegration.

While walking there, I saw a stone upon which a head similar to that of a human was standing. That head moved very slowly, mechanically repeating everything that I considered to say. That head belonged to someone who had already become totally mineralized and who unquestionably was decomposing and disintegrating to finally reduce himself to cosmic dust.

Continuing on my way within the entrails of the planet, I suddenly felt as if a diabolic entity had alighted upon my shoulders. I shook myself forcefully, and that creature fell a little further on the ground.

Thereafter, continuing on the solitary path of tenebrous Tartarus within those frightful profundities where time is terribly long and tedious, I entered into a filthy room where there was a prostitute who, wallowing on the Procrustean bed, was slowly disintegrating. That whore was slowly, little by little, losing fingers, arms, legs, while incessantly copulating with whichever larvae could approach her... Terribly moved, I withdrew from that horrible bedroom...

Last of all, something unusual happened. I saw a pair of witches dressed in black who, slowly soaring over the floor, moved towards a kitchen where these witches prepare their brews, their potions, their spells, in order to cause harm to other unhappy souls from the tenebrous Tartarus...

Time passed by and I began to feel annoyed within such a gross materiality. I longed to emerge from it. I wanted to ascend to the surface of the Earth, to see again the soft light of the day. My longing was not in vain. Soon I was assisted and my Real Being again took me out of those abysses in order to contemplate anew the lovely mountains, the profound seas, the light of the Sun, and the twinkling stars.

Friends, remember the city of Dis in the ninth infernal circle. There, those who have devolved in time exhale their last breath.

Prometheus-Lucifer, the adversary, that abhorred worm that bores through the world, had the most beautiful face, although now he is found chained to the fatal rock of impotence.

OUR INNER PROMETHEUS-LUCIFER, CHAINED TO THE ROCK OF SEX, AND HAVING HIS LIVER EATEN BY AN EAGLE. PAINTING BY JACOB JORDAENS, C. 1640, WALLRAF-RICHARTZ-MUSEUM, COLOGNE, GERMANY.

Let us not think of a dogmatic Lucifer, but of an interior Lucifer within each one of us. Yes, Lucifer is the reflection of the Logos that is found within the inner depth of each person.

It is stated that Lucifer weeps with six eyes. Six is a number that invites us to reflection. 666 is the number of the great whore, and by adding the numbers 6+6+6 we have 18 as a result. Continuing with new additions we arrive at the following synthesis: 1 + 8 = 9, the ninth sphere, the ninth Dantesque circle.

Lucifer is therefore that revolutionary force found in the core of our sexual system, and which wisely handled can transform us into Gods.

To whom would I compare those who do not know how to handle the Luciferic force? I would possibly compare them with the apprentices of electricity or to those unwary ones who—not having such a profession—ignore the danger and dare to play with high tension electrical cables. Undoubtedly they are fulminated and are precipitated into the abyss.

The negative aspect of Prometheus-Lucifer inevitably leads us to failure. This is why it is stated that he is the adversary who dwells within the core of the world.

The antithesis of Lucifer or the superior aspect of Lucifer is the Solar Logos, the Cosmic Christ.

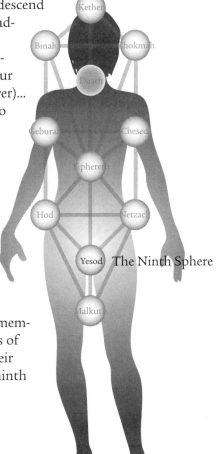

Lucifer is the ladder to descend into the Avernus and the ladder to ascend from it.

Comprehension is indispensable; remember that our motto is Thelema (willpower)...

It is necessary to learn to distinguish between a fall and a descent. We need to descend into the ninth sphere (sex) in order to build the superior existential bodies of the Being and in order to dissolve the ego. The well of the universe is within the ninth circle, the center of the planetary gravity.

It is not irrelevant to remember that the creative organs of the human species have their full representation in the ninth submerged sphere.

No one can ascend without having taken the courage to descend. Any exaltation is preceded by a terrible and dreadful humiliation.

To descend into the ninth sphere is indispensable. Some do it during life by means of their own will, spontaneously, and for their Inner Self-realization. Yet, others, the majority, the multitudes, do it in an unconscious manner when they descend into the abyss of perdition.

Question: Venerable Master, would you be so kind as to explain why sex is also called the ninth sphere? Is it perhaps because this is related with the center of the Earth?

Samael Aun Weor: Friends, it is urgent to comprehend that in the superior dimensions of nature, submerged beneath the epidermis of the Earth, by the law of antithesis there is a ninth circle of glory, where the Initiates of the Universal White Fraternity can see, traced in a concrete manner, the sign of the infinite, the holy eight, set in a horizontal manner. Those who have studied esoteric Kabbalah know very well the inner significance of this magical figure.

The upper part of that symbol represents the brain. The lower part allegorizes sex. The center of that magnificent figure is the atomic point where the nine submerged regions gravitate. Behold there: the brain, heart, and sex of the planetary genie...

Terrible is the struggle: brain against sex, and sex against brain. When sex overcomes the brain, when the brain remains without any control, we are then precipitated headlong into the abyss.

When brain and sex are mutually equilibrated we then realize ourselves intimately.

All creatures that exist upon the face of the Earth have been created in accordance with the holy symbol of the infinite. Now you can explain to yourselves why sex corresponds with the ninth sphere.

The child remains nine months within the maternal womb. For nine ages was humanity within the womb of great nature, Rhea, Cybele, etc. With this explanation I seriously believe that I have answered the question of the gentleman.

Question: Venerable Master, I would like to know how the essence emerges to the light of the Sun, once the ego has been reduced to cosmic dust within this ninth circle of the center of our planet.

Samael Aun Weor: Let us now return into the subject-matter related with the infernal dimensions or infradimensions of nature, after having explained about the sign of the infinite and the superior dimensions of nature.

After the essence exhales its last breath within this region where the throne of Dis is found, the essence without ego, the psychic material, that embryo of soul, is liberated, since as we have already stated, the ego is reduced to cosmic dust. Thus, once the essence is emancipated, it takes up a very beautiful child-like figure, filled with radiant beauty. This is the solemn moment in which the Devas of nature examine the liberated essence. So, after having proved to satiation that the essence no longer possesses any subjective, infrahuman element, they give unto it the token to freedom. What I mean to say with this is that they grant unto the soul the bliss of liberation.

Happy are those moments in which the soul of the dead penetrates through certain luminous atomic doors that immediately grant them departure into the light of the sun.

Thus, once the creature is free and upon the epidermis of our planet, the essence initiates a new evolution. It then becomes a gnome or pygmy of the mineral kingdom. Thereafter it will continue its evolution by ascending through the vegetable and animal levels, until on a faraway day it will re-conquer the intellectual humanoid state that was lost in the past.

Chapter Fourteen

Perpetual Motion

Worthy audience, respectable gentlemen, honorable ladies, our lecture will briefly discuss perpetual motion.

Periodically, in some way or another the intellectual loafers become preoccupied with making a perpetual motion mechanism, on account of which the public opinion becomes intensely agitated. People always get into their heads the challenge of inventing a mechanism that will run perpetually, but this is not possible due to the inevitability of worn-out materials. It is clear that the momentum of any perpetual motion machine ceases if the pieces of the mechanism are worn out. Thus, the outcome of it all is that when trying to discover the law of perpetual motion some people have ended up in insane asylums.

The least that one can do is to laugh when seeing so many wiseacres' machines that fail to fulfill their function. What ingenious and complicated mechanisms have the intellectual loafers not invented? Nonetheless, their problem continues without solution.

Frankly, we have already discovered the law of perpetual motion in the marvelous cylinder of the system of the Archangel Hariton. It is stated:

> "Its chief part is made of amber with platinum hoops and the interior panels of the walls are made of 'anthracite,' 'copper,' and 'ivory' and a very strong 'mastic' unaffectable either by cold, or by heat or by water or even by the radiations of cosmic concentrations."

According to our way of seeing and understanding things, it is obvious that "both the exterior levers and the cogwheels must certainly be renewed from time to time, for although they are made of the strongest metal, yet long use will wear them out."

Unquestionably, we are addressing the Wheel of Samsara, which revolves eternally. All of us, without any exceptions, have

RETRIBUTION

Arcanum 10 of the Tarot

revolved many times along with this great wheel, and if the perpetual motion has not been interrupted, it is exclusively due to the infinite quantity of disposable elements.

Let us think for a moment of the axis of this great wheel. It is stated that it is made of platinum, yet it can also be emphatically affirmed that it is made of silver, since anyone knows that silver and platinum are both of a completely lunar nature. Thus, it is obvious that the axis of the fatal wheel cannot be made from another material.

Now, regarding amber, it is clear that amber is found diluted in the entire creation. We must not forget that the three universal forces are completely unified in this substance. Yes, it is extraordinary that even though each one of the three primary forces of creation works independently, each one on their own accord, nonetheless they are unified thanks to that magnificent substance called "amber."

Again, each of us has not only frequently passed through the mill, but moreover through each cog of the mill's wheels; with the former statement I am emphasizing the fact that we have incessantly revolved through successive eternities within the wheel of the Archangel Hariton, which is the extraordinary Wheel of Samsara. Our egos are the disposable materials which, by descending on the tragic wheel, are disintegrated within the Avernus.

Evolving Anubis always ascends on the right, and devolving Typhon always descends on the left of the wheel.

During all of these lectures we have abundantly repeated that 108 existences are assigned unto each one of us. Thus, it is clear that once the cycle of 108 successive lives finishes, if we have not achieved the self-realization of our inner Being, we descend into the submerged mineral kingdom by revolving on the wheel of the Archangel Hariton. With this statement we want to clearly affirm that evolution reaches a point perfectly defined by nature, where thereafter devolution proceeds. So, evolving, we ascend on the right side of the wheel, and devolving, we descend on the left side of it.

The properly evolving ascension begins from the mineral kingdom. Any esotericist investigator with awakened consciousness can verify the crude reality of the evolving creatures from the superior mineral kingdom. We state 'superior mineral kingdom' in order to differentiate this from the 'submerged inferior mineral kingdom'. Many times, outside of my physical body, when moving within my Eidolon, I have opened rocks or stone fragments in order to study these multiple creatures which inhabit the superior mineral kingdom. Thus, I can tell you without fear of exaggeration that such innocent creatures are beyond good and evil.

Once, when I opened a rock fragment, I saw many ladies and gentlemen elegantly dressed. They were at the most 5 to 10 centimeters tall. Undoubtedly, these types of small mineral elementals like to costume themselves in our humanoid fashion.

While traveling in my car on different roads in Mexico I have seen with mystical surprise other certain superior elementals of the rocks, which have warned me about dangers or have advised me to be cautious on the road. This second type of mineral elementals is unquestionably more advanced than the first type. They assume very similar shapes to those from the intellectual humanoid, although the clothing they wear is of the color of the rocks they inhabit.

The third type of mineral elementals—which are most advanced—are those known by the name of gnomes or pygmies. These types of creatures appear as true dwarves, with long white beards and gray hair. Undoubtedly, this last type knows in depth the alchemy of the metals and cooperates in the alchemical work of nature. Obviously, these are more advanced creatures, which are clearly mentioned by many texts of occultism. It is enough to remember for a moment *The Elementals* of Franz Hartmann, who mentioned these creatures.

So, undoubtedly, the highly developed mineral elementals enter into the vegetable kingdom. Thus, each plant is the physical body of a vegetable elemental. Yes, each tree, each herb, as insignificant as it might be, possesses its particular elemental. Yet, with this statement I do not want to affirm that the elementals of plants, trees, and flowers, etc., are stuck at all hours within their stationary body, since besides being absurd this would also be unjust. Understand that the vegetable elementals have complete liberty to enter and leave their bodies at will. One is astounded when finding them gathered within the fourth coordinate, the fourth vertical.

Normally, the elemental creatures of the plant kingdom are classified in family groups. One is the family of the orange trees, another is the family of peppermint herbs, and another is the family of pine trees. Each family group has its own temple within Eden, within the fourth dimension. Many times, dressed with the Eidolon [Astral Body], I have entered into their paradisiacal temples.

Now, in order to cite something about these paradisiacal temples, I want to address the sanctuary of the family of the orange trees. I found many innocent children within the sanctuary of that vegetable family. These innocent children were busy attending the teachings that their Guru-Deva was imparting to them. That instructor looked like an exquisitely spiritual, feminine beauty wearing a kind of wedding gown, a bridal dress.

I have made similar visits to other vegetable temples located within the Promised Land, that land where the pure rivers of water flow with milk and honey.

Subsequently, the highly developed elementals from the vegetable kingdom enter into the diverse departments of the animal kingdom. These animal creatures are also distributed in multiple families or species. They also have their guides and their temples located within the terrestrial paradise, which is the fourth coordinate, named by the occultists the Ethereal World.

On a certain occasion, while in meditation, I could clearly verify the intelligent meaning of the language of the birds. I clearly remember a certain bird perched on the top of a tree arguing with another bird. The first bird was very quiet, when suddenly its quietude was interrupted by the arrival of the second bird, which, when perching itself on the top of the tree, menacingly uttered many recriminations to the other bird. In meditation, I was on the alert, listening to all that was happening. I clearly remember the improper words of the threatening bird, "A few days ago you hurt my leg, thus because of that fault I have to punish you."

The threatened creature was apologizing, saying, "What happened was not my fault, leave me alone..."

Unfortunately, the aggressor bird did not want to hear apologies, thus while forcefully pecking at his victim, he incessantly remind it of his wounded leg.

On another occasion, also while in profound interior meditation, I heard the barking of two neighboring dogs. The first dog was narrating unto the second dog everything that was happening in his house. The dog said, "My master treats me very badly. In this house everybody constantly hits me and the food is terrible. Everybody, in general, insults me, thus I live a very unhappy life."

The second barking dog answered saying, "Here, everything is much better for me; they give me good food and treat me very well."

The people who were going to and fro on the street only heard the barking of two dogs, since they did not understand the language of animals. Nevertheless, for me, such a language has always been very clear.

On another occasion, a neighbor dog warned me that a big failure awaited me if I took a certain trip towards the north of Mexico. That animal was yelling at me saying, "A failure, a failure, a failure." Yet, I did not pay attention to him. During those days, when arriving at a certain town very close to the desert of Sonora, I told the driver of the vehicle in which we were traveling that it was indispensable for us to find a hotel, since by no means I was going to continue the trip that night. Nonetheless, that gentleman with sleeping consciousness paid no heed to my guidelines. Thus, I warned him in the following manner, "You will be responsible for whatever happens. You are warned. Listen carefully, you are warned."

Hours later, the car swerved off the road and, tumbling, turned over in the desert, and even though there were injured people no one died. I reminded the gentleman of the mistake he committed when not obeying my commands. Undoubtedly, the man acknowledged his crime and asked for forgiveness, yet it was to no avail. The accident already occurred. Regrettably, this is how people with sleeping consciousness are. This is how they wander around the world from birth until they die.

Now, what I am narrating might seem a little odd to you, since by any means when listening you can notice the difference between the singing of two birds, but you would never understand their language, much less two barking dogs. You only hear the sounds of nature, barks, whistles, sings, etc. and nothing else. Something similar might happen to these animal creatures when they listen to the human language. They only perceive higher and lower pitch of voice, sounds more or less high, more or less low, squeaks, roars, neighs, snoring, bellows and clucks. Nonetheless, we understand each other, we have our earthly languages, etc.

Subsequently, the highly developed animal elemental creatures enter into the kingdom of intellectual humanoids. There is no doubt that these tri-brained or tri-centered bipeds are much more dangerous...

We have already repeatedly stated that 108 existences are assigned to every elemental that enters into the kingdom of the rational homunculi, and that the soul who fails, the soul who does not achieve their inner self-realization within their assigned cycle of 108 existences, ceases to return or to reincorporate into humanoid organisms. Hence, that soul is precipitated into devolution within the entrails of the earth, within the infradimensions of nature.

Through our esoteric type of investigations we have been able to verify with completely dazzling clarity what the devolving processes are. Thus, it is clear that we have to go back to square one, to go back down the steps we formerly ascended. So, after recapitulating past humanoid experiences in the Avernus, we must repeat animalistic and vegetative states before total fossilization and the Second Death.

I remember a very interesting case. On a certain occasion I warned a lady of the abyss with the following, "By means of the devolving path that you follow, you will have to be disintegrated within the ninth sphere, in order to become cosmic dust. This is the Second Death."

That lady answered me, "I do not ignore it. We know that, and this is precisely what we want." The demon who accompanied her furiously attacked me with his infernal, psychic powers, thus I had to defend myself with the flaming sword.

Jahveh has made of the entire Wheel of Samsara a mystique, a religion, and his faithful henchmen worship him. When one converses with Jahveh, one can verify that this fallen angel possesses a sparkling intellectuality with which he can totally seduce anyone. All the lectures of Jahveh begin by talking against the Cosmic Christ. Yes, the demon Jahveh is terribly perverse and mortally hate the Solar Logos.

Those who want to attain the realization of their Inner Self with the purpose of avoiding a descent into the infernal worlds must enter the path of the revolution of the consciousness, which means that they must be separated from the Wheel of Samsara, to completely withdraw from the laws of evolution and devolution.

Now you can clearly explain to yourselves why when the Cosmic Christ walked upon the Earth he talked to us about a strait gate and a narrow and difficult path that leads to light...

Understand: the ego has a beginning and an end, it is never immortal. Thus, either we voluntarily annihilate it, or nature will be in charge of disintegrating it within the Avernus. We must choose. We are facing the philosophical dilemma of "to be or not to be." Therefore, those who do not want to listen now, will later on have to suffer the consequences.

The voluntary processes of the dissolution of the "I," here and now, are very interesting. At the beginning, we must eliminate the humanoid weaknesses. Thereafter, we must continue dissolving or disintegrating all those animal or bestial aggregates that we carry within. And much later on, it is indispensable to work with the double-edged axe of ancient mysteries in order to crush and reduce to dust all the lustful and morbid vegetative memories of the past. Finally, we have to work with the tools of the farmer in order to crush the fossil or mineral states of different yesterdays that sleep within the profound depths of the subconsciousness.

What I meant in the former paragraph is that if we truly want to avoid the infernal bitterness, we can do ourselves, here and now, what nature would have to do to us within the abyss.

Question: Beloved Master, when we attain our Inner Self realization and thus separate ourselves from the Wheel of Samsara, does this signify that we cease to revolve within perpetual motion?

Samael Aun Weor: I will gladly answer the question from the audience at once. Respectable gentleman, it is urgent for you comprehend what the perpetual motion of the wheel of Samsara is in each and all of its aspects. Undoubtedly, perpetual motion exists not only in the cylinder of the Angel Hariton, but also within any cosmic cylinder.

You must clearly remember that cosmic days and nights exist. Everything flows and reflows, comes and goes, rises and falls, increases and decreases. There is rhythm in everything. There is electric vibration within the absolute abstract space, and therefore perpetual motion. Frankly, I do not admit absolute immobility. What happens is that there are multiple and infinite forms of perpetual motion.

Question: Beloved Master, you talk to us about three types of elementals, thus I want to know if these exist within the Wheel of Samsara as much in evolution as well as in devolution? Or are they exclusively of evolution?

Samael Aun Weor: Respectable Frater, observe in detail all the phenomena of nature and you will have the answer.

Many believe that apes, monkeys, orangutans, gorillas, etc. are evolving types of animals. Some even suppose that the human comes from the ape. However, that concept resoundingly collapses when we observe the customs of these animalistic species. Place an ape in a laboratory and observe what happens. Unquestionably, the diverse ape families are devolutions that descend from the intellectual humanoid. The humanoid does not come from the ape. The truth about this subject-matter is the reverse: the apes are devolving, degenerating humanoids.

Let us now observe the family of pigs. In the times of Moses, the Israelites who dared to eat the meat of this animal were decapitated. It is clear that this type of elemental is found in a clearly devolving process.

Analogous states of devolution can be discovered in plants and minerals. For example, the copper within the interior of the planetary organism in which we live is the specific center of gravity of all devolving and evolving forces. If we apply the positive force of the universe to copper, we can then behold with the spatial sense multiple marvelous evolving processes. Yet, if we apply the universal negative force to that metal, we will then be able to perceive with integral clairvoyance infinite devolving processes very similar to the devolving processes experienced by the multitudes who inhabit the entrails of the Earth. Now, if we apply the neutral force to copper then the evolving processes as well as the devolving processes remain in a static state.

The laws of evolution and devolution constitute the mechanical axis in all of nature, the silver axis of the Wheel of Samsara. The laws of evolution and devolution work in a coordinated and harmonious manner in everything created.

Obviously, the elementals of the mineral, vegetal, and animal kingdoms evolve and devolve in their own natural scales. Therefore, we can never conceive the disheveled idea that the elementals of nature, because of the fact of having failed within such and such living species, can make the wheel revolve in reverse, meaning, in the opposite direction, that is, to enter into the abyss through the door from which they came out. Thus, I want all of you ladies and gentlemen to comprehend that one enters into the Tartarus through one door and comes out through another door. This signifies, besides other things, that evolving Anubis will always ascend on the right and that devolving Typhon will perpetually descend on the left of the wheel. The chakra of Samsara does not revolve in reverse. Understood?

Question: Venerable Master, regarding certain species of animals, there is a belief among us who understand these laws, thus we would only like if you can give us an explanation regarding the concrete case of crows, rats, and other more or less repugnant species?

Samael Aun Weor: I will gladly answer this question from the audience. Undoubtedly, within nature there are repugnant creatures that indicate a marked devolution. For example, ancient Egyptians hated rats since it is obvious that rats are found in a state of frank devolution. However, another is the state of crows, since even though they feed on death because of the fact that they develop within the Ray of Saturn, they possess certain marvelous powers that indicate evolution.

I have been able to verify what the faculties of the crow are. On a certain occasion, when residing in a small town in Venezuela, in a certain house where a small boy was seriously ill, I astoundingly saw a group of very tranquil crows that had perched upon the roof of that house. Then those simple people declared the following to me, "This child will die." When I asked the reason for that sentence, they then, as an answer, pointed at the black crows. I then comprehended...

The child's sickness did not have a cure, thus the child died. What astonished me the most were the faculties of those elementals. They knew that the child was going to die. Thus, perched upon the roof of that mansion, they were waiting for the supreme moment for their feast... Undoubtedly, the macabre supper never took place because the child received a Christian burial. Nevertheless, the birds arrived and the law was fulfilled.

Question: Very beloved Master; based on the aspects that you have very widely explained unto us, does this imply that all those animal creatures like cats, dogs, pigs, etc. that are found on the path towards disintegration, have previously passed through the human form? Is it possible that these same creatures are found on the path towards human form?

Samael Aun Weor: Respectable brother, allow me to inform you that many elementals of nature already passed through the infernal worlds. In other words, I clarify: after the Second Death every soul becomes an elemental of nature in order to begin again its evolving processes—as I have already stated many times—from the hard rock, thereafter continuing through the vegetal and animal states until reaching the state of intellectual humanoid. In the interim, the elementals of the distinct kingdoms evolve and devolve, but they cannot return into the Avernus since they do not possess ego. Only the humanoids can enter into the Avernus because they have the ego within their interior. Through this explanation I clarified your question and give the answer.

Question: Master, what relationship exists between the essence and the elementals?

Samael Aun Weor: It is good for this honorable audience that listens to me to completely understand that there is no difference between the essence and elementals. It is clear that the essence is the same elemental and the elemental is the same essence. Thus, when the ego is disintegrated within the infernal worlds, we become elementals of nature. However, when the ego is disintegrated here and now by means of conscious work and voluntary sufferings, instead of becoming elementals we become Masters. Behold therefore the importance of the matter.

Question: Master, based on what you have explained, that is, regarding that the elementals are beyond good and evil, and therefore they are innocent, I am curious to know if such an innocence is eventually lost?

Samael Aun Weor: Respectable gentleman, honorable audience who listen to me, I beg to all of you to comprehend my words.

Two types of innocence exist: the innocence of the victors and the innocence of the failures. The soul that after the Second Death escapes from the Avernus in order to become an elemental of nature is obviously a failed soul, even after having re-conquered its innocence. On the other hand, the soul that here and now disintegrates the ego in a voluntary and conscious manner re-conquers its innocence in a victorious manner. This soul becomes a Buddha.

There are elementals that for the first time enter into the wheel of the Archangel Hariton, elementals who have never been humanoids and who long to attain the human state. There are also elementals that before being elementals lived as humanoids and who devolved within the infernal words. Behold the two extremes, the two aspects of elementals:

1. Elementals that begin

2. Elementals that repeat the elemental processes

Question: Very beloved Master, I would like to know—given that we have the opportunity of your wisdom—would you will be so kind as to explain if Self-realization is easier for an elemental that enters for the first time into a human womb, based on the fact that such elemental comes without ego?

Samael Aun Weor: Honorable audience that listens to me tonight, it is urgent for you to know that the essence, the soul that comes from the three inferior kingdoms into a human womb, does not yet have the necessary and indispensable experience that is required in order to achieve the Inner Self realization of the Being. Normally, every essence that enters for the first time into a human organism commits many errors, forms ego, acquires karma, and suffers the unspeakable afterwards. Only later can such a soul achieve Self-realization if this is what she wishes.

Nonetheless, I now repeat what I have already stated in past lectures: not all souls achieve mastery, since for this to happen it is indispensable that there be a certain inner longing. This longing is only possible when the Monad, in other words, the immortal spiritual spark, resolves to truly work on his human soul. It is clear that not all the Monads, Spirits, or Virginal Sparks have interest in attaining mastery, and since we have already stated this in past lectures, it is not necessary to continue given clarifications on this particular subject.

Question: Venerable Master, in any case, I consider that when the ego is voluntarily eliminated, we are really in a process of evolution, because we have always understood that evolution means ascent; consequently I sustain that those who affirm that permanent evolution exists until reaching unitotal perfection are not mistaken. Do you have any objection to this concept?

Samael Aun Weor: I like this question from the audience, obviously this in itself has a completely reactionary basis. Nonetheless, I will answer it at once.

Ladies and gentlemen, do you perhaps think that the ego can evolve? Do you suppose that dissolving the ego is evolution? Any educated clairvoyant can verify the devolving processes of the "I", of the myself, of the self-willed.

It is outstanding to verify how the ego precipitates itself on the devolving path, descending throughout the animal, vegetal, and mineral levels, when we tread the path of the revolution of consciousness.

Or is it my friends that you think that with the voluntary dissolution of the ego, the essence reinitiates a new evolving ascent adhering to the Wheel of Samsara?

Or is that you believe that the Being, the Spirit, will have to perpetually live bottled within the evolving processes of nature and of the cosmos?

We have never denied the laws of evolution and devolution, we only clarify them. The evolving and devolving processes correspond exactly to the great Wheel of Samsara. Such processes cannot be infinitely repeated within the world of the Spirit, because this as a fact would immediately signify perpetual slavery.

Remember friends, that Jesus the great Kabir never wanted to be bottled within the dogma of evolution. That great Hierophant only talked to us about the path of the revolution of consciousness, about the strait, narrow, and difficult path that leads us to light, and few there be that find it.

Gentlemen, when are you going to understand this, in what epoch? When are you going to resolve yourselves to enter through the narrow door and the strait path? Or is it perhaps that you want to correct the doctrine of Jesus Christ?

Those who dissolve the ego reach a radical transformation. This is a total revolution.

Question: Master, it seems to me a concept of total injustice and contrary to the love with which the Great Architect of the Universe is identified, to admit that after having achieved the human state and developed the intellect to the heights upon we find ourselves in—where the advances and wonders of modern scientists are astonishing—that we have to return to the state of horses, dogs, and pigs. How can this concept even appear within the mind of a rational and intelligent human? Frankly, I believe that this insults the eminent dignity of the human being made in the image and likeness of God.

Samael Aun Weor: I see amidst the audience a gentleman who intends to correct the author of the doctrine of the transmigration of souls, that is, to correct the great Avatar Krishna, who lived 1,000 years before Christ.

The great Hindu Avatar never said that the chakra of Samsara revolves backwards, in reverse, he never said that the wheel of the Archangel Hariton processes itself in reverse gear, thus stopping its motion in order to revolve in reverse.

Ladies and gentlemen, the wheel of the Arcanum 10 of the Tarot always follows its forward course. This wheel never turns backwards. Any car can move in reverse, but the Wheel of Samsara can never move in reverse.

Repetition of cycles according to the law of recurrence is different, and this we see verified in the days and nights of Brahma, with its ever incessant repetition. We also see it in the repetition of the seasons of each year, likewise in the diverse cosmological Yugas that never stop repeating themselves, etc. None of this is regression, my friends, all of this moves in accordance with the wheel, all of this forms part of perpetual motion.

Nevertheless, it is necessary to understand that the law of recurrence is repeated sometimes in higher spirals, sometimes in lower spirals. The spiral is the curve of life. Obviously, if we have exhausted the diverse humanoid processes, we must then go up or down. Some ascend, yet others fall into submerged devolution. Those who have dissolved the ego ascend. Those who have not dissolved the ego descend.

The victors transform themselves into Buddhas, into Masters. On the other hand, the failures—after suffering the Second Death announced by our Lord the Christ, by John in the Apocalypse—are transformed into elementals of nature.

Thus, regressions do not exist, but continuity of cycles or periods of cosmic manifestation. We have already stated in past lectures that all these cycles or periods are numbered and in this there is no regression.

The wheel moves forward. The wheel never moves in reverse. One begins with the cycle number one and ends in the cycle three thousand. The counting of cycles or periods of manifestation never marches in the reverse manner. Therefore, mathematics clearly demonstrates that the doctrine of transmigration of souls is exact.

Ladies and gentlemen, it would be very grave for the ego to have no limit, that it could continue developing and unfolding eternally. Think about what it would signify if the evil of the world had no limit. Evil would extend victoriously throughout the infinite spaces in order to dominate all the seven cosmos. In such a case, respectable ladies and gentlemen, there would be injustice indeed. Fortunately, the great Architect of the Universe, cited by the gentleman who asked the question, has made a dam to evil.

Chapter Fifteen

The Dissolution of the Ego

Respectable friends, dear ladies, today, December 9th, in the tenth year of Aquarius, we meet here once again in this place with the longing to profoundly study the theme of the dissolution of the psychological "I."

First of all, it is indispensable for us to carefully analyze this subject-matter about the ego, given that diverse pseudo-esoteric, pseudo-occultist schools emphasize the disheveled idea of the coexistence of a double "I." The first part they call the Superior "I." The second part they qualify as Inferior "I." Yet, we state that superior and inferior are two sections of the same thing.

Yes, they have spoken much about the "Alter-ego," and they even praise it or deify it, considering it divine. Yet, in the name of the truth, it is indispensable to state that the Superior "I" and Inferior "I" are two aspects of the same ego. Therefore, it is undoubtedly incongruent to praise the Superior "I" and belittle the Inferior.

Thus, by directly focusing on this subject-matter, by looking at the ego as it really is in itself and without any types of arbitrary divisions into superior and inferior, it is clear that we then can perform a correct differentiation between what the "I" is and what the Being is.

Nonetheless, it could be objected that such a differentiation is nothing more than another concept elaborated by the intellect. Yes, those who read this will be evasive by affirming that one more or one less philosophical concept is something that does not have the least importance. Moreover, some even give themselves the luxury of reading these affirmations and thereafter forgetting them so they may pay attention to something that for them is indeed considered important.

Yes, people of sleeping consciousness often abandon accounting for these types of affirmations, owing to the fact that they already are tired of so much theory. So, those people say to themselves: What does one more theory matter? What does one less theory matter?

Therefore, we must talk with complete frankness and based on facts, on direct experiences, and not on simple subjective types of opinions. Thus, my friends, I will tell you what I experienced, what I have seen and heard, and if you want to accept my affirmations, you are welcome to do so, yet if you want to reject them, it is your business, since all human beings are free to accept, reject, or interpret the teachings as they wish.

Listen, in the beginning of my present reincarnation, I—like many of you—also had read several pseudo-esoteric and pseudo-occultist books. Thus, searching—as you have—I passed through diverse schools and knew a great quantity of theories. So, it is obvious that because of so much reading and rereading, I also came to believe in the existence of two "I's"—the Superior "I" and the Inferior "I." Then, different preceptors taught me that one has to dominate the Inferior "I" by means of the Superior "I," this, they said, in order to someday achieve Adepthood. Thus, frankly and openly I confess that I was completely convinced of the existence of the so-called two "I's," until fortunately a transcendental mystical event came to intensely shake me at the very bottom of my soul.

So, one night—it does not matter what year, day, or hour—when being present in a completely cognizant and positive manner outside of my physical body, my real Inner Being, the Innermost, came to me. Thus, smiling, the Blessed One said, "You have to die." These words uttered by the Innermost left me perplexed, confused, astounded.

Thus, a little bit scared, I interrogated my Inner Being (Atman), as follows, "Why do I have to die? Let me live a little bit longer; I am working for humanity..."

I still remember the moment when, smiling, the Blessed one repeated unto me for a second time, "You have to die."

Thereafter, within the Astral Light, the Adorable One showed me that which ought to die within myself. Thus, this is how I then saw the pluralized "I" formed by a multitude of tenebrous entities, a true cluster of perverse creatures, distinct types of psychic aggregates, living demons personifying errors.

Thus, my friends, it was in this manner that I came to know that the "I" is not something individual, but a sum of psychic aggregates, a multiple sum of quarrelsome and noisy "I's," some representing anger, others greed, these lust, those envy, these others pride, continuing with those others of laziness, gluttony, together with their infinitude of derivatives. So, indeed, regarding the ego, I did not see anything worthy of being adored, nor any type of divinity, etc.

Anyhow, when arriving at this point of my exposition, it would not be strange that some of our readers will object to my concepts by stating, "It is possible that you, sir, saw your Inferior "I," which is a sum of psychic aggregates [skandhas], as oriental Buddhism categorizes them. However, how different your concept would have been if you had perceived your Superior "I" in all of his greatness."

Yes, my friends, I know very well the diverse forms of intellectualization that you possess, your evasiveness, your elusiveness, your distinct justifications, your reactions, your resistances, the desire of always making everything that has the flavor of ego stand out. It is clear that the ego does not wish to die, and when the ego does not want to continue to exist in its denser and gross forms, it wishes to do so in some exquisitely subtle form. Indeed, nobody wants to see their beloved "I" reduced to cosmic dust, just like that, because any given fellow said it in a lecture hall. So, it is quite normal that the ego does not wish to die and that it looks for comfortable philosophies that will provide it a space in heaven, a place on the altars of churches, or a place filled with infinite happiness within the beyond.

Alas, we truly regret disheartening people, but regarding these very serious matters we have no other choice but to speak bluntly, frankly, and sincerely. Consequently, given that we Gnostics like to talk based on concrete, clear, and definitive facts, now, with the purpose of demonstrating that the Superior "I" does not exist, I have no inconvenience in narrating another unusual event.

Listen, on another given day, while in profound meditation, in accordance with all the rules given in Jnana Yoga, I became immersed within that state that is known as Nirvi-Kalpa-Samadhi. Then I abandoned all my supersensible bodies and thus, converted into a dragon of wisdom, I penetrated within the world of the Solar Logos.

In such Logoic moments, which are beyond the body, the affections, and the mind, I wanted to know something about the life of the great Kabir Jesus. Thus, precisely in those very moments, I witnessed myself transformed into Jesus of Nazareth performing miracles and wonders in the holy land. I still remember the moment when I was baptized by John in the river Jordan. I witnessed myself inside a temple located at the shores of that river. The Precursor was dressed in a beautiful robe, and when approaching him, he steadily looked at me and exclaimed, "Jesus, take off your robe, because I am going to baptize you."

Thus, I walked towards the interior of the sanctuary. Then John, while pouring the anointing oil and a little bit of water upon my head, prayed. Thereafter, I felt myself transformed. What happened afterwards was marvelous. While seated inside a vestibule, I saw three divine suns. The first was blue, which corresponds to the Father. The second was yellow, which corresponds to the Son. And the third was red, which corresponds to the Holy Spirit. Lo and behold, the three Logoi: Brahma, Vishnu, and Shiva.

THE THREE LOGOI ON THE TREE OF LIFE (KABBALAH)

When withdrawing from such a Logoic ecstatic state and returning into my physical body, my confusion was unbearable. "What...? Am I Jesus of Nazareth; am I the Christ?" Bless my soul, oh God, and Hail Mary! How is it that I, a miserable slug from the mud of the Earth, I, who am not even worthy of untying the sandals of the Master Jesus of Nazareth, was transformed just like that into him?

Thus, overwhelmingly absorbed in thought because of all of this, I resolved once again to enter into meditation and repeat that mystical experience. Yet now, only changing in it my longing motive, that is, instead of wanting to know something about the life of Jesus, I was concerned about John and how he baptized the Nazarene.

Thus, the same mystical state unleashed itself within me. Again I abandoned all my supersensible bodies and once more I was within that Logoic state. Thus, abiding within that Logoic state, I fixed my attention with greater intensity on John the Baptist. Then, lo and behold, I witnessed myself transformed into John and performing the activities of the Precursor; that is, baptizing Jesus, etc.

When withdrawing from that Logoic ecstasy and returning into my physical body, I comprehended that within the world of the Logos, in the world of Christ, there does not exist any type of Superior "I" nor Inferior "I." It is urgent for all of those here present to comprehend that within Christ all beings are one, thus the heresy of separation is the worst of heresies.

Thus, friends of mine, everything in this world in which we live is passing by: ideas are passing by, persons are passing by, things are passing by. The only thing that is stable and permanent is the Being, and the reason for the Being to be is to be the Being himself.

Hence, make a distinction between the essential nature of the "I" and the essential nature of the Being.

Question: Master, of what substance are the psychic aggregates which constitute the myself made?

Samael Aun Weor: Ladies and gentlemen, it is indispensable for you to comprehend what the mind and its functions are.

The intellectual animal, mistakenly called human, still does not possess an individual mind, because he has not created it, he has not built it. The Mental Body, properly speaking, can only be created by means of sexual transmutations. I want all of you here present to understand that the Sexual Hydrogen Ti-12 exists within the sacred sperm. Thus, undoubtedly, the esotericist who does not spill the cup of Hermes (who does not ejaculate the semen) in fact originates marvelous transmutations of the libido within his organism, whose outcome is the creation of the individual Mental Body. The Manas, the mental substance, properly speaking, is found in the interior of any individual, yet that mental substance is lacking individuality. That Manas possesses diverse forms, it is found constituted in the shape of aggregates [skandhas]. These have never been unknown to esoteric Buddhism.

Please, I beg this friendly audience who listens to me, to follow in patience the course of my dissertation...

All of those multiple, quarrelsome, and noisy "I's"—which in their conjunction form the myself, the self-willed—are constituted by more or less condensed mental substance. Now you can explain for yourselves the reason why every person is constantly changing opinion. For example: we are real estate salespersons, and some clients approach; we talk to them, we convince them of the necessity of buying a beautiful residence, such fellows become enthusiastic and emphatically affirm that in fact they will buy such residence and that nothing can make them to desist from their decision. Unfortunately, after a few hours, everything changes. The opinion of the client is no longer the same, since another mental "I" is now controlling the brain, and the enthusiastic "I" that a few hours earlier was impassioned with the purchase of the property is now displaced by a new "I" that has nothing to do with such a deal nor with the given word. Thus, this is how the castle of cards falls to the ground and the wretched real estate agent feels deceived.

The "I" that swears eternal love to a woman is displaced tomorrow by another "I" that has nothing to do with the oath. Thus, the man withdraws, leaving the woman disheartened.

The "I" that swears loyalty to the Gnostic Movement is displaced tomorrow by another "I" that has nothing to do with the oath. Thus, the person withdraws from Gnosis, leaving all the brothers and sisters of the sanctuary confused and astounded.

See for yourselves, dear friends of mine, what the infinite forms of the mind are, in what manner they control the capital centers of the brain, and how they play with the human machine.

Question: Master, on this planet on which we live, the "I's" make our life bearable, since it is easy to comprehend that if we dissolve them, we will then withdraw from everything that relates to our desires, thus our life will be terribly sad and boring. Is that not so?

Samael Aun Weor: Respectable ladies and gentlemen, authentic happiness is radically based on the reevaluation of the Being. It is unquestionable that the Being experiences authentic happiness each time he undergoes an intimate reevaluation.

Unfortunately, people of this day and age confuse pleasure as happiness. They bestially enjoy fornication, adultery, alcohol, drugs, money, gambling, etc.

The end of pleasure is pain. Thus, every type of animal pleasure is transformed into bitterness.

Obviously, the elimination of the ego reevaluates the Being, producing happiness as an outcome. Regrettably, the consciousness imprisoned within the ego does not understand, does not comprehend the necessity for the inner reevaluation, and prefers animal enjoyments, because it firmly believes that such is happiness.

Dissolve the pluralized "I" so that you can experience the happiness of the reevaluation of the Being.

Question: Master, based on everything that has been formerly exposed, it seems to us that the necessity to form a Mental Body in order not to have so many minds is evident and unpostponable?

Samael Aun Weor: I will answer the question of the gentleman at once. Indeed, as we have already stated in this lecture, the intellectual animal, mistakenly called human, does not possess an individual mind, since instead of one mind the humanoid has many minds, and this is different. What I am affirming may displease many pseudo-esotericists and pseudo-occultists since they are completely convinced by the theories that they have read. Those theories affirm that the rational homunculus possesses a Mental Body.

Allow us the liberty to dissent against such affirmations. If the intellectual animal had an individual mind, if he truly did not possess those diverse mental aggregates that characterize him, he would have continuity of purpose. Thus, everyone would keep his given word. No one would affirm today and deny tomorrow. The presumed buyer from our former example, after having given his word, would return the following day with cash in hand. To that end, Earth would be a paradise.

Therefore, if we want the authentic reevaluation of the inner Being, it is urgent to create the Mental Body and to dissolve the pluralized "I." Only those sacred reevaluations can grant true happiness unto us.

Question: Venerable Master, is it possible that a person who gives money to the church, who reads the Bible, who goes to confession, who perform works of charity at institutions, who spreads the gospel, who only has one wife and other virtues, can also have "I's?"

Samael Aun Weor: Respectable ladies and gentlemen, allow me to inform you that the "I" disguises itself as a saint, as a martyr, as an apostle, as a good husband, as a good wife, as a mystic, as a penitent, as an anchorite, as charitable, splendid, etc.

Crime is also hidden within the delectable cadence of a verse. Crime is also hidden within the perfumes of the temple. Adultery and fornication is committed at the shadow of the cross, and the worst abject criminals assume pietistic poses, sublime figures, martyr-like features, etc.

It is good to know that many virtuous people possess very strong psychic aggregates. Remember that there is a great deal of virtue within the wicked, and a great deal of evil within the righteous.

There are many mystics, anchorites, penitents within the abyss, within the nine Dantesque circles, who believe that are doing very well. Therefore, do not be surprised that even within the abyss exist exemplary priests who are followed by their devotees.

Question: Master, what is the spiritual value of the good intentions of a sincere person who lives mistakenly?

Samael Aun Weor: Very friends of mine, I will gladly answer this very interesting question from the audience.

Remember that the path that leads to the abyss is paved with good intentions. "For many are called, but few are chosen." (Matthew 22:14)

The wicked from all epochs have had good intentions. Hitler, filled with magnificent intentions, trampled upon many nations, and because of him millions of people died within the gas chambers or in the concentration camps or on the execution walls or within filthy dungeons. Undoubtedly, this monster wanted triumph for great Germany, thus he did not waste any type of efforts to this effect.

Nero burned Rome on behalf of his art, with mystical intentions of making the lyre resound universally. Thus, with the longing of liberating his people from "Christianity," which he considered an epidemic or a scourge, he was throwing the Christians into the Roman circus so that the lions would devour them

The executioner that fulfills an unjust command has magnificent intentions when he kills his fellowman. Millions of heads fell to the guillotine during the French Revolution, and the executioners worked with magnificent intentions because they wanted the triumph of the people. Robespierre, filled with magnificent intentions, led many innocent people to the gallows.

Likewise, we must not forget what the Holy Inquisition was. The inquisitors, with magnificent intentions, condemned many wretched people to the fire, the torture rack, martyrdom.

Thus, I want you, ladies and gentlemen, to comprehend that what is important are the good deeds and not the good intentions that can be more or less mistaken.

The judges of Karma within the tribunals of objective justice judge the souls based on deeds, based on the clear and definitive concrete actions, and not by their good intentions.

Results are what always count. Thus, it is useless to have good intentions if the results of our actions are catastrophic.

Question: Master, what is the procedure to follow in order to liberate ourselves from the psychological defects that so torture our mind?

Samael Aun Weor: Honorable audience, if we truly want to avoid the descent into the infernal worlds, it is urgent, undelayable, and unpostponable to annihilate the ego, to reduce it to ashes in a voluntary and conscious manner.

I want you to know that when in relation with people, when coexisting with our relatives or with our fellow workers, etc., our hidden defects spontaneously emerge, and if we are in a state of alert perception, alert novelty, we see them just as they really are in themselves.

Any discovered defect must be judiciously submitted to analysis through in-depth meditation, with the purpose of comprehended it in a unitotal, integral manner.

It is not enough to comprehend a defect. One has to delve even deeper. It is indispensable to explore ourselves in order to find the intimate roots of the defect that we have comprehended, that is, until apprehending its deep significance.

Any spark of consciousness can immediately illuminate us, and in millionths of a second truly apprehend the deep significance of that comprehended defect.

Elimination is different. Someone can have comprehended some psychological error and even have apprehended its deep significance, and nonetheless continue with that "I" within the different departments of the mind, since without its elimination it is not possible to be free from such and such an error.

Thus, when one wants to die from instant to instant and from moment to moment, elimination is vital, cardinal, and definitive.

Nonetheless, with the mind we cannot extirpate our errors. Listen: by means of our understanding we can only label our diverse psychological defects, thus giving them different names, juggling them from one level into another level of our subconsciousness, hiding them from ourselves, judging them, excusing them, etc., but it is not possible to fundamentally alter them or to extirpate them.

Thus, if what we truly want is to eliminate errors and to die within ourselves here and now, then a power superior to the mind is necessary. Then, we need to appeal to a transcendental power. Fortunately, such a superior power is found latent in all human creatures. I want to address the Kundalini, the igneous serpent of our magical powers.

During complete chemical copulation, we can beg our particular Divine Mother to eliminate the psychological error that we have not only comprehended but also apprehended its deep significance. You can be sure that our particular cosmic mother, holding the spear of Eros, will mortally wound the psychic aggregate that personifies the error that we need to eliminate. This sacred spear, a marvelous emblem of the creative energy, is precisely the weapon with which Devi Kundalini will eliminate from us the defect that we want to annihilate here and now.

Naturally, the elimination of those aggregates is performed in a progressive manner, since many of them are processed within the 49 levels of the subconsciousness. This means that any psychological defect is represented by thousands of psychic aggregates that are begotten and developed within the 49 subconscious levels of the mind.

It could be that someone is not a fornicator in the intellectual zone and nonetheless be a fornicator in the more profound zones of the subconsciousness. Yes, many mystics who were extremely chaste in the merely intellective level, and even within the twentieth or thirtieth subconscious levels, failed when they were subjected to esoteric ordeals within the more profound levels of the subconsciousness. Someone may not be a thief in the merely rational level and even within forty-eight subconscious levels, and nonetheless be a thief within the forty-ninth level.

So, acknowledge that the defects are multifaceted, and that some very holy individuals can be frighteningly perverse in the deepest levels of their subconsciousness. It is by means of eso-

A Hindu symbol of the Divine Mother slaying the Demon-ego with the sacred spear

teric ordeals that the initiates discover themselves, and failures in those ordeals point to, indicate, the diverse, false psychological states within which we find ourselves abiding.

Question: Venerable Master, can you tell us how we bachelors and bachelorettes can perform this work?

Samael Aun Weor: Respectable ladies and gentlemen, the spear of Eros, the holy spear, can always be handled by Devi Kundalini, our own particular Cosmic Divine Mother. Nevertheless, there is a difference between married people and single people, since the spear has a much more superior electrical power when it is handled during the sexual trance. Yet, the spear possesses a marvelous, but inferior power, when it is utilized without the erotic trance.

Bachelors and bachelorettes can also progress, even though their work will be a little slower. However, when they get married, their work will become stronger, more powerful in the complete sense of the word.

Bachelors and bachelorettes can progress until a certain point profoundly defined by nature. Beyond this limit, it is not possible for them to progress without sexual magic.

"How could virtues spring forth from within us, if temptation did not exist?"

Chapter Sixteen
The Devil

Friends of mine, tonight, December 18th, 1972, in the tenth year of Aquarius, we enter into the second part of our dissertations.

Much has been said about the Devil. Indeed, the topic of the Devil has been the cause for a great deal of writings. Nonetheless, those who have actually explained it are few, given that the origin of this myth should be researched within the initiatic crypts of the past and within archaic caverns.

Let us reflect for a moment about what the Sun is. Unquestionably, the king star illuminates us and gives us life. Nonetheless, the sun is in contrast with the darkness. Any sunny day—as bright as it might be—has its shadows, whether under the leafy trees of solitary roads, within the grottos of the mountains, or simply below any mobile or immobile body. Yes, each one of us projects our shadow, here, there, and everywhere. Thus, light and shadow in a harmonious antithesis outline a complete duality, whose extraordinary synthesis is wisdom.

Now, let us survey a little bit further. Let us delve deeper into the profound, unknowable depths of our Being. We know that our internal divine Logos abides beyond the body, the affections, and the mind. Thus, unquestionably, our divine Logos—that which is the ineffable, that which is the reality in us—projects its own reflection, its own shadow, within ourselves, here and now. Undoubtedly, the inner Sun of each one of us also has its shadow, which fulfills a specific mission within the very depths of our own consciousness. Obviously, that shadow, that Logoic reflection, is the psychological tutor, Lucifer, the tempter...

A tutor whose purpose is the development of powers, faculties, extraordinary virtues, etc., is always required in the psychological gymnasium of human existence. Otherwise, how could virtues spring forth from within us, if temptation did not exist? Thus, it is only through struggle, through contrast, through temptation, and through a rigorous esoteric discipline that the flowers of virtue can spring forth from within us.

Therefore, the Devil is not that tenebrous personage created by the dogmatism of some dead sects and against whom the Marquis Eudes de Mirville cast all of his anathemas. Nor is the devil that fabulous entity that deserved to be forgiven, as written by Giovanni Papini in his famous book entitled *The Devil,* which resulted in excommunication for this compassionate writer. We all very well know that Giovanni Papini was the spoiled child of the Vatican, nonetheless in the time of Pious XII they disqualified him. Ladies and gentlemen: Satan, Lucifer, the Devil, is something beyond all of this. The Devil is the reflection of our own inner Being in ourselves and within our own consciousness, here and now.

When revising old mythologies from ancient times, we come to clearly see that the satanic myth was divulged in all of the corners of the world by the priests of the Heliolithic or Heliocentric religion, which in the times of yore was definitely universal. Let us remember that epochs existed in ancient times where temples to the Sun and to the Dragon were built everywhere in all places of the planet Earth. Then, Dragonian cults existed, where the priests of that universal religion named themselves "Children of the Dragon," or simply qualified themselves as "Dragons." They depicted the symbol of the dragon from those gigantic flying reptiles that existed in the epochs of Atlantis and Lemuria. That such a symbol was used in order to allegorize every shadow of the Sun, every reflection of the king star, including the inner particular individual Lucifer of every human being, is indeed remarkable.

In the ancient Egypt of the Pharaohs, the midday Sun, the Sacred Absolute Sun, was always symbolized by Osiris, whilst his shadow, his reflection, his Lucifer, was allegorized by Typhon.

In the Greek mysteries, the spiritual Sun, the Christmas star, the Creator Demiurge, was always represented by Apollo, whilst his shadow, his Lucifer, his Satan, his divine reflection, was definitely allegorized by Python.

ARCHANGEL MICHAEL CONQUERS THE DRAGON

Now, in the Apocalypse of St. John, the resplendent Christ Sun is symbolized by Michael, the warrior divinity, whilst his cosmic shadow is personified by the red dragon.

In the Middle Ages, the Logos was allegorized in the personality of St. George, whilst his shadow is symbolized by the dragon.

So, let us survey what Bel and the dragon, the Sun and its shadow, day and night, signify.

Consequently, the Devil is not that personage that some dead sects have seated on a throne of ignominy in order to frighten the weak. This is why Goethe in his own right placed in the mouth of his God that phrase with which the divinity addresses Mephistopheles:

> *Of all your kind, spirits of negation, who insurrect against mine divine decree; you the least perilous is rated.*

Much has been said about the satanic myth, and some assume that such a myth was exported into the Western world from the land of Egypt. We do not deny at all that many Solar Gods with their corresponding dragons arrived into the land of the Pharaohs, whose origins were from Hindustan. Likewise, we do not deny that the allegory of Osiris and Typhon has been portrayed in old Europe. Nevertheless, we go even further. We have the right to think about the Hyperboreans and their solar cults, together with their dragons and infernos.

So, Pre-Vedic India was not exclusively the only one that sent its Solar Gods and their cults into Egypt. Beyond all doubt, these archaic cults to the Sun and its dragons were also brought to the country of Sais and the banks of the Nile by the submerged Atlantis.

To overcome the dragon, to kill the dragon, is urgent when one wants to be swallowed by the serpent, when one's longing is to be transformed into a serpent. All of this signifies to become triumphant over all the temptations placed by the dragon. To become a victor means to eliminate the ego, to disintegrate all the psychic aggregates that constitute the ego, to reduce all the memories of desire, etc., to cosmic dust.

ST. GEORGE DEFENDS THE VIRTUOUS WOMAN

Indubitably, we are transformed into serpents after we have been devoured by the serpent. Thereafter, the serpent is swallowed by the Eagle, which represents the Third Logos, the Arch-hierophant and Arch-Magi, our Real Being, our Secret Master. Thus, this how we are converted into a Feathered Serpent, into the Mexican Quetzalcoatl, into a Mahatma. Thus, the completion of the work is done.

When arriving at these transcendental heights of the Being, at these inner reevaluations, the reflection of the Logos—that is, the shadow of the Logos within ourselves, the Devil—returns into the Logos, it mixes with Him, it fuses with Him, because deep down He is what He is.

Question: Master, if I ought to forget even the memories of desire, then what stimulus will I utilize in order to work in the flaming forge of Vulcan?

Samael Aun Weor: I will gladly answer this question from the audience. The sacred scriptures emphatically affirm:

> *Howbeit that was not first which is spiritual, but that which is animal; and afterward that which is spiritual.*
> – 1 Corinthians 15:46

Indubitably, when the work in the forge of the Cyclops begins, desire (uste in Sanskrit) is needed, because the profound reevaluations of the Being have not yet been performed. Therefore, it would be impossible to demand beginners to perform the Maithuna, the transcendental sexology, sex yoga, or Kundalini Yoga, with the radical exclusion of desire. Nonetheless, later on, with the dissolution of the psychological "I," it is unquestionable that the factor "desire" becomes unnecessary. The reason: desire cannot radically exist once all the subconscious animal agents are eliminated. When arriving at these transcendental heights of the Being, we can then work in the Ninth Sphere exclusively with the force of Eros—that is, with the power of the Sexual Hydrogen TI-12, which is the transcendental electricity of the zoosperms. Therefore, my friends, as a last resource, desire is not indispensable for the work in the flaming forge of Vulcan.

Question: Beloved Master, since Satan is the reflection of God and therefore Satan is love, is it not incongruent to state that the ego is Satanic?

Samael Aun Weor: Respectable gentleman, friends, ladies, remember that two types of darkness exist. The first we will name darkness of silence and of the august secret of the sages. The second we will call the darkness of ignorance and error. Obviously, the first is the super-darkness. Indubitably, the second is the infra-darkness. This means that the darkness is polarized, and the negative is only the unfoldment of the positive.

Now, by means of simple inductive logic, I invite you to comprehend that Prometheus-Lucifer—chained to the solid rock, sacrificing himself for us, subjected to all the tortures in spite of being the norm of the weight, the giver of light, measure, and number, the Guardian of the seven mansions, who alone dost not allow any to enter therein save the ones anointed by wisdom, and who hold in their right hand the lamp of Hermes—inevitably unfolds himself into the fatal aspect of the egotistic multiplicity, into those sinister psychic aggregates that constitute our "I," and which have been properly studied by Tantric Buddhist esotericism. Gentleman, based on this explanation I expect that you have understood my words.

Question: Master, if the practice of Maithuna-Yoga existed from time immemorial, why then in Vedantic India are complicated erotic stimuli openly offered to the public eye as bas-reliefs on their temples. It seems to me that such stimuli make the practice of the Maithuna even more difficult.

Samael Aun Weor: I will gladly answer with precision the question that with complete clarity a respectable esotericist gentleman has formulated based on a tantric photograph of a sacred sculpture that exists at a very ancient temple and which is portrayed in the Hindustani *Kama Kalpa*. Now, I want to emphatically address that work of sexual magic.

If we carefully observe the photograph from that Hindustani book *Kama Kalpa*, we will see that it portrays a woman standing on her head in Sirsasana, with the extraordinary particularity that her legs are not found in the lotus position, but upwardly opened from right to left so that the femoral parts are horizontal. Although one of her knees is bent, she is barely supported by her head, hands, and arms, as this sacred Asana is known to be performed in the world of Yoga. What is most interesting is the following: a magician, practically squatting between her legs with his phallus forcibly introduced within her uterus, is practicing the Maithuna with her. Undoubtedly, such a tantric woman could not hold herself standing on her head if two female attendants on either side

AN EXAMPLE OF BLACK TANTRA FROM A TEMPLE IN INDIA

were not participating, supporting her legs. One can clearly see a pair of young women helping to hold the body of the female yogi. Those naked auxiliary women feel terrible lust, and this can be clearly seen in their eyes. The magician enjoys himself, caressing the naked breasts of one and then of the other, while keeping his phallus connected to the feminine yoni. Indubitably, this complicated and difficult tantric practice among four persons is unnecessary and is totally rejected by the Universal White Brotherhood.

It is not irrelevant to remind the audience that these complicated sexual practices performed by more than two persons are indeed related to Black Tantra, and this can be evidenced when we study the sinister teachings of the Dag-Dugpa [Drukpa] clan within the church of the red hat priests in the region of the Himalayas, in Eastern Tibet. [Editor's Note: Drukpa comes from the Tibetan འབྲུག་ཡུལ་ ('brug yul), which means "country of Bhutan," and is composed of Druk, "dragon," and pa, "person." See the glossary entry Drukpa for more information.]

It is obvious that the adepts of the Yellow Church, White Tantrics, or true Oordhvareta Yogis, only practice the Sahaja Maithuna according to the rules of the Gnostic Church [sexual union of husband and wife in godly constituted homes].

Therefore, the sexual act or Maithuna among more than two persons, such as it is portrayed by the *Kama Kalpa*, is unquestionably Black Magic. Obviously, Left Tantra is different from White Tantra, hence this illustration from the *Kama Kalpa* is manifestly sinister and tenebrous and could never be accepted by the White Tantric Initiation of the Yellow Buddhist church.

Undoubtedly, the multiple asanas from Black Tantric adepts, instead of awakening the Kundalini or sacred Prana in order to make it to ascend through the spinal canal, stimulate and develop the abominable Kundabuffer organ. Thus, this is how the aspirants end transforming themselves into tenebrous personalities, into black magicians of the worst type.

We know about the *Kama Sutra* and the *Kama Kalpa*. Unfortunately, the *Kama Sutra* has been adulterated in a shameful manner in order to make it widely known in the Western world. Now, regarding the *Kama Kalpa*, it has been tainted with Black Tantra or Sadhanas of the Drukpas.

Let my affirmations be corroborated. Let them be clearly verified through previous surveys of Buddhist canons and occult secret books within subterranean crypts of central Asia. It is clear that I can make these clarifications in a completely conscious and precise manner, since I am an Adept and since I am in a direct contact with the Masters of the White Lodge, such as K.H., Morya, Hilarion, etc.,

Question: Master, how can we differentiate when Lucifer is acting in us and when the ego is acting in us?

Samael Aun Weor: I will gladly answer your question. We have already talked clearly about the Luciferic super-darkness and about the infra-darkness of ignorance and error. Lucifer, the tempter, the great trainer in the psychological gymnasium of existence, works by tempting us, yet these internal impressions tend to be polarized negatively or fatally by means of our egotistical activity.

Indubitably, it is only by means of serene self-reflection and profound, internal meditation that we can make a clear differentiation between inner, direct Luciferic impressions and bestial egotistical impressions.

Normally, people with sleeping consciousness are not properly prepared in order to make such a differentiation of impressions, since this requires a lot of psychological training.

Question: Master, the Devil is always allegorized with the trident. Does this symbol have some special significance?

Samael Aun Weor: This question from the audience reminds me about the trident of the mind that is used by the Brahmins of India and Pakistan. Nonetheless, we go even further, we go into the three primary forces of the universe allegorized by the trident. It is clear that by overcoming the dragon we can crystallize these three forces within ourselves, and in fact we can then be transformed into true Solar Gods. So, if the dragon is the reflection of the Sun, comprehend then what the trident signifies.

Question: Beloved Master, when we are working with Lucifer in the ninth sphere in order to eliminate ego, are we doing it with the positive as well as negative forces of Lucifer?

Samael Aun Weor: Respectable gentleman, ladies, obviously, Lucifer is the stairway to ascend, Lucifer is the stairway to descend, and a power in order to work and in order to dissolve the ego in the laboratory of sexual alchemy. Unquestionably, we can reduce the negative crystallizations of our psyche, the infrahuman elements, the psychic aggregates, the wretched deviations of the luciferic force, to ashes only through the same luciferic force. Thus, friends, this is how the transcendental fohat, the sexual electricity, the marvelous power of Christus-Lucifer, redeems, works, disintegrates, the worthlessness within us, so that the essence, the consciousness, the Buddhata, can be liberated.

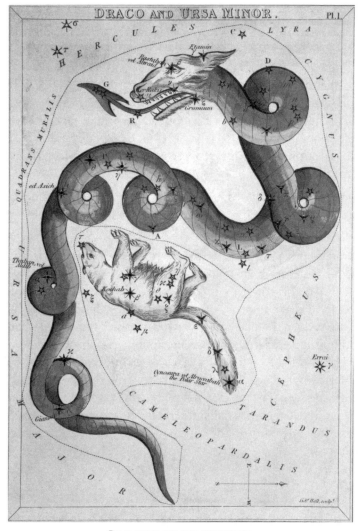

DRACO, THE CONSTELLATION OF THE DRAGON

Chapter Seventeen
The Dragon of Darkness

Friends of mine, we meet here tonight after Christmas 1972 in order to talk a little bit about the dragon of darkness. Remember that these teachings will constitute the Christmas message for the years 1973-1974.

It is necessary to clarify, to specify, to indicate with precision, the crude satanic reality, since, indubitably, in this day and age the subject of the Devil disturbs the public opinion abundantly. Frankly, I do not acknowledge the Devil of dogmatic religions whatsoever, and I think that you cannot acknowledge that fetish of the profane clergy either.

It is obvious that in Atlantis before the second transapalnian devastation, and in the land of Mu, existed a Neptunian type of flying reptile whose skin was covered with scutes or scales. That famous Atlantean amphibian was always utilized by the Chaldeans in order to symbolize the darkness of the night, which is the reflection of the Logos within the universe and within each one of us.

H.P. Blavatsky understood that such a flying reptile is Makara, the tenth sign of the Zodiac. Nonetheless, in regard to this concept we go a little bit further, because specifically I am firmly convinced that such a mysterious creature is completely Neptunian.

The oldest known representation of a dragon. Ishtar Gate. Chaldean.

In any case, this scaly-skinned creature, this flying reptile of the Chaldeans, was later adopted as a symbol by the Hebrews and afterwards robbed by the Christians... What is regrettable about this subject is that this symbolic or allegorical creature has been converted by the Christians into that frightening and horrifying orthodox, maleficent, devil-fetish figure.

Now it is convenient to remember the Gnostic sect called the Naasenians or serpent worshippers. The adepts of this order [knowing that the Dragon has a septenary meaning] symbolized the dragon or reflection of the Logos by the brilliant constellation of seven stars. I am emphatically addressing in a clear and precise manner the constellation of the dragon. Some people suppose that the allegory of the dragon originated with St. John, the seer of the Apocalypse (Revelation), yet in fact such a supposition is mistaken because the dragon relates to Neptune, the symbol of Atlantean magic...

Notwithstanding, (in Revelation) the seven stars of the constellation of the dragon appear held in the right hand of the Alpha and Omega, the Logos of the Apocalypse that revealed himself to John, to show therefore that the Dragon, Lucifer, Prometheus, Satan, or the Devil, in its superior aspect is the same Logos, the "Self-born," the Hindu Aja, which in its inferior aspect is the authentic and legitimate dragon or esoteric devil, and not that fetish from that dogmatic orthodoxy, since every Hierophant, every true, self-realized Master is a dragon of wisdom.

Therefore, my friends, I want you to comprehend what that dogmatic fetish or fantastic orthodox devil is, since due to the false education and mistaken concepts that up until now all of you have received about the Devil, I sense that deep down within some of you, within your own subconsciousness, there is a resistance to acknowledge what the reflection of the Logos, the shadow of God, the true Devil or Lucifer or sacred Prometheus within each one of us is. Indeed, this prejudice that conditions your intellect does not surprise me at all, given that you were taught to believe in a terrible Devil seated on a throne of ignominy, holding a steel trident in his hand and dominating the entire world. Therefore, it is clear that now, when hearing my words, that is, when I tell you that the Devil of dogmatic sects is a mere fantasy, that such a devil does not exist, but what truly exists is the devil of the good law, the shadow of the Spiritual Sun within each one of us, the shadow of the night as an opposition to the day, the shadow of the trees on the side of the roads, etc., it is obvious that this deeply affects you and even surprises you, yet without leaving behind that distrust, which is based on a false belief that was instilled within you from the first years of your childhood.

Listen, how could the shadow of the eternal living God be wicked? Please, reflect on this a little...

Now, a specimen of dragons, "winged and scaled," may be seen in the British Museum, which is certainly very interesting. Likewise, within the mentioned museum, there is a very ancient, archaic image representing the tree of the science of good and evil, the apple tree of Eden... What is very intriguing is to see close to this apple tree the depiction of two figures, a man and a woman, Adam and Eve, sitting on each side of the tree and holding out their hands to the apples with the purpose of devouring them, while at the back of the "tree" is the dragon-serpent, and up above in the clouds appear some beings who curse the tree; they are a living representation of every exoteric profane clergy who is uneducated about the sexual mysteries. Consequently, it is doubtless that the two human beings, man and woman, are before the tree of the science of good and evil, ready for initiation. The serpent-dragon is the initiator, and this is necessary to know how to profoundly understand it. Thus, I will frankly explain it to you, I will clarify what all of this about the serpent-dragon signifies, so that you can understand and march with firmness on the narrow and difficult path that leads the initiate to the final liberation.

Unquestionably, the serpent is the sexual fire that must ascend degree by degree through the spinal medullar canal to the brain. Naturally, this igneous element possesses extraordinary powers, thus when this serpentine fire ascends through the dorsal spine, it transforms us radically.

Now, regarding the dragon, this indubitably is the most extraordinary psychological trainer that each one of us carries within. This is the divine Daimon, mentioned many times by Socrates. The dragon is the very shadow of our individual spirit that leads us into temptations with the purpose of training or educating us, since only in this manner can the precious gems of virtues spring forth from within our psyche.

Consequently, I ask myself and I ask you now: Where is the wickedness of Lucifer? The results speak for themselves, since if there are no temptations, there are no virtues. The stronger the temptations, the greater the virtues. Nonetheless, what is important is to not fall into temptation. Therefore, after this manner we must pray to the Father:

Lead us not into temptation... - Matthew 6:13

Therefore, after having unveiled these two aspects that are hidden behind the tree of the science of good and evil, we arrive at the logical conclusion that the dragon and the serpent or rather—when speaking in synthesis—the serpent-dragon, is undoubtedly the great practical initiator.

We have given the clue of initiation many times and we will not tire of repeating it to satiety: the connection of the phallus and the uterus without ejaculating the semen. So, only in this manner is the sacred fire of sex put in motion. Thus, when this fire is elevated degree by degree, from vertebra to vertebra, throughout the spinal medullar canal, it radically transforms us in the end.

Why does the dragon tempt us during the work? Because it is his duty; because he must make us strong; because he must educate us in the sexual gymnasium; because he must convert us into athletes of sexual magic.

Thereafter, the igneous serpent of our magical powers must swallow us, so that we will be transformed into serpents... Nonetheless, before this extraordinary event, before this banquet of the serpentine fire, we must defeat the dragon. This means that we must victoriously pass all temptations...

In the end, the scaly-skinned dragon, Lucifer, the shadow of the Eternal One, the inner reflection of our true divine Being, will return to Him, will fuse with Him, will shine within Him.

Thus, when reaching this level we will be able to exclaim as the ancient initiates: "I am a Dragon, I am He, He, He."

Question: Master, does the divine Daemon only tempts us in the work with sex or does it also do it in the work of the dissolution of the ego?

Samael Aun Weor: Respectable lady, it is urgent for you to understand that the roots of the ego are found within abuse of sex, within lust, within fornication, within adultery... Now, if we take away the roots from any tree, it is clear that it will eventually die; likewise, something similar will occur to the ego... Yet, unfortunately, Lucifer must educate us in sex. There, in sex, is where we must be submitted to a rigorous training by means of the most severe temptations. Thus, it is clear that if, there, in sex, we victoriously pass all temptations, the disintegration of the ego is inevitably precipitated.

Understand that in my former statement I am not affirming that we must not work on all the psychological defects with the purpose of reducing them to ashes. What I am solely doing is putting certain emphasis on the sexual aspect, given that it is in fornication where we find the original sin.

Question: Venerable Master, we have read in the gospels that the great Kabir Jesus said: "If God were your Father, ye would love me... [but] ye are of your father the devil, and the lusts of your father ye will do." [John 8:42, 43] Can you explain this to us?

Samael Aun Weor: Respectable gentleman, I will gladly answer your question at once. Obviously, all of us are children of the dragon, children of Satan, the Devil, children of the darkness. Yet, when some one wants to become a son of God, he must then defeat the dragon, the tempter, the scaly-skin dragon. If we do it, then we will be transformed into children of God and into Dragons of Wisdom.

Nevertheless, the great Kabir Jesus never cast a curse against his own shadow. In none of the four gospels is it written that Jesus extended his right hand in order to curse his own shadow. It is written that when Jesus, the great Gnostic Priest, was tempted by Satan, he only exclaimed:

Get thee behind me, Satan: for it is written, thou shalt
worship the Lord thy God, and him only shalt thou serve.
– Luke 4:8

Thus, it is clear in the gospels that Satan, Lucifer-
Prometheus, must serve God. His duty is to tempt the Initiate.
It would be absurd that the shadow of the Eternal One tempt
the Eternal One, or in other words, that the Devil tempt God.
The words of the great Kabir Jesus clearly show us that Lucifer
is the minister of the Highest One, the Guardian of the Seven
Mansions, the Servant of Divinity. Therefore, those who anath-
ematize the shadow of the eternal living God are obviously
anathematizing the same God, because God and his shadow
are one. Understood?

Question: Master, it might be that the Devil from dogmatic
orthodoxy with his horns, tail, and trident, exists in reality as
a representation of the psychic aggregates that constitute the
ego.

Samael Aun Weor: Respectable gentleman, I have already
stated in past lectures that we must make a clear differentiation between the essential nature of the divine Daemon and
the essential nature of the ego. Undoubtedly, the ego in itself
with all its psychic aggregates is perverted Astral Light, malignant mind that has nothing to do with the essential nature
of Lucifer. The ego is rather the antithesis of Lucifer, his fatal
opposite.

Question: Master, I understand that the essential nature of the
divine Daemon and the essential nature of the ego are totally
different. However, since the ego is formed by the red devils of
Seth, I therefore believe that the devil with the trident that we
all know could well represent the ego. Don't you think so?

Samael Aun Weor: Respectable gentleman, the basis of your
question is mistaken because it is founded on an error, on a
prejudice. Ladies and gentlemen, I do not see the logic in wanting to convert a flying reptile of ancient Atlantis into a malignant fetish. Therefore, I think that it is incorrect to use such
incongruity as the basis for a question; thus, I do not agree
that a wretched innocent amphibian has to forcibly represent

the perversity of the ego. I agree to symbolize the shadow of the Eternal One with such a reptile, but frankly to allegorize our psychological defects with such a reptile seems to me incongruent. We could allegorize the ego very well in any other figure; let us remember the three classic furies, or the Medusa, etc. So, we can symbolize the ego and its psychic aggregates with such classic figures.

Question: Master, the Catholic religion, for example, does not put the dragon as a devil but represents him as a man with horns, tail, hooves, and trident. What can you tell us about this?

Samael Aun Weor: I will clearly answer this very interesting question that a lady from the audience has elaborated. Ladies and gentlemen, the Devil from the Catholic religion is nothing more than a deviation designed from the same pictorial dragon of the Chaldeans, which in its turn was inspired by a wretched flying reptile from the Atlantean continent. I invite you to comprehend that this innocent animal was later painted in the form of a dragon, and finally, in the most recent figure as that fetish with hooves, horns, and black wings that greatly terrifies ignorant people. So, it is necessary to get rid of ignorance: to inquire, to research, to study.

Question: Venerable Master, when we talk about the science of good and evil, what does evil really mean and what does good mean?

Samael Aun Weor: I am very glad to answer this very interesting question from the audience. Friends, I want you to know that good in the most objective sense of the word is all of that which we consciously do in accordance with the great law. Evil is all of that which after it is done causes remorse within us.

Question: Master, there are many people who do evil, but do not feel any remorse at all. Can you tell us why?

Samael Aun Weor: Respectable lady, your question deserves to be examine in detail. First of all what is remorse? If the transcendental aspects of our Inner Being are confronted with our own Logos or with the Sacred Absolute Sun, then we can verify for ourselves the psychological errors from the inferior parts of our psyche, and this causes remorse within us. Normally, this process is performed within all normal beings; in other words, what I have just stated is that normal beings feel remorse after any wrong action, even if in the physical world they radically ignore it. Nevertheless, the fate of the decidedly perverse is very different, since they have already become too distant from the Sacred Absolute Sun due to their wickedness. Thus, it is clear that these processes are no longer performed within their consciousness, therefore remorse is impossible within them.

Question: Master, you have explained to us that the dragon of the darkness is in synthesis the great trainer in the gymnasium of life, and that we have to defeat him in order to create virtues. Now, when we are defeating the dragon what we are doing is decapitating the ego, and since in this process of decapitation, to work with the igneous serpent of our magical powers—who is undoubtedly our Divine Mother—has a primary importance, I cannot avoid relating the dragon of darkness with our Divine Mother, in other words, with Devi Kundalini. Is this incongruent?

Samael Aun Weor: I understood the question and I will gladly answer it. Ladies and gentlemen, again in these moments I bring forward the Chaldean painting from the British Museum, where the dragon-serpent, which is the effective and practical great Initiator, appears behind the tree of the science of good and evil. Obviously, the dragon only respects the serpent, and this is unquestionable. It is stated that we have to defeat the dragon or kill the dragon; this symbolical affirmation means to triumph over temptation. As we become trained and educated, as the precious gems of virtues are resplendently glowing within the depths of our soul, the ego is becoming dissolved. This is inarguable, irrefutable. In any case, we have to defeat the dragon in order to be devoured by the serpent; blissful is the one who is transformed into a serpent.

Question: Master, can the internal dragon perform a miracle drastically, for example, to perform something spectacular with the purpose of correcting someone?

MAN AND WOMAN COOPERATE TO DEFEAT THE DRAGON. ALCHEMICAL ENGRAVING FROM THE 17TH CENTURY

Samael Aun Weor: My friends, a story from a Gnostic brother from Costa Rica comes into my mind in these moments. His narration is indeed quite interesting. He told us that in a town of his country an unusual and unsuspected event occurred to a prostitute. She used to incessantly get drunk on all types of alcoholic beverages, and in the midst of her drunkenness she used to exclaim, "I do ten or fifteen men a day. Every man who crosses my way, I will do him, and if the Devil crosses my way, I will do him, too..." So, it happened that on a certain occasion a handsome sailor arrived at her door. Thus, as usual, the woman did not have any inconvenience in wallowing with him on her Procrustean bed. After their fornication, the woman sat at the door of the whorehouse, gazing towards the street. Suddenly, the young lad, called her from within the bedroom, saying, "You do not know me. Turn around and look at me so that you can get to know me."

The wretched woman, obeying the instructions of her lover, got up in order to approach once more the interior of her abominable bedroom. Thus, when staring at the one who shortly had been her instrument of pleasure, she saw something horrifyingly terrible and tenebrous. Her scaly-skinned dragon—fashionably disguised in the manner that the orthodox Roman Catholicism represents him—was fixedly staring at her, while a strong smell of sulfur filled the environment...

The woman could not resist the shock, thus while wailing sharply she fell unconscious on the floor.

When the neighbors heard that sharp wailing they came to help her, but the smell of sulfur made them run away terrified.

Three days later, the unhappy woman died in the hospital after narrating what happened to her... The Devil took her away.

The narrator told us that the smell of sulfur persisted for some time within that whorehouse, and because of that smell, people avoided walking on the street where that whorehouse was located.

By judiciously analyzing this narration, we practically discover an operation of moral asepsis, a method of urgency taken by that woman's own interior Lucifer for her sake. Undoubtedly, her inner God commanded his shadow, his Lucifer, his particular interior Dragon, to materialize in such a shape before the wretched woman. So, her inner God commanded his Lucifer to become visible and tangible before her and even to copulate with her... Obviously, her Divine Inner Sun could not have made such an apparition in order to perform that copulation, but his particular shadow could, since it is polarized negatively with respect to the positive light. Thus, it is evident and manifested that Lucifer could do all of this.

Later, the outcome of all of this will be marvelous, given that the wretched female died filled with terror, thus when she once again incorporates, when she is reborn again in this world, when she gets a new physical body, it will be very difficult for her to return to prostitution, since that terror, that psychic shock will remain within her consciousness. So, it is more than likely that in her future existence she will resolve to walk on the straight path, on the path of chastity.

Thus, this is how—in any given moment—the Dragon can work and operate drastically.

Chapter Eighteen

Subterranean Crypts, Serpent's Catacombs

Today, I joyfully see that a very select group of Gnostics are joining us; they are visiting Mexico after having attended the International Gnostic Congress in the Republic of El Salvador. So, together we will continue with our lectures and I hope that all of you will obtain the utmost benefits from them. After this preamble, let us fully enter into the topic that concerns us today.

There were various marvelous catacombs, subterranean crypts, in ancient Chaldaea and in Egypt where the mysteries were cultivated. It is not irrelevant to remember the crypts from Thebes and Memphis; unquestionably, the most renowned of these were the subterranean crypts of Thebes. In those ancient times, there were passages—some of them of a very vast extent—beginning on the western side of the Nile and extended towards the Libyan Desert. It was there, within such crypts, that the secret, sacred mysteries related with the "Kuklos Anankes," the Inevitable Cycle, the Cycle of Necessity, were performed.

In these moments in which we mention this, there comes into my mind the Temple of the Serpents in San Juan Teotihuacán. The esotericist investigator can see there in detail the rattlesnake, chiseled on the rock, and what is the most remarkable about this, is that alongside the sacred viper of the Aztec mysteries, the snail-shell also protrudes, chiseled on the living rock. Various snail-shells stand out, beautifully shining on both sides of the divine serpent.

Undoubtedly, the wisdom of the serpent was really cultivated within the subterranean crypts of Chaldaea, Thebes, and Memphis. Likewise, the transcendental study of the Inevitable Cycle or Circle of Necessity, which processes itself in a spiral (snail-shell manner) during the cosmic manifestation, was also evident. So, observe, dear Gnostic brothers and sisters that accompany me tonight, the eternal, inner relationship between the serpent and the snail-shell. Reflect for a moment on the profound significance that both serpent and snail-shell intrinsically possess.

Obviously, the serpent is the transcendental sexual power, the marvelous power that puts us into existence, since it is the force that originates all life. So, any authentic esotericist knows very well that the sexual serpentine power of the entire universe exercises power over the tattvas and therefore over the elementals of nature. Indeed, the universal serpentine power, Devi Kundalini, originates infinite creations. She creates the Mental Body, the Astral, the Ethereal, and the physical bodies. Now then, if Maha Kundalini, in other words, if the Cosmic Mother, if Mother Nature, has created all the universe or has taken the shape of the world, obviously she has also performed all her processes based on the spiral line, which is so vividly allegorized in the snail-shell. Therefore, any internal progress, every inner development, is based on the spiral of life.

Now, therefore, we can say that each one of us—individually speaking—is a wicked snail-shell within the bosom of the Father. Since the 108 existences that are granted or assigned to every soul for its self-realization are processed now in the higher spirals, now in the lower spirals, lo and behold the snail-shell.

But, dear brothers and sisters who attend our lecture tonight, let us delve a little bit deeper into this topic; let us study the "Kuklos Anankes," the Inevitable Cycle or Circle of Necessity. It is a very remarkable concrete fact that this profound subject-matter was studied solely within those subterranean crypts.

Undoubtedly, the doctrine of transmigration of souls—which later on the Avatar Krishna taught in India—encompasses the same; however, it is noteworthy that the Egyptian "Kuklos Anankes" was even more specific.

Regarding the descent into the infernal worlds, we have already stated, we have already affirmed a great deal about it in our lectures. In them, we have made a certain emphasis on the cycle of 108 lives. We stated that once these 108 lives that are assigned to each soul are completed, if we do not have achieved our self-realization, we then enter into the infernal worlds. Obviously, we frighteningly devolve within these submerged regions until arriving at the ninth circle, located in the core of the world, where the lost ones are disintegrated, where they are reduced to cosmic dust. Thus, after the second death—this is something that we have already stated in our former lectures—the failed soul or souls resurge, reemerge, up to the light of the sun, to once again begin their journey, starting a new evolution, which inevitably has to begin from the lowest rung, which is the mineral kingdom.

Sequentially, the specifications, the diverse analysis and synthesis of the Egyptian "Kuklos Anankes," are precisely remarkable.

It is obvious that through each essence that sprouts from the abyss, its ray has to grow, and whereby its line of particular development has to be considered, since varied are the vegetable families, varied are the animal species, as distinct are the mineral elements, etc. Therefore, the rectors of nature cannot make all the essences that sprout from the abyss pass through the same mineral element, whether this be iron, copper, or silver, etc., or to make them pass through the same specific vegetable family, or through the same determined animal species. Thus, the Gurus-Devas have to wisely distribute life, since some essences can live within the iron, others within the copper, and others within silver, etc., so not all essences pass through the same mineral element.

Likewise, the vegetable elemental families—which are very well organized in the Ethereal World—not all of the vegetable elementals can be pine trees or peppermint plants, since each vegetable family is different. There are Lunar, Mercurial, Venusian, Solar, Martian, Jupiterian, Saturnine plants, etc. Thus, each one of the essences has to relate with their own kind, according to their Ray of Creation, that is, according with this or that vegetable department, and to solve all of this, that is, to know how to distribute them, is something that corresponds to the rectors of Nature.

The animal species are very varied, thus it would be an absurdity to reincorporate determined essences within animal organisms that are not related with their Ray of Creation. Certain essences evolve within the kingdom of birds, others within the quadrupeds, others amongst the fish of the immense sea. Therefore, the rectors of life must know how to wisely handle these currents of elementals in order to avoid confusions, anarchies, unnecessary havoc.

Finally, the entrance of these currents of life into the kingdom of rational humanoids is very delicate. A great deal of wisdom is required in order to avoid catastrophes.

Apprehend therefore what this doctrine about the transmigration of souls is, which was studied in depth by the Egyptians.

Wotan also narrates his expedition through a snake's hole, which he had the bliss of entering. This is, indeed, very suggestive, for the serpent or snake's hole narrated by Wotan here in Mexico is that of the ancient Egyptian and Chaldean crypts [known as the Serpent's Catacombs]. Thus, Wotan's serpent hole is nothing more than a subterranean cave, a crypt of mysteries, where this great initiate triumphantly entered. Wotan states that he was admitted into that serpent hole, a subterranean passage that ran underground the earth, and terminated at the root of the heavens, because he was himself a snake or a serpent.

The Druids from the Celto-Britannic regions also called themselves snakes. It is not irrelevant to remember the Egyptian Karnak and the British Carnac, both living symbols of the serpent's mount. Undoubtedly, my friends, some of you already know very well about the meaning of the serpent. Yes, some of you already have such information, and therefore it seems to me that this report is not new.

Anyway, the Hindustanis clearly talks about the serpent [Kundalini], about a marvelous sexual electric power, the sacred fire that is hidden within each one of us. Undoubtedly, this igneous power or serpentine power looks indeed like a snake; this is how clairvoyants see it. Thus, from the point of view of occult anatomy, I can emphatically affirm unto you that such igneous power looks like a serpent of fire coiled three and a half times within the magnetic center of the coccyx, the fundamental base of the dorsal spine. Even so, sometimes I fear that you have not understood me. Nevertheless, since I know that some of you have read my books, thus based on that it seems that in no way should the teaching that we are imparting tonight astound you.

First of all, the fire has to be awakened and thereafter made to ascend through the medullar canal to the brain; thus, only in this way can we transform ourselves radically.

Then, afterwards—and this is what is the most tremendous—we must be swallowed by the serpent. Only thus can we be transformed into serpents. These are the teachings of Wotan. This is the doctrine of the Mayas and Aztecs.

We can never enjoy the powers of the snake unless first we are swallowed by it. This is something that, regrettably, many pseudo-esoteric and pseudo-occult writers ignore. Nonetheless, I want you to understand that it is not possible to be devoured by the snake without previously having defeated the dragon.

I also cited the dragon in my book entitled *The Three Mountains.* In it, I wanted to make reference to an abominable monster that every human being carries within, along with the three traitors, and which inevitably must be disintegrated within the lunar infernos.

Yet, now I am addressing a different dragon. I am referring to the reflection of the Logos within each one of us, here and now. This is the authentic Devil, the sacred dragon of the Dracontia that has nothing wicked or perverse, as ignorant people suppose.

That sacred dragon is the red dragon, the shadow of the Solar Logos within us, the psychological trainer that each person carries within their interior. That dragon is the one who leads us into the alleys of temptation with the purpose of training us on the path of virtue. We have already stated—and I will not tire of repeating it to satiety—that without temptation there is no virtue. The stronger the temptations, the greater the virtues, if we victoriously overcome them. Temptation is fire. The triumph over temptation is light. Let us therefore not to look with disdain at Typhon Baphomet, the Devil, because every person carries him within, since he is the shadow of our inner God.

Remember, brothers and sisters, that Devil is every contrast: the Devil is the shadow of the Sun, the Devil is the shadow of every tree under the light of the Sun, the King Star; the Devil is the night, etc.

Now, when beholding the Devil from another angle, when considering this Devil from another perspective, as in the reverse and obverse sides of a medal, we can state that the Devil is the reverse side of any medal. Thus, the tenebrous ones, the people that live within the abyss, the demons, consider the angels, the Gods, light, kindness, beauty, as Devils, etc. Thus, if the people who live within the light become terrified when they see demons, it is obvious that the demons are also terrified when they see the people, when they see the angels or the archangels who live within the light.

I am stating something that I have verified, something that I have confirmed, something that I have directly experienced for myself. Many times when I have entered into the infernal worlds, I have seen the tenebrous ones horrified. I have heard them exclaim: "A demon is invading us, let us defend ourselves!" Indeed, they have felt terrified before my presence. I am "a white demon" for them, and they are black demons for me. Therefore, the Devil is a matter of contrasts, of oppositions, etc.

The Dragon was worshipped—in other words, the shadow of the Logos, the Shadow of the Spiritual Sun [the Ain Soph Aur], its reflection in the universe and within us—was worshipped within the Dracontia. Do not forget that behind the Sun that illuminates us is the Phoenician Elon, or the Hebraic Elion, the central sun of this universe in which we live, we move, and have our Being. It is normal for the Sacred Absolute Sun to have its contrasts and oppositions.

Anyhow, Lucifer is the shadow of the Sacred Absolute Sun in us and within us. Lucifer is the great psychological trainer that we have for our own sake. But please, I beg the brothers and sisters that are listening to me to comprehend what I am stating: Do not be afraid, since the resistances that some of you who are listening at this moment have are based on prejudices, on fear, on the mistaken information given by some dogmatic priests. All of us have received a certain false education during our childhood, where erroneous, absurd, negative, and harmful ideas were inculcated in us. We were told that Lucifer was a terrible devil that commanded the entire Earth, who took us into an orthodox hell in order to torture us within dippers and cauldrons with fire, etc. So, I want you, my friends, to know once and for all that such a devil of orthodox religions does not exist, since each one of us carries the true devil within our interior.

The Gnostic sect of Satanians [not the modern Satanists] existed in the Middle Ages, likewise the sect of the Iscariots. The adepts of those sects were burnt alive at the stake during the Inquisition. It is pitiful that the sect of the Satanians was left without any hope of vindication in the present day, due to the concrete fact that their documentation was destroyed. Moreover, the concrete fact causes certain pain that until this date Judas Iscariot has been considered a traitor disciple. [Editor: Many years after this lecture, *The Gospel of Judas* was discovered, which presents Judas as the greatest disciple of Jesus].

If we judiciously analyze the true nature of Satan, the devil, Lucifer, if we comprehend that Satan is only the reflection of God within us, the shadow of the Inner Sun within each one of us, located within the depths of our soul for our own sake, as a fact and by our own right we are doing justice to the ancient Satanian Gnostic community.

Ladies and gentlemen, the orthodox, dogmatic Satan of the clerical sects does not exist. The authentic Lucifer is within each person, and only in this manner should Satan be understood.

Judas Iscariot is another very interesting case. Indeed, this apostle never betrayed Jesus the Christ; he only played a role, and this role was taught to him by his Master Jesus.

Understand, that the cosmic drama—that is, the life, passion and death of our Lord the Christ—was represented by all the great Avatars in ancient times. Before the second transapalnian devastation, the great lord of Atlantis represented in flesh and blood the same drama of Jesus of Nazareth.

On a certain occasion, a Catholic missionary who arrived in China found the same cosmic drama amongst the people of the yellow race. "I believed that we, Christians, were the only ones that knew about this drama," exclaimed the missionary. Thus, confused, he put aside his religious habit.

That drama was brought to Earth by the Elohim. Therefore, any individual who seeks the Inner Self-realization of the Being has to live it, and become the central character of this cosmic play.

So, each one of the twelve apostles of Jesus of Nazareth had to represent their role in the play. Judas did not want to perform the role that was chosen for him; instead he asked for the role of Peter, but Jesus had already firmly established the role that each one of his disciples had to symbolize. Thus, the role that Judas represented had to be learned by memory and this role was taught to him by his Master. Therefore, Judas Iscariot never betrayed his Master.

The gospel of Judas is the gospel of the dissolution of the ego. Without Judas, the cosmic drama is impossible. The apostle Judas is therefore the most exalted, the most elevated adept amongst all the apostles of the Christ Jesus. Indubitably, each one of the twelve had his own gospel. We cannot ignore the gospel of Patar, Peter, since He is the Hierophant of sex, the one who has the keys of the kingdom in his dexterous hand—Peter, the great Initiator. And what can we say about the gospel of Mark, who with so much love guarded the mysteries of the Gnostic unction? And what about Philip, that great enlightened one whose gospel teaches us how to astrally project ourselves and how to travel with the physical body in the Jinn state? And what about the gospel of John that contains the doctrine of the Word? And what about Paul with the philosophy of the Gnostics? It would be very long to narrate here in short everything that is related with the twelve and the Cosmic Drama.

So, the moment has arrived to eliminate from our minds the ignorance and the old religious prejudices. Yes, the moment has arrived to study Christic esotericism in depth.

Question: Master, regarding the demons that they say frighten and torment people on the roads, is that true?

Samael Aun Weor: I will gladly answer this question from the audience. When we do not acknowledge the Devil of dogmatic orthodox sects, we are not denying the existence of the authentic Devil within each person. Likewise, we do not deny the tenebrous demons of the Avernus who torment people. Nevertheless, we must make a clear differentiation between the essential nature of Lucifer, the shadow of the Logos within us, and the essential nature of the demons or psychic aggregates or fallen angels, etc.

Demons exist everywhere, within and outside of us. Our psychic aggregates are demons. The psychic aggregates of the neighbor are demons. Bael, Moloch, Belial are demons, and there are many millions, billions, or trillions more. So, demons exist, inevitably, and we have to fight against them.

Question: Beloved Master, what is the effective manner to defend ourselves from the devils that attack us?

Samael Aun Weor: Friends, many ancient conjurations exist by means of which it is possible to defend ourselves from the attacks of the tenebrous ones. Let us remember the Conjuration of the Seven from Solomon the Sage, the Conjuration of the Four, the Pentagram, etc.

In a very special manner, it is convenient to know that when the pentagram is placed with its superior angle aiming upwards and its two inferior angles aiming downwards, it makes the tenebrous ones scatter.

Question: Master, I want you, sir, to tell me if the fifth Angel—who in righteousness comes and makes war in order to deliver the inner wisdom of the Being—can liberate and give to humanity the great teaching about Judas Iscariot.

Samael Aun Weor: Friends who listen to me tonight, respectable lady who asks this question, listen: certain reactionary elements in the Middle Ages—when comprehending that Samael, my true, internal Being, the fifth of the seven, teaches the occult revolutionary wisdom—gave the shadow of the Logos the name of Samael. To be more precise, they nicknamed me, Samael, as "the Devil" because of the "crime" of my not fitting within their very terribly narrowly mental molds.

Indeed, it is up to me now to unveil, to indicate the path with clarity, to perform a dissection of many words and concepts, in order to see what they have of truth. I am not the only initiate who knows the mysteries of the cosmic drama, neither am I the only one who has the honor of knowing the role of Judas, since we already know that the Gnostic community of the Iscariots existed, which specialized precisely in the gospel of the great Master Judas, faithful disciple of our Lord the Christ.

The learned ignoramuses, the intellectual loafers, the henchmen of many dead sects, have launched themselves against us, the Gnostics, because of the very fact of having divulged these matters. However, we fulfill our duty, and with great pleasure we bestow light within the darkness no matter what the cost might be.

I repeat: the true, just character of Judas has never been correctly presented, in spite of the fact that he was the most exalted of the twelve. What happens is that the elimination of the ego is horribly disliked by this humanity, and since the doctrine of Judas Iscariot is precisely against the "I," against the myself, then it is most natural that even the erudite among the diverse pseudo-esoteric schools and pseudo-occultists mortally hate him.

Anyhow, the four gospels cannot be interpreted to the dead letter, since they are written in code. They have been precisely elaborated by initiates for initiates.

Question: Venerable Master, if Judas Iscariot was the most exalted of the disciples of the great Kabir Jesus, then who was the traitor?

Samael Aun Weor: I will answer this question from the audience. Friends and Gnostic brothers and sister, listen to me: the true traitor of Christ is within each one of you. This means that you not only betrayed the Christ, but moreover you are betraying him daily, from instant to instant, from moment to moment.

The Masonic brothers know very well who the three traitors of Hiram Abiff are. Judas is the demon of desire, who betrays the Inner Christ from second to second. Pilate is the demon of the mind, who always goes around giving excuses, always justifying himself, washing his hands and declaring himself to be innocent, etc. Caiaphas is the demon of evil-will. Each person carries him deep within. He is the one who does not know how to do the will of the Father, the one who always does what he wants, who always does his own whim, who could not care less about the commandments of the Blessed One. These three traitors murdered Hiram Abiff, the secret Master.

Before crystallizing within himself the three primary forces of the universe, Jesus the great Kabir had to eliminate the Inner Judas, as each one of you must do within yourselves.

Thus, having understood this, having comprehended that Judas Iscariot only fulfilled his duty when obeying the Master, when representing the role that he had learned by memory, we must now do justice to this Adept before the solemn verdict of the public conscience.

Question: Master, from the beginning of Christianity, the sacred Bible known as the book of divine truth does not mention the apostles as you denominate them, nor does it teach that Lucifer is the shadow of God. Then why should we give more credit to your words than to the words that are written in the Holy Gospels?

Samael Aun Weor: I will gladly answer the question from the audience. Respectable gentleman, the four gospels were written four hundred years after Christ, not by the apostles, but by disciples of the apostles, and as I have said, they are written in code. Indeed, they are four treatises of Alchemy and Kabbalah. Thus, by judiciously analyzing the words of the great Kabir Jesus, we see within them the Chaldean and Egyptian parable, Pythagorean mathematics, and Buddhist morality. Unquestionably, the great Kabir Jesus traveled through India, Chaldaea, Persia, Greece, Egypt etc.

Only those who have studied Gnosticism, only those who have delved deeper into the Cainite, Satanian, Iscariot, Naasenian, Essenian, Philalethean esotericism, etc. know indeed what the mysteries of Lucifer are, the role that Judas Iscariot performed, and the role that each one of the apostles of the Master Jesus performed in the cosmic drama.

The Bible will not explain the role of each one of the twelve. You must begin, respectable gentleman, by knowing in depth the esotericism of the twelve signs of the zodiac, and thereafter you must guide yourself by means of the study of comparative religions and Gnostic scriptures.

You can intuit very much by studying *The Pistis Sophia.* It is a pity that we only find this book in English; however, I hope that someday it will be translated into Spanish.

Anyhow, we should not study the Bible at the dead letter [literally], since it is written in a symbolic manner. Thus, only the Initiates can understand it.

Question: Master, please explain us why Peter denied the Christ three times?

Samael Aun Weor: I will gladly answer this question. It is stated that Peter denied the Christ three times, and it is convenient to know its significance. Obviously, the three denials are completely symbolic. By means of the three denials we are meant to understand that the initiate falls into temptation once, and once again, whether in the physical world or in the internal worlds. He cries and suffers the unspeakable. Yet, if he perseveres, if he is firm, if at the end he eliminates the ego and reduces it to cosmic dust, he then is transformed into a Master and attains his inner self-realization.

Chapter Nineteen
And There Was War in Heaven

Friends of mine, ladies and gentlemen listen to me, the topic that we will study tonight relates to Revelation 12:7:

And there was war in heaven.

Much has been stated about the great revolt of rebellious angels against the Eternal. Thus, sequentially, Revelation 12:7 affirms:

*Michael and his host of angels fought against the dragon;
and the dragon fought and his angels (or henchmen).*

Albeit, friends of mine, all of this is completely symbolic, and it is necessary to know how to understand it in order to not fall into error.

In our former lectures we gave a broad explanation about the Devil and the dragon, yet now we will delve even further within the whole of this topic.

To begin, between parentheses, I want to tell you and everyone here present that I have a bet with the Devil; this might surprise some of you a little bit.

Listen: on a certain occasion, when the Devil and I were seated at a table face to face—it does not matter the date and the hour—I heard from the lips of my own inner Lucifer the following affirmations, "I will defeat you in chastity, and I will attest this to you. You cannot overpower me."

I said, "Do you want to settle a bet on it with me?"

"Yes," answered Satan, "I am willing to settle a bet."

"How much do we settle the bet for?"

"For this much." And it was done.

Thus, I walked away from that personage, who is nothing more than the reflection of my own Inner Logos. Indeed, I addressed him a little bit unkindly...

Thus, friends of mine, in the name of the truth, I want to tell you that until this moment I am winning the bet, since the Devil has not prevailed against me. By no means has he been able to make me fall into temptation, although I have had to wage tremendous battles against him. The war is therefore tremendous, yet I am defeating the dragon. Thus, I can state that I have prevailed against the dragon.

So, understand that the war in heaven of Michael fighting against Lucifer is the same war that every initiate has to wage against his own dragon. As Michael prevailed against all the rebellious angels, likewise each of us must prevail against and disintegrate all the devil "I's" or psychic aggregates that personify our errors.

Now, when looking at this war in heaven from another angle, we find that this allegory also represents the war that occurred between the primeval adepts of the Aryan race and the sorcerers from Atlantis, the demons from the ocean, etc. It is unquestionable that after the submersion of that ancient Atlantean continent, the black magicians from that ancient land—swallowed by the waters—continued to incessantly attack the adepts of the new race, the Aryan race, to which all of us belong. Therefore, the allegory of "the war in heaven" has different meanings. It can symbolize religious, astronomical, and geological events. Moreover, it possess a very profound cosmological meaning.

Much has been said in the sacred land of the Vedas about the battles of Indra against the demon Vritra. Obviously, Indra is called Vritrahan by the sages, since, just as Michael vanquished the dragon, likewise, the resplendent God Indra is the killer of Vritra, the dragon. It is clear that—like Indra—every initiate that kills or defeats the serpent's dragon is swallowed by the serpent, and—as Wotan—he is immediately converted into a serpent. Nevertheless, the sexual temptations are dreadful. Hence, those who do not fall into temptation are remarkable.

Satan, the dragon, Lucifer, or whatever we want to call him, performs tremendous super-efforts in order to beguile the initiate to fall into temptation. Now, it is clear why almost all fall into temptation, thus this is why it is difficult to find self-realized people, since the weakness of people is found precisely in sex, and it does not matter how strong they feel themselves to be, sooner or later they succumb. Therefore, "the war in heaven" is something dreadful, almost impossible to describe with words, since sexual temptations are not a piece of cake...

Perhaps it is easy to defeat the dragon? What is most critical of all of this is that people have the ego alive. Hence, if the red demons of Seth have not died, then the consciousness of every person is trapped within those sinister aggregates. Thus, indeed it is functioning according to its condition, even justifying itself, washing its hands like Pontius Pilate, or postponing the error by saying, "Today, I could not do it, but later with time I will triumph, etc."

Thus, this is why it is very rare to find Michaels prevailing against the dragon. One needs the lamp of Diogenes in order to find them, since contemporary people are too weak, fragile, ignorant, and absurd.

Now, much has also been written within old texts of classic antiquity about fallen angels, yet this cannot be understood by learned ignoramuses or by intellectual loafers. Listen: any Guru-Deva who falls into animal generation immediately becomes a fallen angel, and even a demon.

It is unquestionable that when any adept commits the crime of spilling the cup of Hermes, [who spills their semen] in fact resurrects within himself all the inhumane elements that he had previously disintegrated. Therefore, for this reason he immediately becomes another demon.

We have now therefore arrived at the root of a very discussed topic, which has been abundantly studied yet rarely comprehended. This is because in order to comprehend this topic, one needs to have lived it. Here, suppositions and vain rationalisms are worthless.

Consequently, given that I lived all of this in a remote archaic past when we, a multitude of Lemurian Bodhisattvas, committed the error of falling into animal generation, this is why now I can give testimony about all of this and crudely explain it as it is, without any kind of suppositions or utopias.

I do not care if people believe me or not. I am stating what I have lived and that is all. As for the rest, let everyone think of their life as they please. Yet regarding myself, I affirm what I have evidenced, what I have been able to see, hear, touch, and experience...

This topic about fallen angels is represented in India in the religious battles between the Iranians and Brahmans, Gods against Demons, Devas against Asuras, as is written in the epic war *The Mahabharata,* etc. Likewise, this topic about the battles against the dragon can be seen in the Scandinavian *Eddas,* where the Ases fight against the ice giants, Asathor [Thor] against Jörmungandr.

Therefore my friends, I want you to comprehend the necessity of fighting against your dragon. I want you to understand that you must prevail against him in the battlefield, if indeed you long to convert yourselves into serpents of wisdom and terribly divine Gods.

Please, I beg you, emerge from within the ignorance in which you confine yourselves. I beseech you to study these books and to live them, since indeed, it hurts me to see all of you converted into weak and miserable shadows.

Question: Master, would you be so kind to explain if a person who is working in the flaming forge of Vulcan [sexual union] falls into temptation during the sexual act, does the "I" or "I's" that she succeeded in disintegrating resurge again within her?

Samael Aun Weor: Respectable Gnostic sister, it is unquestionable that during a sexual fall, some subjective infrahuman element in fact and by its own right immediately resurrects. That is why our Lord Jesus Christ said,

> *The disciple must not allow himself to fall, because the disciple who allows himself to fall has to struggle a lot in order to recover what he lost.*

Question: Master, you talk to us about the war in heaven, and based on the teachings we know that the battles against the secret enemy must be performed within the Avernus, in other words, one must descend into the infernos. Can you please clarify this for me?

Samael Aun Weor: Friends, it is unquestionable that all religious writers—whether they are Christians, Buddhists,

Muslims, etc.—gave an allegorical meaning to their writings. Therefore, when they mention "heavens," they are addressing states of consciousness. Indubitably, our states of consciousness are altered during the fight. Hence, the battle against the secret enemy can lead us to a definite liberation or to a radical failure.

Indeed, it would be incongruent to suppose—even for a moment—that there could be passionate temptations within divine, ineffable regions. Thus, for such reason we must translate the word "heavens" as states of consciousness or as functions of the Essence, etc.

Question: Master, when you mentioned that you made a bet with your own inner Lucifer, can we understand that the prize of this is your own soul?

Samael Aun Weor: Friends, Gnostic brothers and sisters, there are valuations and devaluations of the Being. There also are cosmic capitals equivalent to virtues. Thus, the prize of such a bet is based on a determined cosmic capital. Cosmic capital is appraised in a manner similar to how the currency of the world is appraised. Thus, based on this, if I fail, I would be deprived of a certain sum of virtues and be intimately devalued. Now, I consider that what I have expressed here has been understood by the brothers and sisters and the audience.

Question: Master, we have heard that the ego can be disintegrated when working in the flaming forge of Vulcan. What can you tell us about this?

Samael Aun Weor: Respectable lady, we have already talked very extensively in former lectures about the "modus operandi" for the dissolution of the myself, of the self-willed. Likewise, within our book entitled *The Mystery of the Golden Blossom,* we have given extensive explanations on the same topic. In that book, we stated that it is necessary to work with the lance of Eros during the chemical coitus or metaphysical copulation. Thus, I understand that this audience is no longer unaware of our Gnostic esoteric procedures. What is most important consists precisely in knowing how to pray during the Sahaja Maithuna [sexual union]. In such moments, one has to beseech one's own Divine Mother Kundalini (since each person has their own Divine Mother) so that She will eliminate the error that we need to eradicate or extirpate from within our own psyche. It is unquestionable that the transcendental sexual electricity can reduce any psychological defect to ashes. Indubitably, our Divine Mother Kundalini, when handling the holy lance with dexterity, can turn any psychic aggregate, any inner defect, to dust.

We also stated in former lectures that first of all it is necessary to comprehend the defect that we want to extirpate from within our nature. It is clear that only by means of the technique of meditation can we comprehend any error in an integral manner. Thus, comprehension and elimination are basic for the dissolution of the myself, of the self-willed.

Question: Master, can you explain to us if by spilling the cup of Hermes the Kundabuffer organ is developed?

Samael Aun Weor: Respectable ladies and gentlemen, it is urgent to comprehend that when the cup of Hermes is continuously and habitually spilled, the abominable Kundabuffer organ—the famous Satanic tail of the tenebrous ones, the sinister, negative fohat—also develops, which ultimately leads us down the descending, infrahuman path towards the abyss and the Second Death.

Question: Master, can you please tell us if by working in the flaming forge of Vulcan, without spilling the Cup of Hermes, but without disintegrating the pluralized "I," in the long run also develops the Kundabuffer organ?

Samael Aun Weor: Friends, respectable lady who questions me, it is very necessary to comprehend the necessity of an upright conduct when one is working in the forge of the Cyclops. Those who do not die within themselves, those who do not dissolve their ego, in the end develop the abominable Kundabuffer organ, even if they are working in the flaming forge of Vulcan (Sex Yoga).

We have already stated in former chapters that the abominable organ of all fatalities develops within adulterers, within those who betray the Guru, within the sincerely mistaken ones who are accustomed to justifying their crimes, within the enraged and perverse ones, etc., even if they are working with White Tantra, even if they do not spill the cup of Hermes.

Understand: only by dying within ourselves, and only by truly working in the ninth sphere, and by sacrificing ourselves for our fellowmen, can we develop the igneous serpent of our magical powers [Kundalini] within our inner nature.

Much later, we have to totally prevail against the dragon, if indeed we long to be devoured by the serpent in order to transform ourselves into serpents.

Question: Master, should we understand that the war that the Archangel Michael waged against the dragon and his rebellious angels was performed with the lance of Longinus?

Samael Aun Weor: Friends of mine, the lance of Longinus is the same lance of all magical pacts, the same lance with which St. George wounded the dragon. Undoubtedly, that holy pike, that spear of Achilles, is the marvelous emblem of the sexual energy with which we can to radically incinerate, burn, destroy, the diverse parts of the myself, the ego, the psychological "I."

Question: Venerable Master, what do the rebellious angels allegorize?

Samael Aun Weor: Friends, as it is written that Michael fought against the dragon and his rebellious angels, likewise we have to fight against our inner Lucifer and the psychic aggregates. All of this is related to internal, secret, dreadful, and very painful fights. Each one of us must therefore be transformed into another Michael who will incessantly fight against the dragon and his fatal hosts.

THE ANGEL OF DEATH, BY ÉMILE JEAN-HORACE VERNET

Chapter Twenty
Law of the Eternal Return

My friends who meet at this house this evening, today we are going to study the law of the eternal return of all things.

During the last hours of life, the Angel of Death presides over the deathbed. There are hosts of Angels of Death, and all of them work in accordance with the Great Law.

Three things are sent off to the necropolis or cemetery:

1. First, the physical cadaver

2. Second, the vital body; it escapes from the physical body during its last exhalation. The vital body floats above the sepulcher and slowly decays at the same pace that the physical body disintegrates

3. Third, the ex-personality, which unquestionably can escape from the tomb sometimes and wander around the cemetery or travel to some places that were familiar to it. Undoubtedly, the ex-personality dissolves slowly over time. Thus, the deceased personality's hope for tomorrow does not exist, since this in itself is perishable.

The only element that continues is the element that is not sent into the sepulcher: that is the ego, the myself, the self-willed.

Consequently, death itself is a subtraction of fractions, and the values are the only elements that remain once the mathematical operation is done. Obviously, the summations of those remnant values float in the atmosphere of the world. They attract and repel each other in accordance with the law of universal magnetism. The opened jaws of eternity swallow (these remnant values) the ego and thereafter regurgitates them, expels them, evicts them back into time.

It has been said to us that an electro-psychic design based on the personality of the dead person is projected from him in the precise moment of his death—that is, in the very last moment, when he exhales his last breath. That electro-psychic design continues within the super-sensible regions of nature, and from there this electro-psychic design saturates the fecundated egg. Thus, this is how when our remnant values return, when they reincorporate within a new physical body, we come to possess very similar personal characteristics to those of our previous life.

Therefore, that which continues after death is by no means something very pleasant, since that which is not destroyed like the physical body is nothing more than a bunch of devils, a bunch of psychic aggregates or defects. Within the depth of all of those troglodyte entities that constitute the ego, exists the essence, the psyche, which is the only decent thing that we—as an embryo of soul—have.

The law of karma enters into action when these elements return into the new physical vehicle, since there is no effect without a cause, or a cause without a effect.

The responsibility of the Angels of Life is to connect the silver cord to the fecundating zoosperm. Unquestionably, many millions of zoosperms escape in the moment of copulation, yet only one of them is endowed with the sufficient power to penetrate into the ovum in order to perform the fertilization. This zoosperm's very special type of power is not the outcome of fortuitousness or chance; what occurs is that the zoosperm is propelled from within its inner energy by the Angel of Life, who in those moments performs the connection of the returning essence.

Biologists know very well that the masculine and feminine gametes carry 24 chromosomes, respectively, which when added together give the total sum of 48 chromosomes [official science has only discovered 46 because they ignore the vital or energetic aspect]. Thus, 48 chromosomes come to constitute the germinal cell. This topic about 48 chromosomes comes to remind us of the 48 laws that govern the physical body. Thus, this is how, by means of the silver cord, the essence comes to be connected with the germinal cell.

Now, given that the germinal cell divides itself into two, and the two into four, and the four into eight, and so forth successively through the process of fetal gestation, it is clear that the

sexual energy becomes in fact the basic agent of cellular multi-
plication; this signifies that by no means can the phenomenon
of mitosis be performed without the activity of the creative
energy.

The disembodied remnant values that are ready to occupy a
new physical body do not penetrate the fetus; these only come
to reincorporate themselves in the moment in which the baby
is born, in the precise moment when the baby inhales the first
breath. It is very intriguing that the disembodiment occurs
with the last exhalation and that the reincorporation into a
new organism occurs with the first inhalation.

To affirm that one chooses in a voluntary manner the place
in which one is going to reborn is completely absurd. The facts
are indeed very different. The lords of the law, the agents of
karma, are precisely the ones who select for us the exact place
where we must reincorporate or return—that is, the home, family, nation, etc... If the ego were to choose the country, place,
or family, etc., for its new reincorporation, then the covetous,
proud, avaricious, greedy, would seek palaces, the houses of
millionaires, rich mansions, beds made of roses and feathers.
Then, the world would be completely covered with riches and
sumptuousness. Poor people would not exist. Pain, bitterness
would not exist either. Thus, no one would pay karma. All of
us could commit the worst crimes without the celestial justice
punishing us, etc. Thus, the facts show us the crude reality.
That is, the ego does not have the right to choose the place or
family where it must be born, since each one of us has to pay
what we owe. This is why it is written:

Whosoever sows lightning-bolts will reap tempests.

The law is the law and the law is fulfilled.

It is therefore, very unfortunate that so many famous
writers of contemporary spirituality emphatically affirm that
everyone has the right to choose the place of rebirth.

That which is beyond the sepulcher is something that only
awakened individuals can know. Those individuals are the ones
who have dissolved their ego. They are truly self-cognizant
people.

Many theories exist within the intellectual world, whether spiritualized types of theories or materialized types of theories, since the reasoning of the intellectual humanoids offers a broad scope for many things. Yes, reasoning can create spiritualized theories as well as materialized theories. By means of the most severe logical processes the rational homunculi can elaborate within their cerebral encephalon a materialistic theory as well as a spiritualistic theory. Thus, in one as much as in the other, in the thesis and in the antithesis, the basic logical processes are indeed admirable.

Unquestionably, as a faculty for investigation, reasoning with all its logical processes has a beginning and an end. It is too narrow and limited. Yet, as we have said, it offers a broad scope for many things. It can be applied to everything, whether for the thesis or the antithesis. Thus, clearly the processes of logical cerebration themselves are not convincing because of the concrete fact that any spiritualized or materialized thesis can be elaborated with them. Both theses can demonstrate the same logical vigor, and indeed be very plausible for the reasoning of any humanoid. Therefore, it is not possible for reasoning to truly know anything of what is out of its scope, that which is beyond its scope, which is: that which continues after death.

The great German philosopher Mr. Emmanuel Kant already demonstrated in his great work entitled *Critique of Pure Reason* that reasoning itself cannot know anything about the truth, about reality, about God, etc. Therefore, we are not uttering ideas against the wind a priori, since what I am stating with so much emphasis can be documented with the cited book of this mentioned philosopher. Thus, obviously, as an element of proper cognition for the discovery of reality, reasoning has to be discarded.

Hence, now that we have archived the reasoning processes as proper cognition in regard to this topic of practical metaphysics, we will immediately establish a solid base for the verification of that which is beyond time, that which continues and which cannot be destroyed by the death of the physical body.

I am asseverating something that I have verified, something that I have experienced in the absence of reasoning.

It is not irrelevant to remind this honorable audience that I remember all of my previous lives.

In ancient times, before the submersion of the Atlantean continent, people had developed that faculty of the Being known by the name of "instinctual perception of cosmic truths." After the submersion of that ancient continent, that precious faculty entered into the descending devolving cycle until it was completely lost. Nonetheless, to regenerate that faculty is possible by means of the dissolution of the ego. Thus, once that faculty is attained, we can then verify for ourselves in a self-cognizant manner the law of the eternal return of all things. Indubitably, that mentioned faculty of the Being allows us to experience the reality of that which continues, of that which is beyond death, of that which is beyond the physical body, etc. Hence, since I possess that developed faculty, I can affirm with complete authority what I have verified, what I have experienced with it, which is what is beyond, etc.

Thus, speaking sincerely and straight from the heart, I can state the following: The dead normally live in Limbo, which is the antechamber of hell. Limbo is the region of the dead, the inferior astral plane, a region represented in total by all the grottoes and subterranean caverns of the world, which when united or intimately linked together in their conjunction, form a whole.

The state in which the defunct are found is lamentable. They look like somnambulists since they have their consciousness completely asleep. They wander around everywhere, and firmly believing that they are physically alive, ignoring that they just passed away. Thus, this is why, after disincarnating, the storekeepers continue in their stores, the drunkards in the taverns, the whores in the whorehouses, etc. Hence, it would be impossible for such people, for these types of somnambulists, for these unconscious souls, to give themselves the luxury of choosing the place where they must be reborn. So, it is most obvious that these souls are born without knowing at what hour or how, and subsequently they die, completely unconscious.

Many are the shadows within the deceased ones. Yes, every disincarnated soul is a bunch of unconscious shadows, a bunch of larvae that live in the past, who are not aware of the present, who are bottled within all of their dogmas, within the rancid things of yesterday, within the events of times of yore, within their affections, within sentimentalisms of family, within their egotistical interests, within their animal passions, within their vices, etc.

After being born physically again, the essence expresses itself during the first three or four years of infancy; at that time, the creature is beautiful, sublime, innocent, and happy. Regrettably, when we get closer to the age of seven the ego then begins, little by little, to express itself, and when the new personality has been totally created, the ego comes to totally express itself through us.

It is indispensable to comprehend that the new personality is created precisely during the first seven years of infancy, and thereafter it is strengthened through time and experiences. The personality is energetic. It is not physical as many people assume. After death, the personality slowly decomposes in the cemetery until it becomes radically disintegrated.

This is why, before the new personality is totally formed, the essence can have the luxury of expressing itself with all its beauty, and even make small children be indeed very psychic, sensitive, and pure clairvoyants, etc.

How happy we all would be if we did not have the ego, if only the essence were to express through us! Then, indisputably, pain would not be on the Earth, since it would be a paradise, an Eden, something ineffable and sublime.

Indeed, the return of the ego into this world is truly revolting, horrifying, and abominable, since the ego in itself only radiates unpleasant, tenebrous, and sinister vibratory waves. Therefore, I state that every person, as long as they have not dissolved their ego, is more or less tenebrous, even if they boast of sanctity and righteousness.

The incessant return of all things is a law of life, and we can verify this from instant to instant, from moment to moment. For example: each year when the Earth returns to its original point of departure, we celebrate the new year. All heavenly bodies return to their original point of departure. The atoms within the molecule return to their initial point, the days return, the nights return, the four seasons return: spring, summer, fall and winter; the cycles, Kalpas, Yugas, and Mahamanvantaras return, etc. Hence, the law of eternal return is something indisputable, irrefutable, and inarguable.

Question: Master, you have told us that any hope for tomorrow for the personality of the deceased does not exist, and that the ethereal body disintegrates little by little. I would like to know if the personality lasts longer than the physical body in its disintegration.

Samael Aun Weor: I will gladly answer this interesting question from the audience. Unquestionably, the ex-personality endures its survival longer than the eliminated ethereal body. I am affirming with this that the vital body decomposes itself at the same pace that the physical body disintegrates within the sepulcher. Yet, the personality is different, since it becomes invigorated through time with the different experiences of life, thus obviously the personality lasts longer since it has a more firm energetic note, which usually resists for many years. Therefore, by no means is it an exaggeration to affirm that the discarded personality can survive for entire centuries.

It is intriguing to contemplate various discarded personalities conversing with each other. What I am now addressing might appear bizarre to some of you, yet listen: I have been able to count up to ten discarded personalities corresponding to the same owner; in other words, ten discarded personalities belonging to ten returns of the same ego. Yes, I have seen them, exchanging subjective opinions when meeting together, propelled by psychic affinity.

Nonetheless, I want to clarify this a little bit more in order to avoid confusion. I have stated that one is not born with the personality because one has to develop it. Thus, this is possible during the first seven years of infancy. I have also affirmed that in the moment of death that personality is sent off into the sepulcher and that sometimes it wanders around within its mausoleum or hides within its tomb. Now, think for a moment on an ego that breaks loose from within a physical body after every return. It is clear that each time it breaks loose from within a physical body, it leaves behind a personality. Thus, if we reunite, for example, ten lives of the same ego, we will have then ten different personalities; so, propelled by affinity, these ten different personalities can reunite in order to converse in the cemetery, thus exchanging subjective opinions. Indubitably, those ex-personalities are weakened little by little; they are extinguished extraordinarily until finally becoming radically disintegrated. However, the memories of those personalities continue in the causal world within the Akashic records of nature.

In these moments, on this night in which I am conversing with you about this, there comes into my memory an ancient existence that I had as a military man during the age of the Renaissance in old Europe. Thus, at a given moment, while working as a Causal Man within the world of natural causes, it dawned on me to take the memory of that ex-personality out of the secret archives of that region. The outcome was indeed extraordinary: I saw that military man dressed with the uniform of the age in which he had lived, and then, unsheathing his sword, he violently attacked me. To conjure him was not difficult for me. Thus, I placed him once again within the archives.

This signifies that every memory is alive, it has a reality within the world of natural causes, and this is something that can surprise many esotericist and occultist students.

Question: Master, you told us that the personality is not born with the ego. What can you tell us about the birth of the vital body?

Samael Aun Weor: Friends, I want you to comprehend that the vital body, the basic foundation of organic life, has been designed by the agents of life in accordance with the law of cause and effect. Therefore, those who in their past existence accumulated very critical debts can be born with a defective vital body, and—as it is natural—this will serve as a foundation for a likewise defective physical body.

Liars can be born with a deformed vital body, which as an outcome will give a monstrous or unhealthy physical vehicle.

Vicious people can be born with a manifestly degenerated vital body, which will serve as a foundation for likewise degenerated physical bodies.

For example: The passional abuser of sex in the long run can be born with a vital body polarized wrongly; this will originate an homosexual physical vehicle, which in its feminine form will be lesbian. Thus, indubitably, homosexuals and lesbians are the outcome of sexual abuse in former existences.

The alcoholic can be born with a defective, anomalous vital brain, which can serve as a foundation for a likewise defective physical brain.

The assassin, the murderer, the one who incessantly repeats such a horrendous crime, in the long run can be born with a disability, crippled, quadriplegic, blind from birth, deformed, horrifyingly repulsive, idiotic, or definitively insane. It is good to know that assassination is the worst degree of human corruption; thus, by no means can an assassin return with a healthy physical vehicle.

That is enough for the moment, since it would take too long if we continue talking about this point related with the question that has been formulated.

Question: Master, consequently, those who are born with physical defects are not because of hereditary traits?

Samael Aun Weor: Respectable lady, your question is very important and deserves to be examined in detail. Hereditary traits are clearly subservient to the law of karma. Hereditary traits are the marvelous mechanism by means of which karma is processed. Clearly, heredity is found within the sexual genes; there is where we find it. So, it is by means of the genes—with all the cellular mechanism—that the law of karma works. Thus, it is good to comprehend that the genes control the totality of the human organism. The genes are found within the chromosomes, within the germinal cell, and are the foundation for physical formation. So, when the genes are found in disorder, when their legitimate natural formation does not exist, indisputably they originate a defective body. This is something that has been already demonstrated.

Question: Master, the disincarnated egos that are profoundly asleep in the region of the dead and believe that they are still physically alive, how can they represent the scenes of their life given that they lack a mental body?

Samael Aun Weor: This gentleman's question is mistaken deep down; this means that it is wrongly formulated. Listen, the pluralized ego is mind; we have already clearly stated, we have already said, that the intellectual animal mistakenly called human does not have a mind, but minds. Indubitably, the diverse psychic aggregates that constitute the ego are nothing more than diverse mental forms, a pluralization of understanding, etc. It so happens that when the whole of those minds, or quarrelsome and noisy "I's," return, not all of them succeed incarnating again. Thus, from a sum total of psychic aggregates, some of them enter into the submerged devolution within the mineral kingdom, or they reincorporate within animal organisms, or adhere to specific places, etc.

After death, each one of these aggregates lives within their own scenarios and desires, always in the past, never in the present. Do not forget, my friends, that the "I" is memory, that the "I" is time, that the "I" is a book of many volumes.

Question: Master, based on what you just have said, if we are legions of "I's, then I must conclude that we do not have reality either, since we are only mental forms. Am I right?

Samael Aun Weor: Respectable friend, ladies and gentlemen, you must understand that the intellectual animal mistakenly called human is not yet a well-conceived being; this means that the intellectual animal is just a mathematical point in space, who accedes to serve as a vehicle to determined sums of values. Thus, each person is nothing other than a wretched, thinking animal, condemned to the pain of living as a machine controlled by a multitude of infrahuman, bestial psychic aggregates. The only dignifying element within each of us is the essence, the psychic material, the prima matter in order to fabricate soul, yet regrettably, the essence is bottled within all those inhumane psychic aggregates.

To be a human being is something very different. Yet, to achieve the human level one needs to disintegrate the ego and fabricate the superior existential bodies of the Being. I consider that you have now understood me.

Question: Master, are you then stating that in fact we are nothing but mental forms without any objective reality?

Samael Aun Weor: Friends, please understand me! When I talk about psychic aggregates I am talking about mental forms, since it is clear that such aggregates are indeed crystallizations of the mind. I think that you understand this, thus it seems to me that it is not necessary to continue explaining about it, since it is already clarified.

Question: Master, are you telling us that all those very notable exponents of the magical power of the mind, who emphasize the great importance of having a positive mind, are then mistaken?

Samael Aun Weor: Friends, in these times of Kali Yuga, the Iron Age people have dedicated themselves to mentalism. Thus, within bookstores one finds on one bookshelf, and another bookshelf, and every bookshelf, thousands of books speaking marvels about the donkey of the mind. What is remarkable about all of this is that Jesus, the great Kabir, rode on the donkey of the mind on Palm Sunday in order to enter into the Heavenly Jerusalem. This is how the gospels explain it. This is how the gospels narrate it. Nevertheless, people crucify Jesus the Christ and adore the donkey. Thus, this is how humanity is, my dear brothers and sisters; this is how this epoch of darkness is in which we live.

What do the mentalists want to develop? The mental force? The donkey's power? It would be better for the comprehensive ones to ride on that animal and tame it with the whip of the willpower; thus, in this manner, things would change and we would make of ourselves good Christians, right?

What is that which the mentalists want to develop? The force of the mental ego? It would be better if they disintegrate it, if they reduce it to cosmic dust; thus, this is how their Spirit will become resplendent within each one of them. Regrettably, in this day and age people no longer want anything to do with their Spirit. Now, they kneel down in order to kiss the hooves of the donkey, the ass. Yes, instead of purifying themselves, they corrupt themselves miserably.

If people were to know that they do not have a mental body, and if they were to know that the only thing that they possess is a sum of disgusting, psychic aggregates, which are just mental crystallizations, and if, instead of fortifying and invigorating their bestial "I's" they would disintegrate them, then they would indeed work for the good of their Being and for their own bliss.

Nevertheless, they want to develop the strength of their beast, the sinister power of their mental ego. Thus, the only thing that they attain with it is to become each day more tenebrous and abysmal leftists.

I tell to all my friends, I tell to all the brothers and sisters of the Gnostic Movement, to reduce their mental ego to ashes, to untiringly fight to be free from the mind. Thus, this is how they will attain blissfulness.

Question: Master, don't you think that an essence without an ego will give as an outcome an extremely boring life on this very beautiful planet?

Samael Aun Weor: Friends, the ego considers that existence is boring when it does not get what it desires; nonetheless, when is that ego's desire ever satisfied?

The ego is desire, and desire in the long run becomes frustration, fatigue, boredom, and finally its life becomes boring. So, where is the right for the ego to dare speaking against boredom, when deep down in itself it becomes tediousness, bitterness, disillusion, disenchantment, frustration, and boredom? If the ego does not know anything about blissfulness, then how dare it think that it can express concepts about it?

Unquestionably, when the ego dies, when it is reduced to ashes, the only thing that is left within us is the essence, beauty, and from the essence emerges happiness, love, and blissfulness.

What happens is that the lovers of desire, those who want passional satisfactions, who are superficial people, think incorrectly; thus, they suppose that without ego life would be terribly boring. If those people were not to have ego they would then think in a different manner. They would be then happy and thus they would exclaim: life with ego is frightfully boring!

Friends, do you perhaps think that it is very delightful to perpetually return to this valley of tears in order to cry and suffer incessantly? Comprehend that it is necessary to eliminate the ego in order to liberate ourselves from the wheel of Samsara.

DORJE PHAKMO, A FEMALE REINCARNATE LAMA IN TIBET, CIRCA 1930.

Chapter Twenty-one

Reincarnation

Friends of mine, we have met here in order to study the law of reincarnation. I hope that all of you will get the utmost benefit from these teachings, since it is urgent for all of us to try to integrally comprehend what this great law is.

Indeed, the word reincarnation is very demanding. Let us remember the ten reincarnations of Vishnu, the Cosmic Christ.

Krishna, the great Hindu Avatar, born about one thousand years before Christ, never said that all of the intellectual animals that populate the face of the Earth reincarnate; he only emphatically affirmed that those who reincarnate are the Buddhas, the great Gods, the Devas, the divine Kings, etc. Therefore, let us penetrate into the study of the law of reincarnation in a more detailed manner.

We can state with completely dazzling clarity that reincarnation is impossible for those who do not possess sacred individuality. Unquestionably, only the sacred individuals reincarnate. Thus, this is why human reincarnations were always celebrated with great religious festivities in secret Tibet.

In the name of the truth, I want to clearly, frankly, and openly affirm the crude reality that reincarnation or reincorporation is only possible for those souls who possess the Auric Embryo, the Auric Flower. Thus, by analyzing this matter with great meticulosity, we come to understand that such an embryo must be deliberately fabricated based on conscious works and voluntary sufferings.

The elaboration of the Auric Flower, the Auric Embryo, is possible by means of the psychic material or prima materia, which is found bottled within those infrahuman elements, whose origin—as we already know through the explanations given here in other lectures—is discovered within the merely retrospective field, in a remote past, when human beings developed in their organism the abominable Kundabuffer organ, the Satanic tail. When that organ was eliminated from humanity, its awful consequences remained within the five cylinders of the organic machine, namely: mind, emotion, movement, instinct, and sex. Indubitably, these awful consequences came to constitute a sort of subjective and inhuman second nature that all rational animals carry within. It is unquestionable that the prima matter, the essence with which we can elaborate the Auric Embryo, was bottled within this double nature. Therefore, when there is a serious attempt to elaborate the Auric Flower, the dissolution of the subjective and infrahuman aggregates is imperative.

In times of yore, when the awful consequences of the abominable Kundabuffer organ had not been specifically developed, it was possible—in order to motivate the force or forces that can disintegrate incipient, subjective elements—to appeal to the inner factor that originates the impulses of faith, hope, and love. Regrettably, the basic factor that originates those cited impulses underwent diverse degenerative processes, due to the exorbitant development of the awful consequences of the abominable Kundabuffer organ.

It is indeed painful that the factor that originates the impulses of faith, hope, and love had to radically degenerate. Thus, for that reason we now have to appeal to the only factor that has not yet been lost: I am emphatically addressing the Essence, the psychic material, which is indeed the foundation, the base, of our entire psychic organization.

Hence, the liberation of that Essence is urgent, unpostponable, undelayable, if we seriously want to elaborate the Auric Flower, the Auric Embryo.

Regrettably, this prima materia, this psychic material, does not intervene in the routine activities of our mistakenly named "vigil state." It is a pity that this factor—upon which all of our psychic processes are established—is confined, bottled, within the subconscious zones. This is why it is essential, urgent, and necessary to bring that factor out of its merely subjective state, so it can operate in a self-cognizant and objective manner within the activities of our daily life.

The ego—with all its psychic aggregates—is therefore that double anti-human nature, that infra-human appendage within which the consciousness is bottled.

Thus, if we want to have sacred individuality, then we must rely on the scalpel of self-criticism in order to perform a dissection of all those false values that constitute the "myself." For this, it is indispensable to know in an integral, unitotal manner all of the psychic defects that we possess.

Much has been said about creative comprehension, yet to intellectually comprehend is not enough, since it is indisputable and irrefutable that any psychological defect is processed within 49 subconscious, infraconscious, and even unconscious levels. Thus, the comprehension of our defects in this or that level is not enough. We urgently need to understand our defects in depth. It is indispensable to pierce them, if we really want to exterminate them, to annihilate them.

Nevertheless, even when creative comprehension is urgent and unpostponable, it is not everything. We, the Gnostics, go even further: we want to capture, to apprehend, the deep significance of what we have integrally comprehended, since it is not possible to originate the inner impulses that provoke radical changes within our psyche if we have not been able to capture the deep significance of this or that psychological defect. Obviously, we become duly prepared for this or that inner change when we have comprehended this or that error of our psyche.

Elimination comes afterwards; yet, in order to eliminate, we have to appeal to a superior kind of forces.

For example, someone can have comprehended the defect of anger, and can even have given to himself the luxury of apprehending its deep significance, yet nonetheless continue with it. Thus, to eliminate is different, because the mind can provoke diverse modes of action: it can label the defects, it can move them from one department into another department of understanding, but it cannot fundamentally alter them. This is why if we want to extirpate defects, we need to appeal to a power superior to the mind. Fortunately, such a power exists.

Now, I want to address the serpentine fire, the sacred fire, which normally develops within the body of the ascetic. If, in the times of yore, that igneous power could divide the divine hermaphrodites into opposite sexes, it is then obvious that it can also extirpate from our psyche the inhuman elements, which as appendages constitute a double, sinister, terribly perverse leftist nature within us.

We have already stated in our book entitled *The Mystery of the Golden Blossom* that the "Seminal Pearl" is formed with the first percentages of liberated essence. In that book we have already affirmed that the Seminal Pearl develops and becomes the Auric Embryo, the Auric Flower, in proportion to the different subjective elements of the human being reduced to cosmic dust. Lo and behold, the mystery of the golden blossom.

I have abundantly explained the modus operandi, as much in these lectures as in my former books. I have stated that we must learn to drive the serpentine fire or ray of Kundalini against these or those inhumane aggregates, with the goal of pulverizing them, with the purpose of liberating the Essence. I explained that it is precisely within the flaming forge of Vulcan where we have the opportunity to work with the lance of Achilles. Yes, only with the Holy Pike, a marvelous emblem of the transcendental sexual electricity, can we disintegrate our psychological types of defects.

Whosoever possesses the Auric Embryo, whosoever has elaborated it by means of deliberate works and conscious mortifications, has the right to reincarnate.

It is evident that the Auric Flower grants us sacred individuality. It is indubitable that the Auric Embryo establishes within us a complete equilibrium between the spiritual and the material.

Therefore, comprehend: those who still do not possess the Auric Embryo, return, come back, reincorporate within new organisms, but they do not reincarnate. Let us therefore distinguish between reincarnation and return, since rare are those who reincarnate and millions are those who return.

Question: Master, can you tell us when the Kundabuffer organ was developed in humanity and with what purpose?

Samael Aun Weor: I will gladly answer the question that our Secretary sister has formulated.

During the epoch of the continent Mu or Lemuria, located— as we have already stated in past lectures—in the Pacific Ocean, it was necessary to develop that organ with the purpose of stabilizing the geological crust of the Earth. Since the human machine automatically transforms cosmic energies in order to retransmit them to the interior layers of the planetary organism in which we live, any change that arises in such machines originates determined results within the interior of our planet Earth. It was then, during that epoch, about 18 million years ago, that the Cosmocreators granted complete liberty of action to the internal Lucifer of each one of us, with the goal of developing the tail of the apes—that is, the abominable Kundabuffer organ—in each human organism. Indubitably, based on that procedure of the Cosmocreators, the energetic transformation within the human interior was altered and the Earth was stabilized. Thus, that procedure originated magnificent results for the geological crust of the Earth, but sinister results for humanity. Much later in time, the Gods eliminated that ominous appendage from the human organism, yet they could not eliminate its consequences, since these—as we have already stated—became a second inhumane and perverse nature within each one of us.

Question: Master, does this infer that the Cosmocreators are guilty of the inhumane consequences that humanity carries in their organisms today?

Samael Aun Weor: This question is intriguing to me. The Gods who got involved then committed some mistaken calculations; thus, for such reason they are guilty. I want you to know that the Gods also make mistakes. It is clear, therefore, that those ineffable ones will have to pay their consequent cosmic Karma in a future cosmic day.

Question: Master, since the Essence is the only element that constitutes our psychic organization, and—as you stated—fortunately has not been lost, does this signify that there is a danger for the Essence to be lost?

Samael Aun Weor: I will gladly answer this gentleman's question. First of all, with all due respect, I allow myself to tell the audience who listening to me that the question has been a little bit wrongly formulated, since I have not said that the

Essence is our only psychic organization. I have only affirmed that the Essence is the basic factor of our entire psychic organization, and this is the little difference. Clearly, it is not possible for the Essence to be lost. This is why I affirm that the Essence is the only factor that fortunately cannot be lost.

Even when the Essence—bottled within the ego—has to devolve in time within the infernal worlds, it is evident that it will never be lost, because once the ego is dissolved, the Essence will remain free and ready—as we have stated many times—to enter into new evolving processes.

Question: Venerable Master, you make an emphasis not only in comprehension but also in the apprehension of the deep significance of our psychological defects. I understand that the objective of comprehension is to identify those defects and that the objective of the deep significance is to discover the damage that the defects might cause us as an obstacle for our self-realization. Am I correct?

Samael Aun Weor: It is worthwhile to answer this question from the audience. Listen, comprehension is not identification. Someone can identify a psychological defect without having comprehended it. So, let us therefore distinguish between comprehension and identification.

The essential nature of comprehension is very elastic, because the degrees of comprehension vary. It can be that today we comprehend this or that matter in a certain way and in a certain manner, in a relative and circumstantial manner, yet tomorrow we will comprehend it better.

Now, the apprehension of the deep significance of this or that defect is only possible to by all the parts of our integral Being. Thus, if some parts of our Being have apprehended the deep significance, yet other parts of our same Being have not yet apprehended it, then the integral and deep significance also has not yet been totally apprehended. Therefore, regarding the deep significance of an error, regarding its specific flavor, we must not elaborate preconceptions, since the deep significance of this or that error can only be directly experienced in the precise moment, in the right, given instant. Thus, this is why we must not, by any means, convolute in preconceived ideas about what the deep significance of our psychological errors could be.

Question: Thank you, Master, for this explanation, which reveals to us that comprehension is really a function of the mind, and that the deep significance is a function of the consciousness. Is this correct?

Samael Aun Weor: Friends, the mind with all its functionalisms is feminine, receptive, therefore, it would be absurd to try to make it positive. Thus, it is stubbornness to elaborate ideas, preconceptions, or theories. Therefore, given that the mind is a merely passive instrument by nature, it cannot by itself occupy the place of comprehension.

Distinguish therefore between the essential nature of comprehension and the instrument that we use in order to manifest ourselves in the world. Obviously, comprehension belongs rather to the Essence—that is, to the inner functions of the consciousness, and that is all.

The deep significance of this or that psychological error differs from comprehension by the very fact that it belongs to the diverse perceptions or direct experiences lived by the diverse parts of the unitotal Being.

Question: Master, can the human being who reincarnates choose with awakened consciousness the place and family where he reincarnates?

Samael Aun Weor: I will gladly answer this new question. Allow me to clarify for all of you, present here, that those who possess the Auric Embryo also have in fact an awakened consciousness. Therefore, in their case, it is permissible for them to voluntarily choose the zodiacal sign in which they wish to reincorporate, reincarnate, reborn again; nonetheless, it is not possible for them to alter their karma. This means that they can select diverse types of birth, family, nation, city, etc., yet, always in accordance with their karmic debts. In other words, they could resolve to pay this or that karmic debt in accordance with their free choice, yet by no means can they avoid their karmic debts. They will only have the right to select from their karmic debts which one they want to pay first, and that is all.

Question: Master, do fallen Bodhisattvas lose their Auric Embryo?

Samael Aun Weor: This question is indeed very original; therefore, it is convenient to concretely answer it.

It is necessary to comprehend that the Auric Embryo is imperishable, immortal, eternal. Therefore, fallen Bodhisattvas' egos can be annihilated, even their superior existential bodies of the Being can undergo the process of annihilation within the ninth sphere, and nonetheless, they will never lose their Auric Embryo. Thus, after the radical destruction or definitive annihilation of their ego and their superior existential bodies of the Being, their Auric Embryo would reemerge, resurface, on the face of the Earth, under the light of the Sun, in order to reinitiate or begin a new evolution.

Question: Master, does the consciousness fall asleep in fallen Bodhisattvas?

Samael Aun Weor: Respectable friends, it is clear that when a bodhisattva falls, then the awful consequences of the abominable Kundabuffer organ resurrect within him, and therefore the Auric Embryo, his consciousness, indisputably becomes bottled with those infrahuman factors. Thus, the outcome in this case is that the consciousness loses a good percentage of its habitual lucidity, although it does not radically fall asleep.

Question: Master, does the human who has acquired sacred individuality totally lack desires?

Samael Aun Weor: Friends, when someone has dissolved the ego, that is, when someone has become de-egotized, indisputably he has acquired individualization. Yet, desire is something more profound.

Any of the people here present can radically eliminate the ego, and for such reason acquire sacred individuality, and nonetheless, continue with desire. This might indeed appear paradoxical, contradictory, and even absurd, yet we must analyze this a little bit.

Friends, time claims many things; thus, once the awful consequences of the abominable Kundabuffer organ are annihilated, the Teleoghinooras tapes linger behind, and if one is not concerned with disintegrating them, annihilating them, reducing them to cosmic dust, they can be completely conserved within the supersensible worlds during the entire terrestrial period. Obviously, such tapes are a sort of living movies that certainly correspond to all the scenes of desire, to all of the lustful actions of this life and all of our former lives. Thus, if they are not radically disintegrated, then one hundred percent objective consciousness cannot be achieved either, because within them is bottled part of our consciousness. Clearly, the disintegration of those tapes is a superior type of work that can only be performed with the two-edged axe, which in ancient times appeared within the center of all sacred labyrinths, a symbol that very few have comprehended. Regarding the two-edged axe, some pseudo-esoteric and pseudo-occultist books have been written in a more or less mistaken manner. Anyhow, the transcendental sexual electricity must also reduce the Teleoghinooras tapes to dust.

So, my dear friends, as you are beholding, how difficult it is to give full lucidity and objectivity to the consciousness, since it is lamentable that the Essence is so confined within the many varied subjective and infrahuman elements.

Regrettably, many are those who think that this matter regarding the awakening of the consciousness is something easy. Some of them are constantly writing to me and complaining that they cannot yet project themselves in their Astral body. They protest because after some months they still do not develop powers. They demand—when out of their physical body—to immediately acquire the capacity of being completely lucid, etc. Usually, those who begin our studies are looking for powers, and when they do not immediately transform themselves into omnipotent individuals, then they look for the subjective path of spiritism, or they affiliate themselves to diverse subjective psychic kinds of schools with the purpose of instantaneously acquiring those coveted psychic faculties.

Complete objectivity implies the radical destruction of all of the inhuman elements that we carry within, the annihilation of subconscious atoms, the absolute death of the double infrahuman nature, the radical pulverization of all the memories of desire.

Therefore, dear friends, anyone can have attained sacred individuality, and nonetheless, this does not signify that he is completely free of the process of desire. Thus, to destroy the Teleoghinooras tapes and some other principles which I will address later, signifies to extirpate from our psyche even the most intimate desires.

Question: Master, is it worthwhile to exercise the right of reincarnating when it has been acquired?

Samael Aun Weor: Respectable ladies and gentlemen who listen to me, every longing is acceptable to reincarnating souls. Nevertheless, it is better to exclaim along with Jesus:

> *Father, if thou be willing, remove this cup from me: nevertheless not my will, but thine, be done.* - Luke 22:42

In these moments in which I converse with you, here within the study of my own house which is also yours, something very interesting comes to my memory. It so happens that on a certain night I was telepathically called by a group of Masters from the venerable, great White Lodge. Thus, I withdrew from my physical body and concurred to the call with all the parts of my Innermost Being integrated and dressed with the existential bodies of the Being. In this manner, hovering in space, I softly landed upon the flat roof of a great building. Then the adepts of the occult fraternity received me with jubilant exclamations saying, "The Archangel Samael has arrived." Then, after the customary hugs and greetings, I was interrogated in the following manner, "You, as the Avatar of the new Aquarian age, must answer us about the convenience or inconvenience of delivering cosmic ships to this terrestrial humanity. Your answer embraces a great responsibility."

Then, I went down on my knees, and with my spatial sense I saw the use the earthlings might make of such ships in the future. The eye of Dhagma allowed me to see inside of those ships—in an immediate future—merchants, prostitutes, dictators, etc., traveling to other planets of the solar system, and carrying discord to other corners of the universe, etc.

Therefore, feeling in those moments the responsibility that weighed on my shoulders, I addressed my Father who is in secret, saying, "Father, if thou be willing, remove this cup from me: nevertheless not my will, but thine, be done." Those words vibrated from sphere to sphere, from world to world, within the nine heavens.

Years passed by and everything was resolved. My Father who is in secret gave the right answer: "Selection of human personnel, distribution of these cosmic ships only to certain very select groups of humanity." It is not irrelevant to state to our friends, that already certain isolated human groups possess these types of space vehicles. In an inaccessible region of the Himalayas where Communist invaders can never reach, there is a community of Lamas who received a certain quantity of those cosmic ships, with which they travel to other planets of space. These Lamas—who had the bliss of receiving those precious gifts—are sacred individuals, people who have the Auric Embryo developed, human beings who reincarnate.

Therefore, my friends, we must always do the will of the Father: never ours.

Those who reincarnate can choose the conditions of life that they want, always in accordance with the law of Karma. It is clear that they cannot move away from the karmic law. Yet, it is preferable that our Father who is in secret choose what is most convenient for us.

Question: Master, you have stated that the Gods also make mistakes. Who then is the one who does not make mistakes?

Samael Aun Weor: Friends, for me this question is very important, thus, I will give an appropriate answer; I beg the attention of all the audience.

Only the Father who is in secret does not make mistakes, since He is ineffable, omniscient, and omnipotent. This is why

I insist on the necessity of doing the will of the Father, on Earth as it is done in Heaven. One commits errors when one forgets his Father who is in secret. It is better to consult and leave everything in the hands of the Father.

Question: Master, what is the difference between the Auric Embryo and the consciousness?

Samael Aun Weor: Friends, there is no difference between the Auric Embryo and the consciousness, because the Auric Embryo is the same Essence, but organized, the same consciousness but objectified and radically liberated from any subconscious process.

Question: Master, the Master H.P.B. stated that the only way to stop suffering in this world is to cease reincarnating. What you can tell us with respect to her statement?

Samael Aun Weor: I want you ladies and gentlemen to know that absolute happiness is only achievable when one has God within. One can live in Nirvana, the world of happiness, yet if one does not have God within, one is not happy. Thus, one can cease reincarnating, yet if one does not have God within, one will not be happy either.

However, if one lived within the filthiest dungeon, in the middle of the most terrible ignominy, or even if one were to be within the infernal worlds, if one has God within, one would be infinitely happy.

Concerning this, my friends, it is not irrelevant to remind you that there, within the infernal worlds, live some Masters of compassion who work helping, assisting those souls who are decisively lost, yet since they have God within, they are blissfully happy.

Chapter Twenty-two

Recurrence

Friends of mine, today's lecture will address the law of recurrence.

When the ego returns, when it reincorporates, everything occurs again as it has before, plus the good and bad consequences. So, indubitably, various forms of the great law of recurrence exist. Thus, in this lecture we intend to study the varied forms of recurrence.

Diverse scenes of our previous lives are repeated, at times in more elevated spirals and at other times in lower spirals. The spiral is the curve of life and it is always symbolized by the snail-shell. We are wicked snail-shells within the bosom of the Father. Obviously, we move about, evolve, and devolve on the spiral line of existence.

Another form of recurrence can be evidenced in the history of the Earth and its races.

The first sub-race of our present Aryan root race developed on the central plateau of Asia and had a powerful esoteric civilization.

The second sub-race flourished in the south of Asia, in the Pre-Vedic epoch; then the wisdom of the Rishis from Hindustan was known, as well as the splendors of the ancient empire of China, etc.

The third sub-race developed marvelously in Egypt, Persia, Chaldaea, etc.

The fourth sub-race resplendently glowed among the civilizations of Greece and Rome.

The fifth was perfectly manifested amongst Germany, England, and other countries.

The sixth was the outcome of the mixture of the Spaniards with the autochthonous races from Indo-America.

The seventh is perfectly manifested amongst the outcome of all the diverse mixtures of races, such as today we can evidence in the territory of the United States.

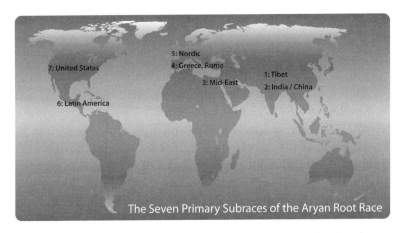

The Seven Primary Subraces of the Aryan Root Race

Obviously, the seven branches of the Aryan trunk already plainly exist and this is absolutely demonstrated.

The studies that we have performed within the causal world have allowed us to correctly verify astounding concrete facts for our present humanity. Given that each of the great root races that have existed in the world have always been terminated by a great cataclysm, we can therefore logically deduce that likewise our Aryan root race is going to be terminated very soon by means of another tremendous cataclysm. In a superior manner, we are talking about the law of recurrence. Thus, let us continue concretizing towards better comprehension.

After the great catastrophe that is approaching, the Earth will again be inhabited by select people. When arriving at this part of our lecture, I must emphatically tell you that the future root race that will populate the face of the Earth is now being intentionally created by the brethren of the occult fraternity. The modus operandi of this new creation is very special. I want you to know that cosmic travelers from other planets visit us constantly; they are already taking select seed from humanoids.

A short time ago in Brazil some newspapers printed a very interesting article about a certain Brazilian peasant who—while working feverishly cultivating the ground—was suddenly surprised by some extraterrestrials who led him into the interior of a cosmic ship, which was resting at a nearby place within the jungle. Then, extraordinary scientists, brethren from the outer space, carefully examined him; they even extracted a little bit of blood from him with the purpose of analyzing it. Thereafter, they placed him within a special room of the ship. Then, the perplexed peasant, astonished, confused, while resting on a bed, waited for something else..? All of a sudden, something unexpected happened: a strange woman with golden hair and yellow skin similar to the skin of Chinese people, lacking eyebrows, lay down beside that peasant and sexually seduced him; once the intercourse was consummated, the peasant was taken out of the ship. Thereafter, the ship soared away throughout the infinite space. Many other similar cases have occurred in diverse parts of our planet.

Moreover, there has been constant discussion about mysterious disappearances of aerial and maritime crews that have been lost forever without any explanation. All of this invites us to reflection; all of this makes us to comprehend that the elder brothers of humanity are taking the earthly seed in order to cross it with people from other planets. Thus, this is how the Holy Gods are already creating the future great root race, the sixth root race which—after the great impending cataclysm— will populate the Earth.

The sixth root race will be a new type of people. They will be the outcome of the mixture of earthlings with extraterrestrials; it will be a resplendent humanity. Lo and behold, respectable brothers and sisters, the selected personnel with whom the future Jerusalem will be created; this is the New Jerusalem mentioned in the Apocalypse of St. John.

It is unquestionable that the glorious esoteric civilizations of ancient times will resurrect in this new root race. By means of the law of recurrence, the powerful cultures of the first Aryan sub-race will emerge from within the chaos, yet in a superior type of spiral during the first sub-race of the future great sixth root race.

The Pre-Vedic civilization that flourished in millenary India and in ancient China will resurrect during the second sub-race of the future great sixth root race.

A new Egypt, new pyramids, a new Nile, and the Egyptian civilization will resurrect during the third sub-race of the future great sixth root race. Then, the ancient pharaohs will reincarnate and thousands of souls from that glorious culture will return from Amente with the purpose of reviving the hieratic mysteries of the sunny country of Khem. Likewise, the mysteries of Chaldaea, Assyria, Babylon, Persia, etc., will again become resplendent in that age yet on a superior spiral within the great spiral line of life.

The mysteries of Greece and Rome will resurrect during the fourth sub-race of that tomorrow's Earth, with the advantage of being in a superior spiral of existence.

Then, during the fifth sub-race a certain dangerous mechanicity will appear again and the civilization of England, Germany, etc., will resurrect once more, etc., with the advantage of being more spiritual, for the concrete fact of being developed on a superior spiral.

During the sixth sub-race of that great root race of tomorrow, something similar to the Latin world will appear, yet within a more elevated, more dignified, more spiritual aspect.

Finally, a very technological civilization will appear in the seventh sub-race of that future root race, although it will not have the gross materialism of this black age of Kali Yuga.

Thus, friends of mine, this is how the law of recurrence works, moving through the spiral of existence.

Now, let us think about the law of recurrence in regards to the planets in the starry spaces, in the unalterable infinite.

Everything that happened in the ancient Moon, in that satellite that illuminates the face of the Earth during nocturnal hours, is right now recurring on our planet Earth. In other words, I affirm the following: all the history of the Earth—along with its races from the dawning of life—is just a repetition of the history of the Selenites who previously inhabited that satellite, Selene; at that time, it was still alive and with abundant life. Lo and behold, ladies and gentlemen, how the law of recurrence works in all the corners of the infinite space.

Now, let us study the modus operandi of this great law in the intellectual animal mistakenly called "human."

When we reincorporate, when we return, when we come back, we repeat in detail all the events of our former and past existences. Subjects exist who are submitted to a rigorous repetition. These are concrete cases of egos that return through many centuries within the bosom of the same family, city, and nation. These are those who—because of incessantly repeating the same things—can predict with absolute clarity that which awaits them in the future. These are those who can say, for instance, "I will get married at the age of 30, my wife will have such a skin color, and such a height, and we will have these amount of children, my father will die at such an age, my mother will die at such an age, my business will prosper or will fail, etc." Thus, it is clear that all of their predictions recur with a surprising exactitude, since these are people who know their role by forcedly repeating so many times the same thing, therefore they do not ignore it, and that is all.

Within this category also enter the child prodigies who astound the people of their era; usually, these are egos that already know their dexterity by memory, thus when they return they marvelously repeat it from the first years of their infancy.

The law of recurrence is astonishing. The normal, common, and ordinary people always repeat their same dramas. The clowns in each of their successive lives, repeat over and over again their same comedies, whereas the perverse continuously reincorporate in order to incessantly repeat their same tragedies. In accordance with the law of cause and effect (Karma), all of these recurrent events that pertain to repeated existences are always accompanied by their good or bad consequences. The assassin will again be involved in the same horrifying event of assassination, yet this time, he will be assassinated. The thief will once again receive the same opportunity of stealing, yet this time, he will be thrown in jail. The bandit will have the same desire of running, of using his legs for crimes, yet this time, he will not have legs, he will be born an invalid or will lose their legs in some tragedy. The one born blind at birth will long to see the things of life, which in a former life possibly led him to cruelty, etc., yet this time, he will not be able to see them. A woman will fall in love with the same husband of her previous life, the one whom she possibly abandoned on the sick bed in order to run off with another man, yet this time, the drama will be repeated inversely—that is, the man she loves will leave her for another woman, leaving her abandoned. The highway bandit reincorporated within a new body—possibly of a feminine nature—will again feel the desire of running, he will feel pursued, he might shout out loud in a state of paranoia, he will have strange deliriums, yet, this time, he will not be able to escape from himself, he will become mentally ill, he will be demented, etc. Thus, friends of mine, this is how the law of recurrence incessantly works.

Question: Master, a country that has been affected many times by violence, is it because of the law of recurrence?

Samael Aun Weor: Obviously, the violence of the multitudes in that country is the repetition of a similar violence that occurred in a chaotic past. Think about the civil wars that occurred in epochs prior to the present, when violence occurred in that country. The war between the left and right political parties repeat themselves in the present as a outcome of the past. Behold the law of recurrence.

Question: Master, if a person has been upright, if he has behaved as a good citizen in the fulfillment of his duties, how does the law of recurrence affect him in his next return?

Samael Aun Weor: Friends, friends, do not tell me that such a fellow has been a model of virtues, a spring of sanctity. As magnificent a citizen as he might have been, he had his very human errors, his scenes, his dramas, etc., and it is clear that there will be repetition of all of this in his new existence, plus the consequences; this is how the law of recurrence operates.

Question: Venerable Master, I have a certain confusion between the law of karma and the law of recurrence, because I have the concept that the law of recurrence terminates when karma is terminated. Can you clarify this point for me?

Samael Aun Weor: Friends, by no means can confusion exist between the laws of recurrence and karma, since they are the same law with a different name. Indubitably, karma works on firm basis. Karma is nothing other than the effect of a cause that we originated. Therefore, the same event has to be repeated, plus its good or bad consequences.

Question: Master, there are people who apparently did not do anything evil to anyone and nonetheless they suffer due to financial problems. Is their problem related to the law of recurrence?

Samael Aun Weor: Respectable friends, ladies and gentlemen, God, the Father who is in secret, can be close to us or far from us. When the child is walking badly, his Father moves away from him; then his child falls into disgrace. He then suffers because of lack of money, he undergoes terrible necessities. The child, by himself, cannot understand the cause of his misery. Obviously, such people believe that they did not do anything bad against anyone. Yet, if they could remember their past lives, then they could evidence for themselves the concrete fact that they treaded on wrong paths. Perhaps they delivered themselves to alcohol, to lust, to adultery, etc.

The Father who is in secret, our own divine Spirit, can give to us or take away from us. He knows very well what we deserve, and if we do not presently have money, it is because He does not want to give it to us. He punishes us for our own good.

Behold, blessed is the man whom God corrects. – Job 5:17

Thus, the Father who loves his child always punishes him for his own good.

The concrete answer for this question is: the victim of such sufferings will repeat the same scenes from the past, plus the consequences, namely, poverty, pain, etc.

Question: Master, does the law of recurrence end when the 108 lives have ended?

Samael Aun Weor: Friends, once the cycle of human existences assigned to every soul concludes, then the law of recurrence also concludes through the repetition of humanoid scenes, animal, vegetal, and mineral states within the infernal worlds. Remember, that before reaching the humanoid state, we went through the mineral, vegetal, and animal states. Thus, once the cycle of 108 humanoid existences is exhausted, we then enter into the abyss in order to repeat anew the animal, vegetal, and mineral states. This is how the law of recurrence works.

Question: Master, the one who attains liberation from the wheel of Samsara no longer repeats the law of recurrence?

Samael Aun Weor: I will gladly answer the question of the lady. I want you ladies and gentlemen to know that the law of recurrence in its superior aspect corresponds to the Law of Katancia or superior karma. From the dawning of every new great cosmic day, the Holy Gods have to repeat cosmic scenes from ancient Mahamanvantaras plus its consequences. Remember that the Gods also make mistakes. Those sacred individuals, who in the present Earth period gave the abominable Kundabuffer organ to humanity, will pay for their mistakes by repeating similar dramas in the future Mahamanvantara.

Our present planet Earth, along with the humanity that populates it, is the outcome of a cosmic karma; the planet is incessantly repeating the historic periods of the ancient moon, along with its cosmic consequences. Any great initiate is capable to verify for himself the concrete, clear, and definitive fact that the ancient inhabitants of Selene were indeed cruel and merciless. Their outcome is before our sight, in the black pages of the black history of our afflicted planet Earth.

Question: Master, who are those who are free from the law of recurrence?

Samael Aun Weor: When looking at the law of recurrence in its superior and inferior aspects of the great life, we can solemnly affirm that only those who are capable of crystallizing within their intimate nature the three primary forces of the universe are the ones who become free from the law of recurrence. The Sacred Absolute Sun wants to crystallize the three primary forces within each one of us. Let us collaborate with Him and His holy designs. Thus, this is how we will become free from the law of recurrence forever.

Chapter Twenty-three

The Snail-Shell of Existence

Today we will mostly talk about the spiral line of life.

Friends of mine, the doctrine of the transmigration of souls, revealed about one thousand years before Jesus Christ by Lord Krishna in the sacred land of the Vedas, has been abundantly debated. All of the processes of the wheel of Samsara have been already explained in our former lectures with absolute clarity. In them we have stated, we have repeated to satiation, that 108 lives are assigned to every soul for the realization of their Inner Self.

Unquestionably, those who fail during any cycle of manifestation—that is, those who do not attain Self-realization within their 108 assigned existences— obviously descend into the submerged mineral kingdom, the Hindustani Avitchi, the Greek Tartarus, the Roman Avernus. It is obvious, it is evident, that devolution within the bowels of the planet on which we live is terribly painful, since indeed, to recapitulate animalistic, vegetaloid, and mineraloid states, in a frankly degenerating manner, is by no means a very pleasant journey.

In our former lectures we also affirmed that after its Second Death, the Essence, which is what we have as an embryo of soul, re-ascends again in an evolutionary manner from the mineral kingdom into the vegetable and animal kingdoms step by step to the intellectual animal, mistakenly called human.

Nevertheless, regarding the law of transmigration of souls, there is something that we have not yet said. We have cited the law of eternal return. We have also mentioned this other great law known as recurrence. Now, we must clarify that these two aforementioned laws develop and unfold upon the spiral line of life. This signifies that within the great spiral line of the universe, every cycle of manifestation is processed in ever higher spirals. However, since this concept is to some extent a little bit abstract, I see the necessity of clarifying it better, so that all of you can profoundly comprehend the teachings.

Listen: after having passed through the Second Death, the Essence escapes from Hell. Then, the Essence once again emerges into the light of the Sun, transformed into a "gnome" [an elemental consciousness related to the mineral kingdom]. There, obviously, it will have to initiate a new, evolving process, but this time within a superior octave. This undoubtedly signifies that the mineral elemental creature will be found breathing within the mineral kingdom, yet this time with a state of consciousness superior to the one it had when it initiated a similar evolution in its previous cycle of manifestation.

Before continuing with these explanations, you must not forget that any cycle of manifestation includes evolutions in the mineral, vegetable, animal, and human kingdoms, and that the 108 existences are only assigned to the human level.

If we examine a snail shell, we will see a curve upon a curve, something similar to a spiral type of ladder. Thus, it is evident that each one of these cycles of manifestation develops in successively higher curves. Now, you will understand why there is a great variety of mineral, vegetable, and animal elementals, and why there are diverse degrees of intelligence among humanoids.

A SNAIL SHELL

Unquestionably, there is a great difference between the mineral elementals that begin for the first time as mineral elementals and those who have repeated the same process many times. We can state the same thing in regards to the vegetable and animal elementals, and likewise regarding humanoids.

Notwithstanding, given that there are always 3,000 cycles of manifestation, indeed, the last one of these is found at a very high octave.

Therefore, those Essences that do not achieve mastery within 3,000 turns of the wheel are absorbed by their virginal sparks in order to definitely submerge themselves within the bosom of the universal Spirit of life.

It is flatly obvious and evident that during our 3,000 cycles of cosmic manifestation, we must pass through all the practical experiences of life. Indubitably, any Essence that has passed through the 3,000 cycles of manifestation has also experienced the horrors of the abyss 3,000 times, and consequently it has improved and acquired self-cognizance. Thus, in fact, those essences have an absolute right to divine happiness. Regrettably, however, they will not enjoy mastery. They do not have it, because they did not acquire it.

We have already stated in our previous lectures that not all the divine Monads or virginal sparks are interested in acquiring mastery. Obviously, the virginal sparks or divine Monads are not the ones who suffer, but their Essences, the embryo of soul that all of us have, which is the emanation of the spark or Monad within each one of us. The pains experienced by every Essence are very well-rewarded indeed, because in return, based on those sufferings, the Essence acquires self-cognizance and happiness without limits. Mastery is different. No one could attain Adepthood without the three factors of the revolution of consciousness, clearly expressed by our Lord the Christ:

> Then said Jesus unto his disciples, "If any man will come after me, let him deny himself, and take up his cross, and follow me." - Matthew 16:24

"To deny himself" signifies dissolution of the "I."

"To take up his cross," to place it on our shoulders, signifies to work with Sex Yoga, the Maithuna, Sexual Magic.

"And follow me" signifies to follow the Christ, which is equivalent to sacrificing one's own life for the sake of humanity, to devote one's life so that others may live.

The virginal sparks that did not achieve mastery during their 3,000 cycles of manifestation perceive the Masters, the Gods, in a manner similar to how ants perceive humanoids.

Aztec traditions state that at the dawning of life, the Gods gathered together in Teotihuacán with the purpose of creating the Sun. They affirm that they lit a great bonfire and thereafter invited the Snail-shell God to hurl himself into the flames, yet after attempting it three times, the Snail-shell God felt a great terror. Then, the sacred songs solemnly affirm that the Purulent God, filled with great courage, hurled himself into the fire. Thus, when the Snail-shell God saw this, he also hurled himself into the fire. Then, the entire assembly of Gods waited silently in order to see what was going to happen.

Legends state that the Purulent God surged forth again from within the living fire, yet transformed into the Sun that illuminates us today. Minutes later, the Snail-shell God surged forth from within the blaze, yet transformed into the Moon that illuminates us at night.

Dear friends, this signifies that we must imitate the Purulent God if we want to be transformed into Solar Gods, into Masters. Thus, we must incinerate the ego, the "I," by means of the sexual fire. Only through the fire can the purulence, the myself, the self-willed, die. Yes, only through fire can we be transformed into tremendously divine solar Gods.

Regrettably, not all virginal sparks are interested in acquiring Mastery. The majority, the millions of creatures that live on the face of the Earth, prefer the path of the snail-shell: the lunar path.

Question: Venerable Master, at the beginning of this important dissertation, you told us that animalistic, vegetaloid, and mineraloid states are recapitulated during the descent of the Essence into the infernal worlds. Would you be so kind as to explain the word recapitulate?

Samael Aun Weor: I will gladly answer this gentleman's question. Friends of mine, I want you to comprehend very well what the animalistic, vegetaloid, and mineraloid abysmal recapitulations are.

The devolving descent into the entrails of the submerged world is radically different from the evolving ascension over the surface of the Earth. The animalistic recapitulation within the abyss is a degenerative, devolving, painful type of descent. The vegetaloid recapitulation within the entrails of the Earth is frightening. Those who undergo such processes seem rather like shadows that drift away amongst unutterable sufferings here, there, and everywhere. The devolving mineraloid recapitulative descent within the entrails of the world in which we live is more bitter that death itself. In it, the creatures fossilize themselves, they mineralize themselves, and slowly disintegrate amongst torments that are impossible to describe with words. After the Second Death, the Essence escapes, reemerges into the light of the Sun, in order to recapitulate similar processes, yet in an evolving, ascending, innocent, and happy manner. Lo and behold friends of mine, the difference between the devolving and evolving recapitulations.

Anyhow, all of these infinite devolving and evolving processes are exclusively of a lunar type and are clearly developed within the universal snail-shell.

Question: Master, you have explained that in each cycle of existences the elementals who are in the evolving process are awakening consciousness because they are processing themselves within more elevated octaves. Is this awakening of the consciousness the outcome of the sufferings of devolution or the outcome of the evolving ascending process?

Samael Aun Weor: Respectable friend, it is good for you to understand that the consciousness suffers as much as in the evolving processes as well as in the devolving processes. Therefore, the consciousness awakens progressively based on these efforts and sacrifices.

Millions of humanoids have their consciousness profoundly asleep, yet when they enter into the abyss after the 108 existences of any cycle of manifestation, they inevitably awaken in evil and for evil. The remarkable aspect on this case is that at least they awaken, even though only to justify their errors within the infernal worlds.

Any enlightened clairvoyant will evidence for himself the fact that the innocent elementals are awakening in a positive, evolving sense.

Therefore, there are several types of awakened consciousness:

1. First: the awakened consciousness of the innocent creatures of nature.

2. Second: the awakened consciousness of the devolving humanoids of the abyss.

3. There is a third type of awakened consciousness. I am addressing the consciousness of Masters, the Gods. Yet, in this precise moment we are not occupying ourselves with them.

Unquestionably, rotating around the wheel of Samsara are those with innocent, awakened consciousness, and also devolving abysmal creatures awakened in evil and for evil.

Question: Master, it disturbs me when you mention this matter about more elevated octaves within higher spirals, because I am accustomed to think of octaves in relation to musical notes, which are related with the transmutation of the serpentine fire. Can you please clarify this for me?

Samael Aun Weor: Indubitably, the octaves of the snail-shell are musically processed in a gradual manner with the notes Do, Re, Mi, Fa, Sol, La, Ti.

If we carefully observe a spiral ladder, we will see a succession of curves that are successively higher, in such a manner that they are preceded by lower ones. This formation, this distribution of curves in the shape of any spiral, is enough in order to comprehend that there are musical pauses between octave and octave. The abysmal descent corresponds to each one of these pauses.

Therefore, the 3,000 turns of the wheel incessantly resound as a unique whole within the rhythms of Mahavan and Chotavan that sustain the universe firmly in its march.

Question: Master, if the Essence is good, why does it has to come to suffer in this world?

Samael Aun Weor: Friends of mine, the Essence in itself is beyond good and evil; it is absolutely innocent, pure, and vigorous. But when the Essence is bottled within the ego it suffers, and when the ego is dissolved, the suffering of the Essence ceases.

Due to a mistake of the Gods, the Essences of the planet Earth certainly remained bottled within the myself. Regarding this mistake, we have already stated in past lectures that certain sacred individuals gave this humanity the abominable Kundabuffer organ with the purpose of stabilizing the geological crust of our planet. When that organ disappeared, its awful consequences remained within each person. These awful consequences crystallized and became the ego, a type of second nature within which, lamentably, the Essence remained bottled. If that second nature did not exist, the Essence would be free and happy. Regrettably, it exists, as an outcome of the abominable Kundabuffer organ.

Question: Master, it is stated that we are children of God and that God is perfect. Why did God send his children to suffer?

Samael Aun Weor: I will gladly answer this question from the audience. Ladies and gentlemen, the hour has arrived to acknowledge that all of us are children of the devil. Please, I beg you, do not be frightened. We already know that for our own sake the Lord Satan or Prometheus-Lucifer is exclusively the projected shadow of our own internal divinity within ourselves. Yes, it is evident that Lucifer is the great coach that we carry within. This is why in its depths the sexual impulse is Luciferic.

Therefore, as we have already explained in past lectures, the Devil is not that fabulous personage that some dogmatic sects present to us, but the very personal coach of each one of us. Hence, the Luciferic sexual force is what impels the humanoids to triumph or to fail, to degenerate or regenerate. Thus, from this point of view we can affirm that we are children of the devil. This has been already stated by our Lord the Christ. The great Master said:

> *Ye are of your father the devil... If ye were God's children, ye would do the works of God.* - John 8: 44, 39 [Note: the original text says "Abraham's children." In Kabbalah, Abraham represents the sephirah Chesed, our own Inner God]

It is necessary for us to become children of God, and this is only possible by means of the three factors of the revolution of the consciousness, as we have already stated in this lecture.

A child of God is one who reaches resurrection.

So, reflect on these words and do not boast of being saints or righteous, because all of you are children of the Devil.

Friends, God never sends us to suffer. It is we who through successive births and through our own mistakes have created these sufferings.

Question: Master, if we are children of the Devil, who has more power over us, the Devil or God?

EVEN THE GREATEST ANGEL CAN FALL. LUCIFER FALLING FROM HEAVEN.

Samael Aun Weor: I will gladly answer this question. We have stated that within each one of us the dragon is the shadow of our Inner God. It is evident that each one of us is a child of that shadow, of that dragon; thus, logically in the present state in which we find ourselves, the dragon is absolutely controlling us. Therefore, from this relative and circumstantial point of view in which we find ourselves, the Devil has more power over us than God. Nevertheless, this does not signify that the Devil is more powerful than God.

When the immortal spark resurrects within us, when we transform ourselves into children of God, then everything will be different; in those days we will have overcome the dragon.

Question: Master, what can you tell us about the Angels, Bodhisattvas, and fallen Masters? How do they relate to the spiral of life?

Samael Aun Weor: Respectable friends, a supreme moment exists for all the millions of Essences that populate the face of the Earth. I am emphatically addressing that supreme moment in which for the first time they resolve to enter the solar path, which is indeed very different from the lunar path. So, the precise moment, the critical hour arrives for all the millions or trillions of virginal sparks in which they have to define themselves for the solar path or for the lunar snail-shell path.

Once someone deliberately chooses the path of the razor's edge, their fate is cast; after this moment, there is no turning back. Those who attain mastery and thereafter want to step back in order to enter into the lunar path will have to undergo frightening eternities within the infernal worlds, until obtaining—after many billions or trillions of years—the annihilation of the superior existential bodies of the Being and the destruction of the animal ego. This signifies that the greater degree of consciousness, the greater degree of responsibility, and he who increases wisdom increases sorrow.

Unquestionably, the fallen Bodhisattvas—the dark angels, the tenebrous archangels, in other words—the angelic or divine creatures who are submerged within the abyss for the crime of wanting to take the lunar path after having defined themselves for the solar path, will have to suffer millions of times more intensely than the common and ordinary souls.

Anyhow, once the disintegration of their solar vehicles and their egos has been obtained, they will have to restart their evolving journey from the mineral kingdom, but with a golden embryo and therefore with a greater consciousness than the other elementals of nature, until reaching anew the humanoid state. Once this objective has been attained, since they possess the golden embryo, those beings will have to return to the solar path again in order to create their superior existential bodies, thus, re-conquering the angelic or archangelic state, etc. that they previously rejected.

So, fate is different for the virginal sparks that in their 3000 cycles never chose the solar path. Transformed into simple elementals of nature, they submerge with their Essence into the universal ocean of life, free in its movement. These are beings who preferred the elemental life, who never aspired to mastery, who always enjoyed being within the bosom of great nature, and who now, as sparks of divinity, return forever into its bosom.

Chapter Twenty-four

Karmic Transactions

Friends of mine, tonight in this gathering we will very seriously study the matter of karmic transactions. Allow me the liberty to tell you that I am not going to talk about profane transactions; I will emphatically address the transactions of karma.

First of all it is necessary that people understand what the Sanskrit word "Karma" means. It is not irrelevant to affirm that the word Karma implies the law of action and consequence. Obviously, there is no cause without an effect, nor an effect without a cause. Thus, any action of our life, whether good or bad, has consequences.

Today, I have been reflecting on the misfortune of our world. How happy these intellectual humanoids would be if they never had that which is called ego,(the "I", the myself, the self-willed) since the ego indubitably perpetrates countless mistakes whose outcome is sorrow. If present rational humanoids were devoid of ego, they would simply be beautiful, innocent, pure, and infinitely happy natural elementals. Thus, dear friends, imagine for a moment an Earth populated by millions of innocent humanoids, devoid of ego, and governed by Divine Kings, Gods, Hierophants, Devas, etc. Obviously a world like this would indeed be paradise, a blissful planet.

No humanoid can be forced to transform into a human being. Thus, all of those millions of humanoids—even though they are not human beings in the most complete sense of the word—could have been infinitely happy if that second, malignant, and terribly perverse nature had not emerged within their interior.

Regrettably, as we have already profusely stated in these lectures, due to a mistake committed by certain sacred individuals, something abnormal appeared within each individual—that is, certain inhuman elements appeared, within which the consciousness is bottled up. It is clear that such inhuman elements emerged as an outcome of the awful consequences of the abominable Kundabuffer organ. Thus, this is how, beloved friends of mine, this planetary humanity failed; this is how it became frightfully malignant. It would have been better if those sacred individuals had not given that infamous, abominable organ to these wretched tri-brained or tri-centered bipeds.

Let us think for a moment about the multitude of humanoids that populate the face of the Earth. They suffer the unspeakable, being victims of their own errors. If they did not have ego, they would not have those errors, nor would they suffer their consequences.

In past lectures, we stated that not all Virginal Sparks, not all humanoids, are interested in Mastery; nonetheless, this is not an obstacle for authentic happiness. Within the infinite space there are many blissful dwellings for elemental humanoids who do not have interest in Mastery, since unquestionably, the 3,000 cycles or periods of time assigned to any Essence, to any Monad for their cosmic manifestation, are developed not only here on our planet Earth, but also on other planets of the starry space. Thus, dear friends, by beholding all of this you can understand that many mansions of happiness exist for the Souls, and that by no means is Mastery indispensable in order to have the right to the authentic bliss of the Pure Spirit. The unique thing that is required in order for us to have the right to true happiness is first of all to not have ego. Indeed, when the psychological aggregates, the inhuman elements that make us so horrible and wicked, do not exist within us, there is no Karma to pay; thus the outcome is bliss.

Not all of the happy creatures that live on all of the planets of infinite space have reached Mastery. Nonetheless, they are found in tune with the cosmic order because they do not have ego, since when one lives according to upright thought, upright feeling, and upright action, the consequences are usually blissful. Regrettably, upright thought, upright feeling and upright action, etc., are impossible when a second inhumane nature breathes in us, acts within us and through us, here and now.

Now we must avoid falling into confusion about what we have already stated, since it is obvious that amongst the multitudes, few are those who aspire to Adepthood, to the realization of their Inner Being. Unquestionably, these few souls are transformed into true kings of the universe and into terribly divine Gods, whereas the multitudes—after their 3,000 cycles of manifestation—return into the Universal Spirit of life as simple, blissful elementals.

What is unpleasant about these millions of earthling humanoid elementals is that they have created within themselves a second infrahuman nature. That inhuman nature has made them not only perverse, but moreover and worse, a disgrace. If it were not for their egotistical self, none of them would be irate, none of them would covet the goods of their neighbor, none of them would be lustful, envious, proud, lazy, gluttonous, etc.

Alas, I regret very much to have to state that the fate reserved in the future great cosmic day for the Archangel Sakaki and his high commission of sacred individuals (who, in archaic times gave the abominable Kundabuffer organ unto humanity) holds unutterable bitterness, a blood-curdling karma, since there is no doubt that due to their mistake, this humanity lost its happiness and became monstrous. May the holy Gods forgive me for uttering such an affirmation, but facts speak for themselves and before such evidence we have to surrender, whatever the cost. Fortunately my dear friends, justice and mercy are the two principal columns of the Universal White Fraternity. Justice without mercy is tyranny; mercy without justice is tolerance, complacency with crime.

In this world of misfortune in which we find ourselves, it is necessary to learn how to handle our own karmic transactions, in order to maneuver the ship of our existence through the diverse scales of our life. Karma is negotiable, and this is something that may very much surprise the followers of diverse orthodox schools. Indeed, some pseudo-esotericists and pseudo-occultists have become too pessimistic in relation with the law of action and consequence, since they mistakenly suppose that karma develops in a mechanical, automatic, and cruel manner. Those erudites believe that it is not possible to alter that law. I very sincerely regret to have to dissent from their way of thinking. If the law of action and consequence, if the nemesis of existence, were not negotiable, then where would divine mercy be? Frankly, I cannot accept cruelty within divinity. The reality, that which is all perfection, that which has diverse names, such as Tao, Aum, Inri, Zen, Allah, Brahma, God, or better said Gods, etc., by no means can be without mercy, something cruel, tyrannical, etc. Therefore, I emphatically repeat that karma is negotiable.

When an inferior law is transcended by a superior law, the superior law washes away the inferior law.

Perform good deeds so that you may pay your debts. The lion of the law is fought with the scales.

Whosoever has capital with which to pay, pays and does well in business; however, the one who does not have any capital shall pay with pain.

If our good deeds are placed on one plate and our bad deeds on the other plate of the cosmic scales, it is evident that our karma will depend on the weight that is on the scales. If the plate of bad deeds weighs more, the outcome will be bitterness. However, it is possible to increase the weight of the good deeds on the other plate of the equal-arm-beam of the scales. Thus, in this manner we will cancel out our karma without undergoing suffering. All that we need is to do good deeds in order to increase the weight of the plate of good deeds.

Now good friends of mine, you will comprehend how marvelous it is to do good. There is no doubt that upright thought, upright feeling, and upright action are the best transactions. Thus, we must never protest against karma. What is important is to know how to negotiate it.

Regrettably, the only thing that occurs to people when they undergo a great bitter sorrow is to wash their hands like Pontius Pilate, and to say that they did not do anything bad, that they are not guilty, that they are righteous souls, etc.

I tell those who are in misery, to examine their conduct, to judge themselves, to sit down at least for a moment on the bench of the accused. Thus, after a brief analysis of themselves,

they should modify their behavior. If those who find themselves unemployed would become chaste, infinitely charitable,
peaceful, one hundred percent helpful, it is obvious that they
will radically alter the cause of their misfortune; thus as a consequence, they modify the effect.

To alter an effect is not possible if, firstly, the cause that
produced it has not been radically modified, since as we have
already stated, an effect without a cause does not exist, nor a
cause without an effect.

There is no doubt that poverty has its causes in drunkenness, in disgusting lust, in violence, in adulteries, in squandering, and in avarice, etc.

It is not possible for someone to live in poverty when the
Father who is in secret is present here and now. I will illustrate
this with a story:

On a certain occasion, my real inner Being, my immortal
Monad, took me out of my physical body in order to give
me instructions about a certain disciple. Once the instructions concluded, I did not hesitate to address my Lord, my
Innermost, with the following words. "I am tired of having a
body, thus I would like to disincarnate."

In those moments the Lord of perfections, my inner God,
answered me with a solemn voice, "Why are you complaining? I
am giving you food, clothing, and shelter, and nonetheless you
still complain? Remember how in the final days of your past
existence you were barefoot, old and sick, wandering around
on the streets of Mexico wearing a torn suit, in the most frightful poverty and how you passed away within a filthy hut. At
that point in time, I was absent."

In those moments, the countenance of my Lord shone, and
his blue eyes reflected the infinite heaven, his glorious white
robe reached his feet; everything in Him was perfection.

Then, I told him, "Lord, I have come to kiss your hand and
receive your benediction." Thus the adorable one blessed me
and I kissed his right hand. Subsequently, when I returned into
my physical body I entered into meditation. Indeed my dear
brethren, when the child misbehaves the Father withdraws,
thus the child falls into disgrace.

My dear friends, I think you now comprehend better what poverty is, and why and how it arrives.

The Father who is in secret has enough power in order to provide for us, as well as to take away from us.

Behold, blessed is the man whom God corrects. – Job 5:17

So, karma is a medicine that is prescribed to us for our own sake.

Regrettably, people protest, blaspheme, they justify themselves instead of bending down reverently before the living eternal God. Yes, people justify themselves stubbornly, thus like Pontius Pilate they wash their hands. Yet, karma is not modified with complaints. On the contrary, it becomes harder and more severe.

We demand fidelity from our spouse when we ourselves have been adulterers in this life or in former lives. Yes, we want to be loved when we have been merciless and cruel.

We demand comprehension when we have never known how to comprehend anyone, when we have never learned how to see the point of view of our neighbor.

We long for immense bliss when we have always been the cause for much disgrace.

We would have liked to have been born in a very beautiful home with many comforts, yet in past lives we did not know how to provide a home and beauty for our children.

We protest against insulters when we have always insulted everyone who surrounds us.

We want our children to obey us when we have never known how to obey our parents.

Slander annoys us terribly, yet we have filled the world with pain due to our slandering.

Gossip upsets us, we do not want anyone to gossip about us, and nonetheless, we are always involved in gossip and chit-chat, talking badly against our neighbor, mortifying the lives of others.

To that end, we always demand what we have never given. We were evil in all of our former lives, thus we deserve the worst. Nevertheless, we expect the best should be offered to us.

Instead of worrying so much about their sickness, the sick should work for others; they should do works of charity, should try to heal others, console the afflicted, take to the doctor those people who cannot afford to pay the doctor, to give away medicine, etc. Thus, in this manner they will cancel their karma and they will become totally healed.

Those who suffer in their home should multiply their humility, patience, and serenity. They must not answer with insults. They must not tyrannize their neighbor, must not upset those who surround them, must know how to forgive the defects of their neighbor with patience infinitely multiplied. Thus, this is how they will cancel out their karma and will become better.

Regrettably, my dear friends, that ego that each one of us carries within does exactly the contrary of what we are stating here. Thus, for that reason, I consider that it is urgent, unpostponable, and imperative to reduce "the myself" to cosmic dust.

Question: Venerable Master, do you consider your mission accomplished if you achieve that the intellectual humanoids transform themselves into innocent elementals?

Samael Aun Weor: I will gladly answer this question. Many prophets, great Avatars, and Masters fought in ancient times against the awful consequences of the abominable Kundabuffer organ. Thus, this is a popular type of mission, whose purpose is to make this humanity return to its total innocence. Those saints, in ancient times, also had their esoteric circle for those devotees of the direct path, for those who in all ages aspired to attain the mastery. Behold therefore, friends, the two circles, the exoteric or public, and the esoteric or secret. It is not irrelevant to remind you that the great confessional religions fill precisely these two needs. Any confessional religion serves the multitudes as well as the initiates. I think that now you will completely understand the meaning of my mission upon the face of this afflicted planet on which we live.

Question: Master, is any type suffering that one is undergoing attributed to the absence of the Father?

Samael Aun Weor: Friends, there are voluntary and involuntary sufferings. The first are processed within those who follow the direct path, the solar path; the second is the outcome of our own karma. It is obvious that when the child misbehaves the Father withdraws, thus the consequence is pain.

Question: Master, in regard to Nemesis or Karma, is it possible for any suffering to be negotiable before the lords of Karma?

Samael Aun Weor: Dear friends, I want you to comprehend that when this or that karma has been utterly developed and unfolded, it inevitably has to reach its end. This signifies that it is only possible to radically modify karma when repentance is total and when every possibility of repeating the error that produced it has radically disappeared. When Kamaduro reaches its end, it is always catastrophic. Not all karma is negotiable. Likewise, it is good to know that when we have radically eliminated the ego, the possibility of delinquency has also been annihilated; thus, as a consequence, karma can be forgiven.

Chapter Twenty-five
Direct Experience

Respectable friends, we meet today, March 19th 1973, the eleventh year of Aquarius in order to conclude these lectures. Unquestionably, for the sake of the great cause these lectures will be published as a book. Thus, I want to conclude by emphasizing the necessity of directly experiencing everything that we have explained, since the experience of reality is cardinal and definitive for creative comprehension.

Indeed, the hour has arrived to clearly understand that we possess a definitive psychological factor, by means of which it is possible to verify what we have stated in all of these lectures. With great solemnity I am addressing the Essence. The Essence is the very foundation of our psychic organization, which is that element that has not yet been lost.

It is indubitable that the Buddha, the doctrine, religion, and wisdom are endowed within the Essence, within the consciousness. In synthesis, we can affirm that the Essence, the consciousness, is endowed with the indispensable data for regeneration, inner self-realization, and for the living completion of everything that we have stated in these lectures. This means that if the basic principles of regeneration are endowed within that primary element, which is the primordial foundation of all our psychic organization, obviously the first thing that we need to do is to destroy, to annihilate our second nature, which is that infernal type of nature within which the Essence is imprisoned.

It is completely evident that the Essence radically awakens when it is disembottled, when the Essence is liberated. Thus, as you can see, there are multiple advantages that an awakened consciousness can provide. Amongst such advantages the first is magnificent in itself, since it has the capacity of fundamentally guiding us by wisely directing our steps along the path of the razor's edge, which will lead us towards final liberation.

The second advantage guides us along the path of those varied direct experiences to the total verification of each and every one of the affirmations that we have taught in these lectures. Thus, the modus operandi of a disembottled, awakened, self-cognizant Essence is integral illumination, luminous experience, and practical confirmation.

Therefore, the complete annihilation of all undesirable elements that constitute the myself, the self-willed is undoubtedly urgent and unpostponable.

We need to learn how to voluntarily direct all the functionalisms of our psyche. It is not good that we continue living under bondage. We must become leaders and lords of ourselves.

Our consciousness awakens at same pace that our undesirable elements are eliminated. Nonetheless, we need to become serious. Up to now we have not been serious people, since presently each one of us is nothing more than a log upon the boisterous waves of the sea of existence. Again: we need to become serious. This affirmation implies a tremendous self-vigilance from instant to instant, from moment to moment.

Remember what we have already stated in our previous lectures: the defects that we carry hidden within burst forth spontaneously in relation to our neighbors, and if we are alert and vigilant like a watchman in times of war, we will discover them. In every self-discovery there also exists self-revelation. A discovered defect must be rigorously analyzed and studied in all the levels of our mind and integrally comprehended through the diverse processes of profound internal meditation. Afterwards, when the defect that we have analyzed has been integrally understood, we proceed with supplications to Devi Kundalini, our particular Divine Cosmic Mother, with the purpose that She eliminate and disintegrate the defect in question.

My respectable brethren, this work is very profound, frightfully serious. Indeed, it is extremely profound. Thus, only in this manner is it possible to extirpate, to eradicate from our psyche, the many undesirable, infrahuman, tenebrous elements within which the Essence is imprisoned.

As the consciousness is increasingly awakened, the possibilities of direct experience become successively more lucid and continuous. Above all, my dear friends, I want you to learn how to practically handle the diverse sparks of an awakened consciousness.

In practical life we can carefully detect the concrete fact that all people live with their consciousness asleep.

In these moments, the memories of something remarkable come into my mind. On one occasion about seventeen or eighteen years ago, it so happened that I was in a market in the Federal suburb with my priestess-wife Litelantes. During the moments when we were picking up a watch that she had sent to be repaired in a jewelry store, we were suddenly shaken by violent explosive dynamite.

Litelantes was horrified, thus she asked me to return home immediately. My answer was a blunt no, since I knew that a second explosion was about to occur and by no means did I want to endanger our lives. So, all her pleading was in vain...

The sirens and bells of the "smoke-eaters" or firemen resounded in those moments. Quickly, those humble and martyr-servers of humanity hurried towards the scene of the explosion... "Of all those firemen who are right now enter-ing that catastrophic stage, not one will come out safe and sound; all of them will die!" Those were my words. Horrified, Litelantes kept silent.

Moments later, Mexico City was shaken terribly by a second explosion, whose outcome was death for all those humble fire-men, since they were instantaneously disintegrated. Nothing was found of them, not even their cadavers. The only thing that could be found was one sergeant's boot.

Frankly, I was astounded when I realized the degree of unconsciousness of those firemen. If they had been awakened, by no means would they have perished.

I still remember the desperate weeping of the women who rushed away from that market, as well as their children who, horrified, grabbed the skirts of their mothers.

If I had not been awake, obviously I would have perished, because hundreds of people died at the very bus stop where I board the bus to return home.

I still cannot forget the many cadavers strewn about the street. They were laid out at the edge of the sidewalk covered with newspapers. Unquestionably, these were victims of their own curiosity. Yes, they were curious people, unconscious, asleep people, who after the first explosion had rushed to the place of the explosion in order to contemplate the spectacle. If those people had been awake, they would never have curiously rushed to the place of the explosion. Regrettably, they were profoundly sleeping; thus, this is how they encountered their death.

When we returned to our home located at the "Colonia Caracol," our neighbors were alarmed because they had supposed that we had been killed in the explosions. Indeed, they were astounded, since despite being so close to the place of the catastrophe, we were able to return home alive and unharmed. Lo and behold the advantages of being awakened.

Friends, we have to awaken, and to learn how to live alert from moment to moment, from second to second.

It is unpostponable to always divide our attention into three parts:

1. Subject

2. Object

3. Location

SUBJECT: We must not forget ourselves. We must watch ourselves every second, every moment. This implies a state of alertness in relation to our thoughts, gestures, actions, emotions, habits, words, etc.

OBJECT: Detailed observation of all those objects or representations that reach our mind through our senses. Never become identified with such things, because this is how one falls into the fascination and sleep of the consciousness.

LOCATION: Daily observation of our home, our bedroom, as if it was something new. Daily questioning of ourselves: "Why did I arrive here, at this place, at this market, at this office, at this temple, etc.?"

These three divided aspects of our attention by no means constitute another chapter, or something different from the process of the dissolution of the "I," since we undoubtedly need to study, to observe ourselves from moment to moment, if indeed what we want is to discover our own psychological defects. We have already stated that the defects that we carry hidden within burst forth naturally, spontaneously, in relation to our neighbors.

Subject, is not merely self-observing the steps that we take, nor the positions of the body, etc. Vigilance upon ourself as subject implies a silent and serene study of all our inner psychological processes, emotions, passions, thoughts, words, etc.

The detailed observation of objects without identification will allow us to know the processes of covetousness, attachments, ambition, etc. It is irrefutable that a covetous person will struggle greatly in order to not become identified with a diamond ring or with some banknotes, etc.

The observation of location will allow us to know how far our attachments and fascinations go in relation to diverse places.

This triple set of attention is therefore a complete exercise in order to discover ourselves and in order to awaken our consciousness.

When I was still very young, a tender adolescent, I instinctively practiced this marvelous exercise. In these moments, two special cases come to mind, which for the sake of this lecture I will narrate for you.

First case: One night, I entered through the doors of a marvelous mansion. Silently, I passed through a beautiful garden, until I arrived at a fastuous family room. Moved by an inner impulse, I walked a little further and fearlessly entered an attorney's office. Seated at the desk, I found a lady of average height, with gray hair, a pale face, thin lips, and small pointed nose. That respectable lady was of medium height. Her body was not very thin yet it was not too fat either. Her look was somewhat melancholic and serene. Then, with a sweet and quiet voice, the lady invited me to sit in front of the desk. All of a sudden, something unexpected occurred. On top of the desk I saw two butterflies made of glass come to life. They moved their wings, breathed, looked around, etc. Indeed, such a phenomenon seemed extremely exotic and odd to me: two butterflies made of glass and with life of their own?

As I was accustomed to dividing my attention into three parts, I firstly did not forget myself. Secondly, I did not become identified with those glass butterflies. Thirdly, I carefully observed the place.

When contemplating those insects made of glass, I told myself, "This cannot be a phenomenon of the physical world, because in the tridimensional region of Euclid, I have never known glass butterflies with a life of their own. Unquestionably, this can only be a phenomenon of the Astral world."

I then looked around and asked myself the following questions, "Why am I in this place? Why did I come here? What am I doing here?"

I then addressed the lady and spoke to her in the following manner, "Ma'am, can you excuse me for a moment while I go out to the garden? I will soon return." The lady nodded her head in acknowledgment, thus I left the office for a moment.

Once outside in the garden, I executed a little stretched-out jump with the intention of hovering in the surrounding environment. Great was my astonishment when I hovered. I verified for myself that indeed I was out of my physical body. Then I comprehended that I was in the Astral world. At that moment, I remembered that quite long ago, several hours ago, I had left my physical body; unquestionably, my physical body was sleeping in my bed.

Once I made this unique verification, I returned to the office where the lady awaited me. Then, I wanted to convince her that she was outside of her physical body. "Ma'am," I said, "you and I are outside of our physical bodies. I want you to remember that quite a few hours ago you laid down to sleep in your bed. Thus, now you are to be found here outside of your physical body and conversing with me, since it is well known that when the physical body sleeps, the consciousness, the Essence, unfortunately trapped within the ego, wanders around outside of our corporeal body."

Once I uttered these words, the lady looked at me with the eyes of a somnambulist. Sadly, she did not understand. I comprehended that her consciousness was asleep... I did not want to insist anymore, thus I bade her farewell and left that place. Thereafter, I soared towards California, with the purpose of performing certain important investigations...

On the road, I caught sight of a disembodied soul who in life had been a loader of heavy bundles in public markets. This unhappy soul was carrying an enormous bundle on his back; he seemed to suffer the unspeakable. Thus I approached the defunct and said to him, "My friend, what is going on with you? Why are you carrying such a heavy bundle upon your painful shoulders?" Then, the wretched soul looked at me with the eyes of a somnambulist and said, "I am working."

"But sir," I insisted, "you died a long time ago. The bundle you are carrying upon your shoulders is nothing more than a mental form, so cast it away."

I tried everything, but to no avail. This wretched defunct soul did not understand me; he had his consciousness extremely asleep. Thus, performing a last effort in order to help him, I soared around him in the surrounding environment with the purpose of alarming him, of making him understand that something odd was happening in his existence, to make him realize in some way that he was dead, etc. Sadly, it was all useless.

Afterwards, once I performed the necessary important investigations, I returned to my physical vehicle that lay sleeping in my bed.

Question: Master, do you mean to say that the possibility of a direct experience, as you have explained it in your lectures, is not possible without the dissolution of our psychological defects?

Samael Aun Weor: I will answer this question in detail for the audience. Listen to me friends, ladies and gentlemen. Any direct experience is to be found associated with the percentages of awakened consciousness. Normally people only possess 3% awakened consciousness and 97% subconsciousness or sleepy consciousness. Unquestionably, the first sparks of direct experience begin when one reaches 4 or 5% awakened consciousness. Now, let us distinguish between sparks and total plenitude, which are different. For example, someone who possesses 10%

of awakened consciousness will have a greater percentage of lucidity than those who possess 4 or 5%. Anyhow, the capacity for direct investigation will also be increased in a progressive and orderly manner as the Essence is liberated, as the ego begins to be dissolved.

The exercise of the three divided aspects of our attention (as we have already explained in this lecture) will allow us to thoroughly evidence the percentage of consciousness acquired.

Notwithstanding, the consciousness becomes totally awakened when the ego has been radically annihilated. Thus, in these circumstances we can descend at will into the infernal worlds, with the purpose of seeing, hearing, touching, and experiencing the crude reality of those submerged regions. Since these types of investigations are very advanced, they can only be satisfactorily performed with an absolutely awakened consciousness.

Question: Master, you mentioned two advantages that derive from the Essence: first, the Essence can guide us in order to live adequately. Second, the Essence grants us direct experience. In regard to your experience with that tremendous explosion in the federal district market, which of these two faculties of the Essence granted you the capacity of saving your life?

Samael Aun Weor: Noble sir, allow me to tell you that the second of those qualities of the consciousness (direct experience) allowed me to know beforehand about the event that was going to occur—the death of the firemen.

Question: Master, can you explain the difference between projections of the mind and authentic experiences?

Samael Aun Weor: I will gladly answer this new question from the audience. Allow me to tell you, ladies and gentlemen, that the character of mental projections is completely subjective, whereas the character of authentic experiences is completely objective, thus indeed they are very different.

Mental projections are creations that the mind has subconsciously elaborated. A mind identified with such projections falls into fascination and into the typical dreams of the unconsciousness. Yet, in authentic experiences, the mind has exhausted the process of thinking; it does not project, it is open to the new. It receives without identification and in absence of all fascination and every dreamlike process.

In order to illustrate my answer, I will narrate a supersensible experience that I had. After having astrally projected myself from my physical body in the moments when my body was falling profoundly asleep on the bed, I invoked a certain disembodied soul who, indeed, in life was a close relative of my family. The defunct presented himself dressed with a gray suit that he wore in life; he came alone, laughing. He indeed seemed to be a somnambulist, thus he spoke nonsense (something that he heard from someone else...) Useless were my efforts in order to make him recognize me. That wretched person's consciousness slept profoundly; he definitely did not see me. Deep down, he exclusively perceived his own mental forms; thus, he laughed like a raving lunatic, like an idiot.

Behold these two aspects that come to clarify the essential aspect of this question. This defunct man projected his own mental forms, he dreamed with them, he was absolutely fascinated by them, and thus he did not even perceive me. I, on the other hand, was completely cognizant, awakened. I knew that my physical body had remained asleep in the bed. My mind was not projecting. I had exhausted the thinking process. I was open to the new. I perceived the disembodied soul, I was investigating that soul, and became aware of the deplorable state of that soul...

Thus, with this narration I have illustrated the answer to the question from the audience.

Question: Venerable Master, regarding the exercise about the three divided aspects of our attention that we perform here in this physical world, how is it possible that it can be repeated in the Astral world, when these worlds are completely different?

Samael Aun Weor: My friends, if we observe our life within normal and ordinary dreams we can evidence the concrete fact that many scenes of those dreams correspond to the events of our daily life; in other words, those dreams correspond to the events, to the actions of each moment that right here—in this physical world—we have lived. Thus, as a direct consequence, we can emphasize the fact that if we physically perform the exercise of the three divided aspects of our attention, this will be also repeated (as in the case of dreams) during those hours when the Essence (bottled within the ego) is found outside of the physical body. I do not think that you ignore the fact that when the physical body sleeps, the essence bottled up within "the myself," withdraws from the physical body.

Therefore, if we habituate ourselves to the practice of such an exercise from instant to instant and from moment to moment, here in the physical world, we will then instinctively repeat it during the hours of sleep. Thus, the outcome will be the awakening of the consciousness. This is how we will be able to see, hear, touch, and experience all of what we have been stating in these lectures in relation to hell, the devil, and karma.

Our consciousness awakens at the same pace that our ego is dissolved. This awakening can be evidenced by means of the execution of the exercise about the three divided aspects of our attention that we taught here. Once the ego is absolutely dissolved, such an exercise will allow us to use our consciousness voluntarily in order to investigate the great realities.

Question: Master, how could the profane comprehend the differences between what is real and what is unreal? What is illusory from what is real? The objective from the subjective?

Samael Aun Weor: The audience has formulated a very interesting question which I will immediately answer.

Friends of mine, some nights ago we were watching certain scientific news on television. By means of the diverse representations on the screen, the public was informed about some experiments that present scientists are performing on the brain. By connecting certain nodules to the brain, scientists can control diverse sections of the brain. Under these conditions the human machine can be controlled by means of waves. This has already been absolutely demonstrated. Likewise, experiments were performed in the bullfight plaza; a scientist can stop the bull by means of such a system. The scientist made the bull cease to attack in precisely the moments in which he was about to charge the cape. Thus, with this experiment, it has been perfectly demonstrated that every organism is a machine that is susceptible of being controlled like any other machine.

Now, in the case of the humanoid machine, it is obvious that the diverse psychic inhumane aggregates take turns (one psychic aggregate after another) controlling the various cerebral zones at different times. Thus, the diverse psychic inhumane aggregates integrally replace the cerebral nodules, the waves and the automatic machines with which scientists can control brains. In other words, we will state that by means of their electrical systems, the scientists at specific moments execute the same role as the psychic aggregates; that is, by means of their scientific experimentation, they are demonstrating the reality of such aggregates.

Someone has to control the brain in order for it to execute actions, whether the brain is controlled by the psychic aggregates or it is controlled by the scientists through special electrical systems. Anyhow, these investigations have totally confirmed what we now state: the intellectual humanoid is an unconscious automaton, a subconscious machine. Thus, how can an unconscious machine accept that it is asleep? How can such a machine affirm that the world is Maya (illusion), etc.?

The humanoid machine dreams because of the very fact that it is a machine, but the humanoid machine ignores it. It is in denial of its dreaming state, and firmly believes that it is awakened; thus, the humanoid machine would never accept the thesis that it is asleep. This is why the automaton, the mechanized humanoid, is not capable of differentiating the objective from the subjective, because of the very fact that it is a mechanized creature; thus, the humanoid machine perceives what is objective as subjective and vice-versa.

The sleeping machine, the humanoid automaton, is very far from comprehending the difference between objective consciousness and subjective consciousness, given that the humanoid machine has its own theses that are precisely based on the profound sleep of its consciousness. Thus, by all means it is not possible to make a profane person—who is asleep—comprehend the difference between consciousness and subconsciousness, between objectivity and subjectivity, between sleep and vigil, etc, since only by awakening consciousness is it possible to acknowledge those differences.

Regrettably, any profane person believes they are awakened and even becomes offended if someone tells him that his consciousness is asleep. Talking in Socratic language we would say that the learned ignoramus, the asleep profaner, the unconscious machine, not only ignores but also ignores that he ignores. Not only does he not know, but moreover and worse, he does not know that he does not know.

My friends, it is necessary to stop being machines. When someone accepts that he is a machine, he begins to cease being a machine. Thereafter, the veil of illusions is torn to pieces.

We need to be transformed into human beings and this is only possible by destroying, by annihilating the psychic aggregates that incessantly alternate among themselves in order to control the organic machine.

It is indispensable to acquire reality, to stop being mere automatons moved by waves or by aggregates, which is the same, and to be transformed into true, responsible, cognizant individuals.

Question: Master, what are the differences between the three divided aspects of our attention exercise and the dissolution of the ego in order to awaken consciousness?

Samael Aun Weor: Ladies and gentlemen, throughout all these lectures we have been especially interested in the dissolution of the ego, in the complete destruction of all those psychic aggregates within which our consciousness is flasked, bottled up. It seems to me that we have spoken very clearly, that we have given a perfect didactic for the absolute annihilation of the myself, the self-willed. We have completely explained that we can only liberate, awaken the Essence, by means of the radical annihilation of the inhumane elements that we carry within.

In today's lecture, we taught a specific, explicit exercise. We spoke about the three divided aspects of our attention with the purpose of utilizing the diverse percentages of awakened consciousness each moment (that we are attaining by means of the death of the myself) more perfectly.

In the first case, we have taught the complete doctrine related with the annihilation of the myself. In the second case, we taught a marvelous exercise, which is a practice that will allow us to use the consciousness (which we will successionally liberate) perfectly, clearly, and precisely.

At any rate, it is necessary to be truly transformed into competent investigators of esotericism and of pure occultism. This is our longing, these are our intentions, and this is why we have taught the indispensable doctrine through these lectures.

Glossary

Arcanum: (Latin. plural: arcana). A secret, a mystery. The root of the term "ark" as in the Ark of Noah and the Ark of the Covenent.

Astral: This term is derived from "pertaining to or proceeding from the stars," but in the esoteric knowledge it refers to the emotional aspect of the fifth dimension, which in Hebrew is called Hod.

Astral Body: What is commonly called the Astral Body is not the true Astral Body, it is rather the Lunar Protoplasmatic Body, also known as the Kama Rupa (Sanskrit, "body of desires") or "dream body" (Tibetan rmi-lam-gyi lus). The true Astral Body is Solar (being superior to Lunar Nature) and must be created, as the Master Jesus indicated in the Gospel of John 3:5-6, "Except a man be born of water and of the Spirit, he cannot enter into the kingdom of God. That which is born of the flesh is flesh; and that which is born of the Spirit is spirit." The Solar Astral Body is created as a result of the Third Initiation of Major Mysteries (Serpents of Fire), and is perfected in the Third Serpent of Light. In Tibetan Buddhism, the Solar Astral Body is known as the illusory body (sgyu-lus). This body is related to the emotional center and to the sephirah Hod.

"Really, only those who have worked with the Maithuna (White Tantra) for many years can possess the Astral Body." - Samael Aun Weor, *The Elimination of Satan's Tail*

Auric embryo: The symbiosis of the forces of heaven and the earth crystallized within the superlative consciousness of the Being by means of their Self-realization.

"When the ego is destroyed, the Auric Embryo is formed; then the immortal principles enter into the Initiate..." - Samael Aun Weor, *Tarot and Kabbalah*

Centers, Seven: The human being has seven centers of psychological activity. The first five are the Intellectual, Emotional, Motor, Instinctive, and Sexual Centers. However, through inner development one learns how to utilize the Superior Emotional and Superior Intellectual Centers. Most people do not use these two at all.

Chakra: (Sanskrit) Literally, "wheel." The chakras are subtle centers of energetic transformation. There are hundreds of chakras in our hidden physiology, but seven primary ones related to the awakening of consciousness.

"The chakras are points of connection through which the divine energy circulates from one to another vehicle of the human being." - Samael Aun Weor, *Aztec Christic Magic*

Consciousness: "Wherever there is life, there exists the consciousness. Consciousness is inherent to life as humidity is inherent to water." - Samael Aun Weor, *Fundamental Notions of Endocrinology and Criminology*

From various dictionaries: 1. The state of being conscious; knowledge of one's own existence, condition, sensations, mental operations, acts, etc. 2. Immediate knowledge or perception of the presence of any object, state, or sensation. 3. An alert cognitive state in which you are aware of yourself and your situation. In Universal Gnosticism, the range of potential consciousness is allegorized in the Ladder of Jacob, upon which the angels ascend and descend. Thus there are higher and lower levels of consciousness, from the level of demons at the bottom, to highly realized angels in the heights.

"It is vital to understand and develop the conviction that consciousness has the potential to increase to an infinite degree." - The 14th Dalai Lama.

"Light and consciousness are two phenomena of the same thing; to a lesser degree of consciousness, corresponds a lesser degree of light; to a greater degree of consciousness, a greater degree of light." - Samael Aun Weor, *The Esoteric Treatise of Hermetic Astrology*

Demiurge: (Greek, for "worker" or "craftsman") The Demiurgos or Artificer; the supernal power that built the universe. Freemasons derive from this word their phrase "Supreme Architect." Also the name given by Plato in a passage in the Timaeus to the creator God.

"Esotericism admits the existence of a Logos, or a collective Creator of the universe, a Demiurge architect. It is unquestionable that such a Demiurge is not a personal deity as many mistakenly suppose, but rather a host of Dhyan Chohans, Angels, Archangels, and other forces." - Samael Aun Weor, *The Three Mountains*

"It is impossible to symbolize or allegorize the Unknowable One. Nevertheless, the Manifested One, the Knowable Elohim, can be allegorized or symbolized. The Manifested Elohim is constituted by the Demiurge Creator of the Universe. [...] The great invisible Forefather is Aelohim, the Unknowable Divinity. The great Triple-Powered God is the Demiurge Creator of the Universe: Multiple Perfect Unity. The Creator Logos is the Holy Triamatzikamno. The Verb, the Great Word. The three spaces of the First Mystery are the regions of the Demiurge Creator." - Samael Aun Weor, *The Pistis Sophia Unveiled*

"The Demiurge Architect of the Universe is not a human or divine individual; rather, it is Multiple Perfect Unity, the Platonic Logos." - Samael Aun Weor, *Gnostic Anthropology*

Devachan: In the lecture "The Mysteries of Life and Death," Samael Aun Weor describes the Devachan as "a region of ineffable happiness in the World of the Universal Superior Mind." And in "Mental Representations," he says, "The dead commonly waste much time in the Devachan. I will not deny that this Devachan is a place of happiness and delights, but the figures that make life in the Devachan agreeable are merely living representations of the families, parents, and friends they left on Earth. In one word, the forms of the Devachan are living mental representations, or effigies. They result in a bizarre nature, that is why I say they waste too much time in the Devachan, but they are happy in this place. They feel accompanied by the loved ones they left on Earth. They do not even remotely notice that this world of happiness is full of mental effigies. If they noticed, they would lose the Devachan for themselves."

Devolution: (Latin) From devolvere: backwards evolution, degeneration. The natural mechanical inclination for all matter and energy in nature to return towards their state of inert uniformity. Related to the Arcanum Ten: Retribution, the Wheel of Samsara. Devolution is the inverse process of evolution. As evolution is the complication of matter or energy, devolution is the slow process of nature to simplify matter or energy by applying forces to it. Through devolution, protoplasmic matter and energy descend, degrade, and increase in density within the infradimensions of nature to finally reach the center of the earth where they attain their ultimate state of inert uniformity. Devolution transfers the psyche, moral values, consciousness, or psychological responsibilities to inferior degradable organisms (Klipoth) through the surrendering of our psychological values to animal behaviors, especially sexual degeneration.

Divine Mother: "Among the Aztecs, she was known as Tonantzin, among the Greeks as chaste Diana. In Egypt she was Isis, the Divine Mother, whose veil no mortal has lifted. There is no doubt at all that esoteric Christianity has never forsaken the worship of the Divine Mother Kundalini. Obviously she is Marah, or better said, RAM-IO, MARY. What orthodox religions did not specify, at least with regard to the exoteric or public circle, is the aspect of Isis in her individual human form. Clearly, it was taught only in secret to the Initiates that this Divine Mother exists individually within each human being. It cannot be emphasized enough that Mother-God, Rhea, Cybele, Adonia, or whatever we wish to call her, is a variant of our own individual Being in the here and now. Stated explicitly, each of us has our own particular, individual Divine Mother." - Samael Aun Weor, *The Great Rebellion*

"Devi Kundalini, the Consecrated Queen of Shiva, our personal Divine Cosmic Individual Mother, assumes five transcendental mystic aspects in every creature, which we must enumerate:

1. The unmanifested Prakriti

2. The chaste Diana, Isis, Tonantzin, Maria or better said Ram-Io

3. The terrible Hecate, Persephone, Coatlicue, queen of the infernos and death; terror of love and law

4. The special individual Mother Nature, creator and architect of our physical organism

5. The Elemental Enchantress to whom we owe every vital impulse, every instinct." - Samael Aun Weor, *The Mystery of the Golden Blossom*

Drukpa: (Also known variously as Druk-pa, Dugpa, Brugpa, Dag dugpa or Dad dugpa) The term Drukpa comes from from Dzongkha and Tibetan འབྲུག་ཡུལ ('brug yul), which means "country of Bhutan," and is composed of Druk, "dragon," and pa, "person." In Asia, the word refers to the people of Bhutan, a country between India and Tibet. Drukpa can also refer to a large sect of Buddhism which broke from the Kagyug-pa "the Ones of the Oral Tradition." They considered themselves as the heirs of the indian Gurus: their teaching, which goes back to Vajradhara, was conveyed through Dakini, from Naropa to Marpa and then to the ascetic and mystic poet Milarepa. Later on, Milarepa's disciples founded new monasteries, and new threads appeared, among which are the Karmapa and the Drukpa. All those schools form the Kagyug-pa order, in spite of episodic internal quarrels and extreme differences in practice. The Drukpa sect is recognized by their ceremonial large red hats, but it should be known that they are not the only "Red Hat" group (the Nyingmas, founded by Padmasambhava, also use red hats). The Drukpas have established a particular worship of the Dorje (Vajra, or thunderbolt, a symbol of the phallus). Samael Aun Weor wrote repeatedly in many books that the "Drukpas" practice and teach Black Tantra, by means of the expelling of the sexual energy. If we analyze the word, it is clear that he is referring to "Black Dragons," or people who practice Black Tantra. He was not referring to all the people of Bhutan, or all members of the Buddhist Drukpa sect. Such a broad condemnation would be as ridiculous as the one made by those who condemn all Jews for the crucifixion of Jesus.

Ego: The multiplicity of contradictory psychological elements that we have inside are in their sum the "ego." Each one is also called "an ego" or an "I." Every ego is a psychological defect which produces suffering. The ego is three (related to our Three Brains or three centers of psychological processing), seven (capital sins), and legion (in their infinite variations).

"The ego is the root of ignorance and pain." - Samael Aun Weor, *The Esoteric Treatise of Hermetic Astrology*

"The Being and the ego are incompatible. The Being and the ego are like water and oil. They can never be mixed... The annihilation of the psychic aggregates (egos) can be made possible only by radically comprehending our errors through meditation and by the evident Self-reflection of the Being." - Samael Aun Weor, *The Pistis Sophia Unveiled*

Essence: "Without question the Essence, or Consciousness, which is the same thing, sleeps deeply... The Essence in itself is very beautiful. It came from above, from the stars. Lamentably, it is smothered deep within all these "I's" we carry inside. By contrast, the Essence can retrace its steps, return to the point of origin, go back to the stars, but first it must liberate itself from its evil companions, who have trapped it within the slums of perdition. Human beings have three percent free Essence, and the other ninety-seven percent is imprisoned within the "I's"." - Samael Aun Weor, *The Great Rebellion*

"A percentage of psychic Essence is liberated when a defect is disintegrated. Thus, the psychic Essence which is bottled up within our defects will be completely liberated when we disintegrate each and every one of our false values, in other words, our defects. Thus, the radical transformation of ourselves will occur when the totality of our Essence is liberated. Then, in that precise moment, the eternal values of the Being will express themselves through us. Unquestionably, this would be marvelous not only for us, but also for all of humanity." - Samael Aun Weor, *The Revolution of the Dialectic*

Evolution: "It is not possible for the true Human Being (the Self-realized Being) to appear through the mechanics of evolution. We know very well that evolution and its twin sister devolution are nothing else but two laws which constitute the mechanical axis of all Nature. One evolves to a certain perfectly defined point, and then the devolving process follows. Every ascent is followed by a descent and vice-versa." - Samael Aun Weor, *Revolutionary Psychology*. "Evolution is a process of complication of energy." - Samael Aun Weor, *The Perfect Matrimony*

Fohat: (Theosophical/Tibetan) A term used by H.P. Blavatsky to represent the active (male) potency of the Shakti (female sexual power) in nature, the essence of cosmic electricity, vital force. As explained in *The Secret Doctrine*, "He (Fohat) is, metaphysically, the objectivised thought of the gods; the "Word made flesh" on a lower scale, and the messenger of Cosmic and human ideations: the active force in Universal Life.... In India, Fohat is connected with Vishnu and Surya in the early character of the (first) God; for Vishnu is not a high god in the Rig Veda. The name Vishnu is from the root vish, "to pervade," and Fohat is called the "Pervader" and the Manufacturer, because he shapes the atoms from crude material..." The term fohat has recently been linked with the Tibetan verb phro-wa and the noun spros-pa. These two terms are listed in Jäschke's Tibetan-English Dictionary (1881) as, for phro-wa, "to proceed, issue, emanate from, to spread, in most cases from rays of light..." while for spros-pa he gives "business, employment, activity."

Fornication: Originally, the term fornication was derived from the Indo-European word gwher, whose meanings relate to heat and burning. Fornication means to make the heat (solar fire) of the seed (sexual power) leave the body through voluntary orgasm. Any voluntary orgasm is fornication, whether between a married man and woman, or an unmarried man and woman, or through masturbation, or in any other case; this is explained by Moses: "A man from whom there is a discharge of semen, shall immerse all his flesh in water, and he shall remain unclean until evening. And any garment or any leather [object] which has semen on it, shall be immersed in water, and shall remain unclean until evening. A woman with whom a man cohabits, whereby there was [a discharge of] semen, they shall immerse in water, and they shall remain unclean until evening." - Leviticus 15:16-18

To fornicate is to spill the sexual energy through the orgasm. Those who "deny themselves" restrain the sexual energy, and "walk in the midst of the fire" without being burned. Those who restrain the sexual energy, who renounce the orgasm, remember God in themselves, and do not defile themselves with animal passion, "for the temple of God is holy, which temple ye are."

"Whosoever is born of God doth not commit sin; for his seed remaineth in him: and he cannot sin, because he is born of God." - 1 John 3:9

This is why neophytes always took a vow of sexual abstention, so that they could prepare themselves for marriage, in which they would have sexual relations but not release the sexual energy through the orgasm. This is why Paul advised:

"...they that have wives be as though they had none..." - I Corinthians 7:29

"A fornicator is an individual who has intensely accustomed his genital organs to copulate (with orgasm). Yet, if the same individual changes his custom of copulation to the custom of no copulation, then he transforms himself into a chaste person. We have as an example the astonishing case of Mary Magdalene, who was a famous prostitute. Mary Magdalene became the famous Saint Mary Magdalene, the repented prostitute. Mary Magdalene became the chaste disciple of Christ." - Samael Aun Weor, *The Revolution of Beelzebub*

Gnosis: (Greek) Knowledge.

1. The word Gnosis refers to the knowledge we acquire through our own experience, as opposed to knowledge that we are told or believe in. Gnosis - by whatever name in history or culture - is conscious, experiential knowledge, not merely intellectual or conceptual knowledge, belief, or theory. This term is synonymous with the Hebrew "daath" and the Sanskrit "jna."

2. The tradition that embodies the core wisdom or knowledge of humanity.

"Gnosis is the flame from which all religions sprouted, because in its depth Gnosis is religion. The word "religion" comes from the Latin word "religare," which implies "to link the Soul to God"; so Gnosis is the very pure flame from where all religions sprout, because Gnosis is Knowledge, Gnosis is Wisdom." - Samael Aun Weor, *The Esoteric Path*

"The secret science of the Sufis and of the Whirling Dervishes is within Gnosis. The secret doctrine of Buddhism and of Taoism is within Gnosis. The sacred magic of the Nordics is within Gnosis. The wisdom of Hermes, Buddha, Confucius, Mohammed and Quetzalcoatl, etc., etc., is within Gnosis. Gnosis is the Doctrine of Christ." - Samael Aun Weor, *The Revolution of Beelzebub*

Hydrogen: (From *hydro*- water, *gen*- generate, genes, genesis, etc.) The hydrogen is the simplest element on the periodic table and in Gnosticism it is recognized as the element that is the building block of all forms of matter. Hydrogen is a packet of solar light. The solar light (the light that comes from the sun) is the reflection of the Okidanok, the Cosmic Christ, which creates and sustains every world. This element is the fecundated water, generated water (hydro). The water is the source of all life. Everything that we eat, breathe and all of the impressions that we receive are in the form of various structures of hydrogen. Samael Aun Weor often will place a note (Do, Re, Mi...) and a number related with the vibration and atomic weight (level of complexity) with a particular hydrogen. For example, Samael Aun Weor constantly refers to the Hydrogen Si-12. "Si" is the highest note in the octave and it is the result of the notes that come before it. This particular hydrogen is always related to the forces of Yesod, which is the synthesis and coagulation of all food, air and impressions that we have previously received. Food begins at Do-768, air begins at Do-384, and impressions begin at Do-48.

Initiation: The process whereby the Innermost (the Inner Father) receives recognition, empowerment and greater responsibilities in the Internal Worlds, and little by little approaches His goal: complete Self-realization, or in other words, the return into the Absolute. Initiation NEVER applies to the "I" or our terrestrial personality.

"Nine Initiations of Minor Mysteries and seven great Initiations of Major Mysteries exist. The INNERMOST is the one who receives all of these Initiations. The Testament of Wisdom says: "Before the dawning of the false aurora upon the earth, the ones who survived the hurricane and the tempest were praising the INNERMOST, and the heralds of the aurora appeared unto them." The psychological "I" does not receives Initiations. The human personality does not receive anything. Nonetheless, the "I" of some Initiates becomes filled with pride when saying 'I am a Master, I have such Initiations.' Thus, this is how the "I" believes itself to be an Initiate and keeps reincarnating in order to "perfect itself", but, the "I" never ever perfects itself. The "I" only reincarnates in order to satisfy desires. That is all." - Samael Aun Weor, *The Aquarian Message*

Internal Worlds: The many dimensions beyond the physical world. These dimensions are both subjective and objective. To know the objective internal worlds (the Astral Plane, or Nirvana, or the Klipoth) one must first know one's own personal, subjective internal worlds, because the two are intimately associated.

"Whosoever truly wants to know the internal worlds of the planet Earth or of the solar system or of the galaxy in which we live, must previously know his intimate world, his individual, internal life, his own internal worlds. Man, know thyself, and thou wilt know the Universe and its Gods. The more we explore this internal world called "myself," the more we will comprehend that we simultaneously live in two worlds, in two realities, in two confines: the external and the internal. In the same way that it is indispensable for one to learn how to walk in the external world so as not to fall down into a precipice, or not get lost in the streets of the city, or to select one's friends, or not associate with the perverse ones, or not eat poison, etc.; likewise, through the psychological work upon oneself we learn how to walk in the internal world, which is explorable only through Self-observation." - Samael Aun Weor, *Revolutionary Psychology*

Through the work in Self-observation, we develop the capacity to awaken where previously we were asleep: including in the objective internal worlds.

Karma: (Sanskrit, literally "deed"; derived from kri, "to do...") The Law of Cause and Effect.

"Be not deceived; God is not mocked: for whatsoever a man soweth, that shall he also reap." - Galatians 6:7

Kaya: (Sanskrit) Mahayana Buddhism describes perfect Buddhahood in terms of kayas or bodies. There are varying ways of understanding the kayas.

1. Dharmakaya: Truth-body, or Formless body, related to the Absolute and visible only to inhabitants of its realm.

2. Rupakaya (body of Form) which is divided into two more:

a. Sambogokaya (Body of Perfect Enjoyment), the "spontaneous clarity" aspect of the buddha, which is perceptible only to highly-realized beings.

b. Nirmanakaya (Body of Manifestation), the compassionate aspect of the buddha, which appears in the world.

Kundalini: "Kundalini, the serpent power or mystic fire, is the primordial energy or Sakti that lies dormant or sleeping in the Muladhara Chakra, the centre of the body. It is called the serpentine or annular power on account of serpentine form. It is an electric fiery occult power, the great pristine force which underlies all organic and inorganic matter. Kundalini is the cosmic power in individual bodies. It is not a material force like electricity, magnetism, centripetal or centrifugal force. It is a spiritual potential Sakti or cosmic power. In reality it has no form. [...] O Divine Mother Kundalini, the Divine Cosmic Energy that is hidden in men! Thou art Kali, Durga, Adisakti, Rajarajeswari, Tripurasundari, Maha-Lakshmi, Maha-Sarasvati! Thou hast put on all these names and forms. Thou hast manifested as Prana, electricity, force, magnetism, cohesion, gravitation in this universe. This whole universe rests in Thy bosom. Crores of salutations unto thee. O Mother of this world! Lead me on to open the Sushumna Nadi and take Thee along the Chakras to Sahasrara Chakra and to merge myself in Thee and Thy consort, Lord Siva. Kundalini Yoga is that Yoga which treats of Kundalini Sakti, the six centres of spiritual energy (Shat Chakras), the arousing of the sleeping Kundalini Sakti and its union with Lord Siva in Sahasrara Chakra, at the crown of the head. This is an exact science. This is also known as Laya Yoga. The six centres are pierced (Chakra Bheda) by the passing of Kundalini Sakti to the top of the head. 'Kundala' means 'coiled'. Her form is like a coiled serpent. Hence the name Kundalini." - Swami Sivananda, *Kundalini Yoga*

Logos: (Greek, plural Logoi) means Verb or Word. In Greek and Hebrew metaphysics, the unifying principle of the world. The Logos is the manifested deity of every nation and people; the outward expression or the effect of the cause which is ever concealed. (Speech is the "logos" of thought). The Logos has three aspects, known universally as the Trinity or Trimurti. The First Logos is the Father, Brahma. The Second Logos is the Son, Vishnu. The Third Logos is the Holy Spirit, Shiva. One who incarnates the Logos becomes a Logos.

"The Logos is not an individual. The Logos is an army of ineffable beings." - Samael Aun Weor, *Endocrinology & Criminology*

Magic: The word magic is derived from the ancient word "mag" that means priest. Real magic is the work of a priest. A real magician is a priest.

"Magic, according to Novalis, is the art of influencing the inner world consciously." - Samael Aun Weor, *The Mystery of the Golden Blossom*

"When magic is explained as it really is, it seems to make no sense to fanatical people. They prefer to follow their world of illusions." - Samael Aun Weor, *The Revolution of Beelzebub*

Master: Like many terms related to spirituality, this one is grossly misunderstood. Samael Aun Weor wrote while describing the Germanic Edda, "In this Genesis of creation we discover Sexual Alchemy. The Fire fecundated the cold waters of chaos. The masculine principle Alfadur fecundated the feminine principle Niffleheim, dominated by Surtur (the Darkness), to bring forth life. That is how Ymir is born, the father of the giants, the Internal God of every human being, the Master." Therefore, the Master is the Innermost, Atman, the Father.

"The only one who is truly great is the Spirit, the Innermost. We, the intellectual animals, are leaves that the wind tosses about... No student of occultism is a Master. True Masters are only those who have reached the Fifth Initiation of Major Mysteries. Before the Fifth Initiation nobody is a Master." - Samael Aun Weor, *The Perfect Matrimony*

Meditation: "When the esotericist submerges himself into meditation, what he seeks is information." - Samael Aun Weor

"It is urgent to know how to meditate in order to comprehend any psychic aggregate, or in other words, any psychological defect. It is indispensable to know how to work with all our heart and with all our soul, if we want the elimination to occur." - Samael Aun Weor, *The Pistis Sophia Unveiled*

"1. The Gnostic must first attain the ability to stop the course of his thoughts, the capacity to not think. Indeed, only the one who achieves that capacity will hear the Voice of the Silence.

"2. When the Gnostic disciple attains the capacity to not think, then he must learn to concentrate his thoughts on only one thing.

"3. The third step is correct meditation. This brings the first flashes of the new consciousness into the mind.

"4. The fourth step is contemplation, ecstasy or Samadhi. This is the state of Turiya (perfect clairvoyance). - Samael Aun Weor, *The Perfect Matrimony*

Monad: (Latin) From monas, "unity; a unit, monad." The Monad is the Being, the Innermost, our own inner Spirit.

"We must distinguish between Monads and Souls. A Monad, in other words, a Spirit, is; a Soul is acquired. Distinguish between the Monad of a world and the Soul of a world; between the Monad of a human and the Soul of a human; between the Monad of an ant and the Soul of an ant. The human organism, in final synthesis, is constituted by billions and trillions of infinitesimal Monads. There are several types and orders of primary elements of all existence, of every organism, in the manner of germs of all the phenomena of nature; we can call the latter Monads, employing the term of Leibnitz, in the absence of a more descriptive term to indicate the simplicity of the simplest existence. An atom, as a vehicle of action, corresponds to each of these genii or Monads. The Monads attract each other, combine, transform themselves, giving form to every organism, world, micro-organism, etc. Hierarchies exist among the Monads; the Inferior Monads must obey the Superior ones that is the Law. Inferior Monads belong to the Superior ones. All the trillions of Monads that animate the human organism have to obey the owner, the chief, the Principal Monad. The regulating Monad, the Primordial Monad permits the activity of all of its subordinates inside the human organism, until the time indicated by the Law of Karma." - Samael Aun Weor, *The Esoteric Treatise of Hermetic Astrology*

"(The number) one is the Monad, the Unity, Iod-Heve or Jehovah, the Father who is in secret. It is the Divine Triad that is not incarnated within a Master who has not killed the ego. He is Osiris, the same God, the Word." - Samael Aun Weor, *Tarot and Kabbalah*

"When spoken of, the Monad is referred to as Osiris. He is the one who has to Self-realize Himself... Our own particular Monad needs us and we need it. Once, while speaking with my Monad, my Monad told me, 'I am self-realizing Thee; what I am doing, I am doing for Thee.' Otherwise, why are we living? The Monad wants to Self-realize and that is why we are here. This is our objective." - Samael Aun Weor, *Tarot and Kabbalah*

"The Monads or Vital Genii are not exclusive to the physical organism; within the atoms of the Internal Bodies there are found imprisoned many orders and categories of living Monads. The existence of any physical or supersensible, Angelic or Diabolical, Solar or Lunar body, has billions and trillions of Monads as their foundation." - Samael Aun Weor, *The Esoteric Treatise of Hermetic Astrology*

Mountain of Initiation: The first of three symbolic mountains that represent stages of spiritual development. The first mountain is a series of initiations achieved by the Monad, in which the soul is created and prepared for the remainder of the work. See *The Three Mountains* by Samael Aun Weor.

Mountain of Resurrection: The second of three symbolic mountains that represent stages of spiritual development. The second mountain is a process of psychological refinement in which the initiate cleanses the psyche of all impurity and prepares for resurrection. See *The Three Mountains* by Samael Aun Weor.

Nirmanakaya: See: Kaya

Nirvana: (Sanskrit, "extinction" or "cessation"; Tibetan: nyangde, literally "the state beyond sorrow") In general use, refers to the permanent cessation of suffering and its causes, and therefore refers to a state of consciousness rather than a place. Yet, the term can also apply to heavenly realms, whose vibration is directed related to the cessation of suffering. In other words, if your mind-stream has liberated itself from the causes of suffering, it will naturally vibrate at the level of Nirvana (heaven).

"When the Soul fuses with the Inner Master, then it becomes free from Nature and enters into the supreme happiness of absolute existence. This state of happiness is called Nirvana. Nirvana can be attained through millions of births and deaths, but it can also be attained by means of a shorter path; this is the path of "initiation." The Initiate can reach Nirvana in one single life if he so wants it." - Samael Aun Weor, *The Zodiacal Course*

Objective: [See: Subjective]

Ray of Creation: The light of the Ain Soph Aur, also known as the Okidanokh, Quetzalcoatl, Kulkulcan, Krestos, and Christ. This Ray descends as a lightning bolt, creating and illuminating all the levels of existence.

"The proper arrangement of the Ray of Creation is as follows:

1. Absolute - Protocosmos

2. All the worlds from all of the clusters of Galaxies - Ayocosmos

3. A Galaxy or group of Suns - Macrocosmos

4. The Sun, Solar System - Deuterocosmos

5. The Earth, or any of the planets - Mesocosmos

6. The Philosophical Earth, Human Being - Microcosmos

7. The Abyss, Hell - Tritocosmos

"The brothers and sisters of the Gnostic Movement must deeply comprehend the esoteric knowledge which we give in this Christmas Message, in order for them to exactly know the place that they occupy in the Ray of Creation." - Samael Aun Weor, *The Elimination of Satan's Tail*

Sambogakaya: See: Kaya

Samsara: (Sanskrit; Tibetan khorwa) Cyclic, conditioned existence whose defining characteristic is suffering. It is contrasted with nirvana.

Self-realization: The achievement of perfect knowledge. This phrase is better stated as, "The realization of the Innermost Self," or "The realization of the true nature of self." At the ultimate level, this is the experiential, conscious knowledge of the Absolute, which is synonymous with Emptiness, Shunyata, or Non-being.

Subjective: "What do modern psychologists understand as 'objective?' They understand it to be that which is external to the mind: the physical, the tangible, the material.

"Yet, they are totally mistaken, because when analysing the term "subjective," we see that it signifies "sub, under," that which is below the range of our perceptions. What is below our perceptions? Is it not perhaps the Infernal Worlds? Is it not perhaps subjective that which is in the physical or beneath the physical? So, what is truly subjective is what is below the limits of our perceptions.

"Psychologists do not know how to use the former terms correctly.

"Objective: the light, the resplendence; it is that which contains the Truth, clarity, lucidity.

"Subjective: the darkness, the tenebrous. The subjective elements of perception are the outcome of seeing, hearing, touching, smelling and tasting. All of these are perceptions of what we see in the third dimension. For example, in one cube we see only length, width and height. We do not see the fourth dimension because we are bottled up within the ego. The subjective elements of perception are constituted by the ego with all of its "I's." - Samael Aun Weor, *Tarot and Kabbalah*

Tantra: Sanskrit for "continuum" or "unbroken stream." This refers first (1) to the continuum of vital energy that sustains all existence, and second (2) to the class of knowledge and practices that harnesses that vital energy, thereby transforming the practitioner. There are many schools of Tantra, but they can be classified in three types: White, Grey and Black. Tantra has long been known in the West as Alchemy.

"In the view of Tantra, the body's vital energies are the vehicles of the mind. When the vital energies are pure and subtle, one's state of mind will be accordingly affected. By transforming these bodily energies we transform the state of consciousness." -The 14th Dalai Lama

Trogoautoegocrat: The law of nature that balances the reciprocal nourishment of all organisms. This law is the equilibrium of nature, within which all creatures receive what they need to survive, and give to others what they need to survive. Everything in nature must conform to this law in order to live.

Oordhvareta: (or Urdhvareta. Sanskrit; urdhva means "upwards")

"In India, sexual magic (Arcanum A.Z.F.) is known by the Sanskrit term 'Oordhvareta [Urdhvareta].' People who practice the Arcanum A.Z.F. in India are called Oordhvareta yogis. The Great Arcanum is found in a Hindustani book entitled Secrets of Yoga. The author is a yogi from Southern India." - Samael Aun Weor, *The Yellow Book*

Also, a perfect initiate whose sexual fluid is completely sublimated.

Vajroli mudra: In this book, the author is referring to a technique presented in *Tibetan Exercises of Rejuvenation*.

Wheel of Samsara: (Sanskrit, bhavachakra; Tibetan, srid pa'i 'khor lo / Shri Pa'i Korlho) The world of illusion; the cycle of birth and death. Related to the Tenth Arcanum: Retribution.

In Buddhism, the Wheel of Life is depicted as a great cycle held in the claws of Yama, the lord of death. The wheel illustrates the cyclical nature of karmic conditioning within which all beings are migrating.

White Lodge or Brotherhood: That ancient collection of pure souls who maintain the highest and most sacred of sciences: White Magic or White Tantra. It is called White due to its purity and cleanliness. This "Brotherhood" or "Lodge" includes human beings of the highest order from every race, culture, creed and religion, and of both sexes.

Yoga: (Sanskrit) "union." Similar to the Latin "religare," the root of the word "religion." In Tibetan, it is "rnal-'byor" which means "union with the fundamental nature of reality."

"The word YOGA comes from the root Yuj which means to join, and in its spiritual sense, it is that process by which the human spirit is brought into near and conscious communion with, or is merged in, the Divine Spirit, according as the nature of the human spirit is held to be separate from (Dvaita, Visishtadvaita) or one with (Advaita) the Divine Spirit." - Swami Sivananda, *Kundalini Yoga*

"Patanjali defines Yoga as the suspension of all the functions of the mind. As such, any book on Yoga, which does not deal with these three aspects of the subject, viz., mind, its functions and the method of suspending them, can be safely laid aside as unreliable and incomplete." - Swami Sivananda, *Practical Lessons In Yoga*

"The word yoga means in general to join one's mind with an actual fact..." - The 14th Dalai Lama

"The soul aspires for the union with his Innermost, and the Innermost aspires for the union with his Glorian." - Samael Aun Weor, *The Revolution of Beelzebub*

"All of the seven schools of Yoga are within Gnosis, yet they are in a synthesized and absolutely practical way. There is Tantric Hatha Yoga in the practices of the Maithuna (Sexual Magic). There is practical Raja Yoga in the work with the chakras. There is Gnana Yoga in our practices and mental disciplines which we have cultivated in secrecy for millions of years. We have Bhakti Yoga in our prayers and Rituals. We have Laya Yoga in our meditation and respiratory exercises. Samadhi exists in our practices with the Maithuna and during our deep meditations. We live the path of Karma Yoga in our upright actions, in our upright thoughts, in our upright feelings, etc." - Samael Aun Weor, *The Revolution of Beelzebub*

"The Yoga that we require today is actually ancient Gnostic Christian Yoga, which absolutely rejects the idea of Hatha Yoga. We do not recommend Hatha Yoga simply because, spiritually speaking, the acrobatics of this discipline are fruitless; they should be left to the acrobats of the circus." - Samael Aun Weor, *The Yellow Book*

"Yoga has been taught very badly in the Western World. Multitudes of pseudo-sapient Yogis have spread the false belief that the true Yogi must be an infrasexual (an enemy of sex). Some of these false yogis have never even visited India; they are infrasexual pseudo-yogis. These ignoramuses believe that they are going to achieve in-depth realization only with the yogic exercises, such as asanas, pranayamas, etc. Not only do they have such false beliefs, but what is worse is that they propagate them; thus, they misguide many people away from the difficult, straight, and narrow door that leads unto the light. No authentically Initiated Yogi from India would ever think that he could achieve his inner self-realization with pranayamas or asanas, etc. Any legitimate Yogi from India knows very well that such yogic exercises are only co-assistants that are very useful for their health and for the development of their powers, etc. Only the Westerners and pseudo-yogis have within their minds the belief that they can achieve Self-realization with such exercises. Sexual Magic is practiced very secretly within the Ashrams of India. Any True Yogi Initiate from India works with the Arcanum A.Z.F. This is taught by the Great Yogis from India that have visited the Western world, and if it has not been taught by these great, Initiated Hindustani Yogis, if it has not been published in their books of Yoga, it was in order to avoid scandals. You can be absolutely sure that the Yogis who do not practice Sexual Magic will never achieve birth in the Superior Worlds. Thus, whosoever affirms the contrary is a liar, an impostor." - Samael Aun Weor, *Alchemy & Kabbalah*

Index

Frauds, 117
Fraudulent, 102, 118
Freedom, 17, 19, 22, 37, 39, 146
Freemasons, 284
French Revolution, 171
Friars, 135
Fruitless, 295
Fruits, 50, 106
Fulminated, 141, 144
Funerary, 112
Furies, 193
Fury, 53
Future, 14, 27, 47, 54, 116, 196, 235,
    241, 244-247, 250, 263
Galatians, 290
Galaxies, 15-17, 24, 39, 95, 19, 289,
    293
Gallows, 171
Gambling, 75, 80, 118, 169
Games, 118
Gametes, 218
Garden, 137, 273-274
Garment, 44, 110, 287
Generation, 131, 211
Generosity, 73, 93-94
Genes, 225, 288
Genesis, 288, 291
Genie, 145
Geologic, 71, 129, 131
Geological, 83, 91, 99, 101-102, 111,
    119, 210, 235, 256
German, 220, 291
Germany, 143, 171, 243, 246
Germinal, 17, 19, 218, 225
Germinate, 35, 108
Gestas, 126
Gestation, 218
Giacopo Rusticcuci, 65
Giants, 86, 212, 291
Gift, 118, 241
Giovanni Papini, 178
Glands, 126
Glass, 273-274
Globe, 139
Gluttons, 65-67, 69, 77-78
Gluttony, 70, 165, 263
Gnome, 146, 252

Gnomes, 150
Gnosis, 45, 115, 169, 288, 295
Gnostic, 2, 11, 38, 44, 109, 115, 118,
    123, 137-138, 169, 183, 188,
    191, 195, 197, 203-204, 206,
    208, 212-213, 228, 284, 291,
    293, 295
Gnostic Church, 183
Gnostic Movement, 2, 11, 109, 123,
    138, 169, 228, 293
Gnostic Priest, 191
Gnosticism, 115, 208, 284, 288
Gnostics, 46, 116, 165, 197, 204,
    206, 233
Goal, 234-235, 289
Goddess, 65, 138
Gods, 4, 14, 123, 134, 138, 143, 179-
    180, 185, 202, 212, 231, 235,
    241, 245, 250, 253-256, 261,
    263-264, 287, 289
Goethe, 179
Golden, 31, 44, 213, 234, 245, 260,
    285, 291
Good, 1-2, 5, 7, 9, 14, 23, 31, 33, 38,
    46, 49, 60, 65-66, 73, 77, 79,
    85, 91, 93, 103, 111, 115-117,
    119, 126, 128, 131, 135, 137,
    139, 150, 152, 158, 170-172,
    189-190, 193-194, 225, 227-
    228, 238, 243, 247-249, 255-
    256, 261, 264, 268, 270
Goodwill, 79
Gorillas, 155
Gospel, 32, 38, 79, 126, 170, 203-
    204, 206, 283
Gospel of Judas, 203-204
Gospels, 32, 191-192, 206-207, 227
Gossip, 266
Govern, 80, 87, 218
Governed, 15-17, 20-21, 23, 57, 63,
    108, 126, 261
Government, 117
Governs, 23, 119
Grail, 133
Grain, 35
Gravitate, 10, 145
Gravitation, 16, 290

Tears, 36, 49-51, 70, 229
Technique, 214, 294
Technological, 246
Tedious, 91, 142, 228
Teeth, 32, 129, 131
Tegghiaio, 65, 107
Teleoghinooras, 239-240
Telepathically, 240
Telescopes, 16
Television, 278
Tempests, 219, 289
Temple, 21, 107, 115, 118, 151, 166, 170, 182, 197, 272, 287
Temples, 107, 129, 151, 178, 182
Tempt, 60, 190, 192
Temptation, 176-178, 190, 194, 201, 208-210, 212
Temptations, 180, 190-191, 201, 210-211, 213
Tempted, 191
Tempter, 177, 184, 191
Tempting, 123-124, 126-129, 131, 184
Tempts, 176, 191
Ten, 91, 195, 223-224, 231, 285
Tenorio, 138
Tension, 144
Tenth, 121, 163, 177, 187
Teotihuacán, 197, 253
Teric, 175
Terminated, 200, 244, 248
Terrestrial, 9, 12, 19, 27, 55, 62, 71, 83, 121, 151, 239-240, 289
Tertium Organum, 10
Testimony, 141, 211
Tests, 139
Text, 56, 257
Texts, 139, 150, 211
Thanatos, 46
Theban, 111
Thebes, 197
Thelema, 144
Theogonies, 54
Theories, 164, 170, 220, 237
Theory, 163-164, 220, 288
Theosophical, 34, 287
Theosophical Society, 34

Theosophists, 49
Theosophy, 24
Therapy, 106
Thief, 126, 173, 247
Thieves, 127
Think, 5, 7-8, 12, 21, 24, 31, 37-38, 59, 71, 75, 77, 91, 95, 104, 115, 118-119, 143, 149, 160, 162, 180, 187, 192, 211, 223, 227-229, 239, 246, 248, 256, 262, 266-267, 278, 291, 295
Thinking, 12, 30, 226, 264, 277
Thinks, 26, 31
Third, 9-10, 15, 17, 22, 63, 65-67, 69, 77, 86, 108, 123, 150, 166, 180, 217, 243, 245, 255, 283, 290-291, 294
Third Logos, 108, 123, 180, 290
Thirst, 69
Thirteen, 133
Thirtieth, 173
Thor, 212
Thought, 10, 61, 167, 262, 264, 287, 290
Thoughts, 272-273, 291, 295
Thousand, 30, 162, 231, 251
Thousands, 30, 87, 173, 227, 246
Thread, 12-13
Threads, 286
Three, 1, 9, 11, 13-17, 21-24, 80, 83, 96, 121, 126, 131, 134, 149, 155, 159, 162, 166, 185, 193, 196, 201, 207-208, 217, 222, 250, 253, 257, 272, 274, 276-278, 280, 284, 286, 290, 292, 294-295
Three Aspects, 9, 11, 13, 290, 295
Three Brains, 96, 286
Three-brained, 56, 58, 61
Three-centered, 56, 58, 61
Three-fold, 69
Three-headed, 63
Three Logoi, 166
Three Mountains, 83, 126, 201, 284, 292
Three Traitors, 134, 201, 207
Throat, 69

Glorian Publishing is a non-profit publisher dedicated to spreading the sacred universal doctrine to suffering humanity. All of our works are made possible by the kindness and generosity of sponsors. If you would like to make a tax-deductible donation, you may send it to the address below, or visit our website for other alternatives. If you would like to sponsor the publication of a book, please contact us at 877-726-2359 or help@gnosticteachings.org.

Glorian Publishing
PO Box 110225
Brooklyn, NY 11211 US
Phone: 877-726-2359

VISIT US ONLINE AT:

gnosticteachings.org